CAREER COUNSELING

THE BROOKS/COLE SERIES IN COUNSELING
PSYCHOLOGY
John M. Whiteley, University of California at Irvine
Arthur Resnikoff, Washington University
Series Editors

COUNSELING ADULTS
Editors: Nancy K. Schlossberg, University of Maryland
        Alan D. Entine, State University of New York at Stony Brook

CAREER COUNSELING
Editors: John M. Whiteley, University of California at Irvine
        Arthur Resnikoff, Washington University

APPROACHES TO ASSERTION TRAINING
Editors: John M. Whiteley, University of California at Irvine
        John V. Flowers, University of California at Irvine

COUNSELING WOMEN
Editors: Lenore W. Harmon, University of Wisconsin—Milwaukee
        Janice M. Birk, University of Maryland
        Laurine E. Fitzgerald, University of Wisconsin—Oshkosh
        Mary Faith Tanney, University of Maryland

CAREER COUNSELING

EDITED BY

JOHN M. WHITELEY
UNIVERSITY OF CALIFORNIA AT IRVINE

ARTHUR RESNIKOFF
WASHINGTON UNIVERSITY

BROOKS/COLE PUBLISHING COMPANY

Monterey, California

A Division of Wadsworth Publishing Company, Inc.

Acquisition Editor: *Charles T. Hendrix*
Project Development Editor: *Claire Verduin*
Production Editor: *Marilu Uland*
Interior Design: *Laurie Cook*
Cover Design: *Sharon Marie Bird*
Typesetting: *Instant Type, Monterey, California*

Printed in the United States of America

10 9 8 7 6 5 4 3 2 1

Much of the material in this book originally appeared in *The Counseling Psychologist,* the official publication of the Division of Counseling Psychology of the American Psychological Association.

Library of Congress Cataloging in Publication Data

Main entry under title:

Career counseling.

   (The Brooks/Cole series in counseling
psychology)
       Includes index.
       1. Vocational guidance—Addresses, essays,
lectures.   I. Whiteley, John M.   II. Resnikoff,
Arthur.
HF5381.C2652   331.7'02   77-25908
ISBN 0-8185-0255-X

SERIES FOREWORD

The books in the Brooks/Cole Series in Counseling Psychology reflect the significant developments that have occurred in the counseling field over the past several decades. No longer is it possible for a single author to cover the complexity and scope of counseling as it is practiced today. Our approach has been to incorporate within the Brooks/Cole Series the viewpoints of different authors having quite diverse training and perspectives.

Over the past decades, too, the counseling field has expanded its theoretical basis, the problems of human living to which it addresses itself, the methods it uses to advance scientifically, and the range of persons who practice it successfully—from competent and skillful paraprofessionals to doctoral-level practitioners in counseling, psychology, education, social work, and psychiatry.

The books in the Brooks/Cole Series are intended for instructors and both graduate and undergraduate students alike who want the most stimulating in current thinking. Each volume may be used independently as a text to focus in detail on an individual topic, or the books may be used in combination to highlight the growth and breadth of the profession. However they are used, the books explore the many new skills that are available to counselors as they struggle to help people learn to change their behavior and gain self-understanding. Single volumes also lend themselves as background reading for workshops or in-service training, as well as in regular semester or quarter classes.

The intent of all the books in the Brooks/Cole Series is to stimulate the reader's thinking about the field, about the assumptions made regarding the basic nature of people, about the normal course of human development and the progressive growth tasks that everyone faces, about how behavior is acquired, and about what different approaches to counseling postulate concerning how human beings can help one another.

John M. Whiteley
Arthur Resnikoff

PREFACE

This text presents the contents of two issues of *The Counseling Psychologist* that were devoted to career counseling. The decision to republish these articles reflects the importance that both Brooks/Cole and the Editorial Board of *The Counseling Psychologist* attach to career counseling in its many facets.

For those readers for whom this is an initial contact with the subject, Chapters 1-3 provide an introduction to the various approaches to career counseling. The first chapter briefly outlines the key points from each of the succeeding chapters and provides a list of key questions for which authors of the other chapters have quite different answers. Chapter 2 is a summary and comparison of five basic approaches to career counseling: the trait and factor, the developmental, the psychodynamic, the client-centered, and the behavioral. These different approaches are compared on the bases of whether they use diagnosis (and, if diagnosis is used, what form it takes), the process career counseling takes in each approach, the desired outcomes each approach specifies, what interview techniques are employed, how (and whether) tests are used, and the use made of occupational information. Chapter 3 provides critiques of the summary and comparison of the five basic approaches. Taken together, Chapters 1-3 will provide a common denominator of understanding of the basic approaches to career counseling from which the remaining sections of the book may be investigated.

Three different approaches to career counseling—Crites' comprehensive model, Krumboltz and associates' social-learning model, and Holland's person/environment typology model—are presented in Chapters 4-7. The concluding chapters, 8-11, are more specialized. Two of them examine research priorities and conceptual frameworks for career awareness, and two discuss the application of behavioral self-control theory and cognitive-developmental theory to career counseling.

This book is intended for use by undergraduates, beginning graduate students, and participants in in-service training programs. The later parts of the book also can be used by advanced graduate students and practicing professionals.

John M. Whiteley
Arthur Resnikoff

CONTENTS

CAREER COUNSELING

CAREER COUNSELING: AN OVERVIEW

JOHN M. WHITELEY
University of California Irvine

The purpose of this chapter is to introduce the reader to the important issues covered in this book. Career counseling is, on the one hand, based on decades of research, with many approaches already reflecting established methodologies, instruments, and counseling practices. On the other hand, there is fundamental disagreement about which of the established methodologies, instruments, and counseling practices are most effective with clients. Further, there are new approaches being developed all the time, with two being introduced in this book: behavioral self-control (Chapter 8) and the cognitive-developmental approach (Chapter 11).

Within this book, there are alternative answers posited to fundamental questions facing the career-counseling field. Consider the following important questions:

Is one approach to career counseling applicable to different client populations in diverse situations?

Is it possible to create a system of career counseling that will reflect the uniqueness of both counselor and client?

Will it be possible to meet society's needs for career-counseling services within the framework of the approaches that exist today?

Is differential treatment of clients based on a diagnosis of their needs a viable approach?

Do the tools exist for counselors to use in creating efficient systems for serving client needs?

Is one-to-one career counseling an anachronism?

How pervasive is sex bias in career counseling, and how influential to the outcome of counseling is the sex of the counselor?

Are there such things as a good vocational choice and a preferred way to make a vocational choice?

Why do people make the original career decisions they do, change those decisions throughout their life span, and express different interests at different stages of life?

How are career-related preferences acquired, and how are career decisions made?

How do genetic factors, environmental conditions, learning experiences, cognitive and emotional responses, and skills interact in the progress of a person's career?

Does the social-learning approach lack the career (vocational) content and organizational structure (as a delivery system) necessary for practical career-counseling applications?

Are career-counseling theories necessarily more useful for either classification of known data or understanding of future client change and development?

Should career counseling be viewed as the approach of last resort?

Do most people's careers basically remain within related occupational groups?

What are the characteristics of persons who remain undecided about career choices?

Why do people change jobs, and what factors affect their search for a new job?

Can a typological model such as Holland's give adequate consideration to career decisions and problems from a developmental perspective?

Are developmental theories adequately able to deal with how people interact with environments, predict achievement and satisfaction, and organize work histories?

Is Holland's person/environment typology equally applicable from adolescence through retirement?

Is the proper role of the counselor in career counseling that of the "engineer," helping clients "engineer" their decisions?

What research approach will be the most productive for generating increased knowledge about career counseling?

Do the original applications to career counseling of behavioral self-control and cognitive-developmental theory presented in this book hold promise for generating useful career-related research and practical applications?

Some of the questions stated above have been raised explicitly by authors in this book; others are implicit in the differing conceptions of career counseling. But all the questions have one important characteristic in common: different authors in this book would give quite conflicting answers to them. The reader will find these experts in fundamental disagreement.

While this may at first seem disconcerting, it reflects the state of the career-counseling field: it is in active turmoil but exploring many fruitful lines of inquiry and not attempting to apply static answers to the changing career problems facing clients.

In the remainder of this introductory chapter, the key points of each author's contribution will be addressed. The questions posed earlier in this chapter will serve as useful organizers of the central issues as the reader weighs the merits of each approach.

John Crites compares and contrasts five different approaches to career counseling across common dimensions of theory and technique. His intent is to identify their respective strengths and weaknesses as a prelude to synthesizing a "conceptual and experiential basis for formulating a comprehensive approach to career counseling," which is the subject of Chapter 4.

An important assumption underlying Crites' analysis is that it is unlikely that any one approach to career counseling will be applicable in diverse populations and situations. The analogy he makes is to psychotherapy, wherein he cites Kiesler (1966) to support the statement that no one system is universally effective. Another assumption Crites makes is that what is needed by the career counselor is a system of career counseling that is "comprehensive." He describes a "comprehensive" system as one that "approximates as closely as possible the uniqueness of each client-counselor dyad."

The taxonomy developed by Crites has two bases for comparison of the several theories: models and methods. Models is subdivided into diagnosis, process, and outcome; methods, into interview techniques, test interpretation, and the use of occupational information. The theories that were subjected to this method of analysis were the Trait-and-Factor theory (Paterson & Darley, 1936; Darley, 1950; Williamson, 1939a, 1939b), the Client-Centered theory (Patterson, 1964), the Psychodynamic theory (Bordin, 1968; King & Bennington, 1972), the Developmental theory (Super, 1942, 1954, 1955, 1957a, 1957b; Super & Overstreet, 1960), and the Behavioral or Social-Learning theory (Goodstein, 1972; Krumboltz & Thoresen, 1969; Krumboltz & Baker, 1973).

The third chapter includes responses to the Crites article by John Holland, Louise Vetter, and Lenore Harmon and her associates. Holland is the founder of a major approach to career counseling not reviewed by Crites and does not share the assumptions underlying the Crites article—namely, that one approach cannot be applicable in many diverse populations and that what a counselor needs is a "comprehensive" approach.

Holland's critique extends beyond the intellectual and scientific weaknesses of the current approaches to career counseling to what he feels are societal, financial, organizational, and practical weaknesses. Holland does not believe that the current approaches have met society's needs for service, nor does he believe that they can if they are applied only in one-to-one counseling. Differential treatment based on diagnosis he sees as largely a myth, with the individual counselor's "predilections" acting as a more powerful determinant of what the client actually receives than the person's "special needs." He sees career counseling as rendered in an uncoordinated manner. Solutions to client problems are approached through the realms of listening and talking rather than through a broader approach. What we need, he believes, are more counselors who are interested in "creating systems of efficient service" and then "managing and evaluating such services." After reviewing briefly new developments and trends, Holland outlines seven characteristics of current approaches that are promising and that constitute part of a "renovation" of vocational counseling. He concludes by specifying six goals for the future, including focus on the vocational problems in society, emphasis on those services that help the most people at the lowest cost, greater organization of delivery in order to develop a more rational and effective set of services, greater awareness by career counselors of the scientific heritage of their profession, more regular evaluation and monitoring of career counseling, and less effort spent on individual vocational counseling.

Vetter draws attention to the importance of gender—for both clients and counselors. She cites some of the research documenting sex biases, including the counselor's lack of information about the realities of women's careers. She reports that some forms of career information can be more of a problem than a solution for clients. Another source of limitation to the counselor's work, as Vetter sees it, has been a failure to benefit from the career-related literature from the fields of sociology and economics, in particular, and the social sciences, in general.

Harmon has asked four graduate students in a master's-level class to comment on the Crites paper. John Kapellusch notes that, as much as there is a need for a good general theory of career counseling, more than a taxonomy is required. A taxonomy could result in the use of a special approach without the benefit of the specialized theory behind it. Finally, he cautions that unless Crites can solve specific counseling problems in his next article, he will end up producing a "mildly eclectic approach," wasting "his time (and ours)." Yvonne R. Porter indicates that, while all the major approaches to career counseling assume that there is such a thing as a "good vocational choice," they fail to recommend a "concrete course of action." One possible reason she suggests is that not enough is known yet about the meaning of work in people's lives and about what "decisions will probably be more beneficial to our clients." Thomas J. Meyer draws attention to the fact that the technical use of language in the Crites chapter will serve to limit its readership. The choice of language will exclude most clients from understanding and perhaps benefitting from it, and it will not even be as useful as it could be to the people in the profession. He also calls for a greater attention to "job strategies," helping the client develop a way of coping with and adapting to the job situation. Our theories do not go far enough toward helping "the beleaguered person on the job." Lorraine Jacobs indicates that, in choosing among the many theories of career development, the counselor must keep in mind the specific problem to be dealt with and the amount of time available to spend with the client. Some problems and populations are not dealt with adequately by existing theories, and the approaches covered by Crites do not take adequate account of the time constraints under which most counselors work.

In formulating Chapter 4, the comprehensive career-counseling model, John Crites draws on three sources: his earlier article in this book (Chapter 2) in which he reviewed five major approaches to career counseling; systems of counseling and psychotherapy covered in Ford and Urban (1963) and Corsini (1973); and his personal experiences as a supervisor and career counselor. The model, as Crites presents it, has been derived "experientially as well as logically," blending the "theoretical and pragmatic as meaningfully as possible."

Under the rubric of diagnosis, the central issue is whether or not to diagnose. Only client-centered counseling has eschewed diagnosis, on the grounds that it shifted responsibility away from the client. Crites points out what he considers to be inconsistencies in the client-centered position, reviews the key positions of other approaches on the question of diagnosis, then offers his own synthesis. The key points of the diagnosis synthesis are as follows: (1) do a differential diagnosis of the problem, its antecedents, and contingencies; (2) determine how "career mature" in choice attitudes and competencies the client is and how these attitudes and competencies relate to the choice problem; (3) draw conclusions about what the problem is, how it occurred, how it is being dealt with, and what career counseling processes may be most appropriate.

The synthesis of process in career counseling consists of a first stage of diagnosis, a second stage of problem clarification and specification (with the counselor and client working collaboratively), and a third stage of problem resolution. The focus in this third stage is on instrumental learning and the generalization of what has been learned in career counseling to the resolution of other life problems. The synthesis of outcome in career counseling as seen by Crites involves examination of the impact of the counseling on the client's philosophy of life, interpersonal relationships, self-concept, and so on.

In terms of methods of career counseling, the primary vehicle is the interview technique, by which the models of diagnosis, process, and outcome are realized. Crites' comprehensive approach employs the client-centered and developmental approaches during the beginning problem exploration, the psychodynamic approach characterized by "interpretive" counselor responses during the middle stage, and the trait-and-factor and behavioral approaches during the final period of review and reinforcement of the problem resolution. Crites' chapter concludes with sections on the role of test interpretation, occupational information, and materials in comprehensive career counseling.

In Chapter 5, John Krumboltz, Anita Mitchell, and G. Brian Jones address themselves to a social-learning-theory analysis of such important questions as:

> Why do people happen to enter the particular educational programs or occupations they do?
>
> How or why is it that they change from one educational program or occupation to another at various points throughout their lives?
>
> How can it be explained that they express different preferences for various programs or occupations at different times in their lives?

The theory as they present it attempts to explain "how educational and occupational preferences and skills are acquired" and "how selections of courses, occupations, and fields of work are made." The theory they present also identifies the "interactions of genetic factors, environmental conditions, learning experiences, cognitive and emotional responses, and performance skills" that produce progress along one or another career path.

In terms of how these various influences interact, Krumboltz and his associates identify three important consequences. The first of these are self-observation generalizations. Self-observation generalizations refer to individual self-statements evaluating how one's own real or perceived performance compares to known standards. The single most important self-observation generalization for career decision making consists of preferences, which are the outcome of learning experiences. The second important consequence is task-approach skills, defined by the authors as "cognitive and performance abilities and emotional predispositions for coping with the environment, interpreting it in relation to self-observation generalizations, and making covert or overt predictions about future events." Career decision-making skills are included in this category. The third important consequence is action, and a social-learning approach to career decision making is specifically concerned with entry behaviors, which are defined as actions that represent "an overt step in a career progression." In what is a highly useful section for both researchers and practitioners, the authors suggest several of a number of the testable propositions in their theory and mention possible testable hypotheses. Chapter 5 concludes with the implications of the social-learning approach for both counselors and clients.

Chapter 6 consists of commentaries on the Chapter 4 contribution by Crites and the Chapter 5 contribution by Krumboltz and associates and includes a rejoinder by Krumboltz. The first commentary is by John Holland. He describes himself as feeling like a "hungry ant who had discovered the remains of a picnic created by a group of gourmets" in terms of deciding where to begin, because "every time I reviewed these papers I discovered more ideas I wanted to write about." He found the application of social-learning principles to vocational questions to be "helpful, stimulating, and always clear," with social-learning principles seen as congenial with "most of our speculations about vocational life." The substantial deficiencies he sees are its weak organizational value and its lack of parallel typologies of persons and work environments. In summary, Holland sees the social-learning approach as lacking "both the organizational property and vocational content necessary for most practical applications."

Holland notes that theories of personality, interest, or vocational decision making require a classification to describe and organize what we know about jobs and people, as well as speculations that will explain change and personal development. Holland observes that "theories and speculations about vocational choice, careers, and vocational adjustment are always much more useful for one of these purposes than both." He estimates that social-learning ideas will be most helpful for (1) filling in the blank spaces in other speculations about vocational life and (2) designing comprehensive programs of vocational assistance. Social-learning principles are seen as having little to add to the practice of one-to-one vocational counseling apart from the application of general learning principles.

Crites' synthesis is seen by Holland as having a "marked resemblance to the old trait-and-factor model" with "no persuasive evidence that his particular synthesis is unique, valid, or effective . . . ." This is in the context of a broader view of Holland's that vocational counseling should be "the treatment of last resort," the only other valuable use being to sensitize counselors and researchers about vocational problems and interpersonal relations.

Holland raised a difficult dilemma—the desire by clients to confirm one or more vocational alternatives and the approach suggested by counselors of helping clients in acquiring decision-making skills and enhanced general adjustment. The dilemma is the inherent conflict in pressing for the attainment of all three goals. Holland describes himself as reluctantly resolving the dilemma by letting the client direct the treatment. Further, the long-range value of decision-making training remains untested. The Crites description of the "process" of vocational counseling is seen by Holland as a "reasonable integration of what most counselors understand." The synthesis of interviewing methods, however, is a "smorgasbord." Holland considers it hard to believe that it would not "confuse and block many users." Another basic viewpoint of Holland is that there is little value in trying to renovate traditional vocational counseling.

Anne Roe found the Krumboltz and associates article to be a "thorough analysis," "comprehensive," and "well organized." She did bring attention to the fact that, while technological developments have produced job opportunities, they have also rendered obsolete a number of jobs. She also mentioned that chance is not discussed in the Krumboltz et al. article, although her own research has revealed the importance many people attribute to chance as a factor in their careers.

Roe considers the Crites paper to be a "thoughtful analysis" of the models, methods, and syntheses. She did mention the limitation inherent in confining his discussion to career counseling that has been sought by the client and to the counselor/client interaction. There is no suggestion of how a client can be helped in any other situation.

John Krumboltz wrote a rejoinder to the Holland and Roe critiques entitled "This Chevrolet Can't Float or Fly." Krumboltz began by focusing on Holland's assertion that the social-learning theory of career selection lacks the organizational property and vocational content necessary for most practical applications." He said in part:

> We do not yet have a table of organization for self-observation generalizations, for instrumental or associative learning experiences, or for task approach skills related to each possible occupation. Nor do we know how to organize the infinite sequence of learning activities so as to produce a coherent account of precisely what occupational preferences will result.

The basic point he made was that the social-learning theory, as he presented it, is not intended to supply such organizational property or vocational content. It is intended to be a "first step toward understanding more precisely what specific kinds of learning experiences contribute to the development of occupational preferences." Krumboltz offered a very succinct and important summary statement about the characteristics of the social-learning approach: "It posits certain environmental and cultural events that facilitate or inhibit the reinforcing and punishing consequences which contribute to various occupational preferences."

The social-learning approach was designed to accomplish two tasks singled out by Krumboltz. The first is to make explicit how, as a result of genetic endowment and learning experiences in a cultural context, decision making and other task-approach skills are developed. The second task of the social-learning approach is to show how skills and preferences from past learning interact with social, cultural, and economic forces in the present to result in specific occupational-entry behaviors. One purpose of the theory is to explain the "cause of occupational preferences and behaviors."

If evidence from research supports the propositions of social-learning theory, Krumboltz sees the practice of career counseling affected in the following directions:

1. Decision making will be taught as a skill.
2. Criteria of vocational-counseling success will be different in the direction, for example, of seeing whether certain decision-making processes are used in a variety of settings.
3. Occupational preferences and skills will be developed more systematically.

As a guide to future investigation, Krumboltz closes his rejoinder by identifying a number of areas in which the social-learning approach is incomplete. It is not yet able to specify how learning experiences combine to yield certain preferences. A useful goal for the future would be to specify how people cognitively process experiences to generate preferences. Social-learning theory cannot currently specify what behavioral or cognitive processes represent effective decision-making skills. Nor is it clear how people associate occupations with particular activities.

In Chapter 7, John Holland and Gary Gottfredson have extended and clarified the basic formulations in the Holland (1973) typology of persons and environments. The typology developed by Holland is a vehicle for organizing occupational materials and experiences, for explaining and interpreting vocational data and behavior, and for planning remedial activities. In Holland's approach, a person's classification as one of six personality types is related to his or her classification in one of six occupational environments. A hexagonal model arranges personality and occupation according to their psychological similarities and differences.

The Holland and Gottfredson article assumes a basic knowledge of Holland's theory and will be most useful to the reader if Holland (1973) has been read first, along with some of the reviews (Campbell, 1974; Harmon, 1974; Osipow, 1973; Walsh, 1973; Warnath, 1974) of the theory. Holland states that his theory attempts to answer four questions:

1. How do personal development, initial vocational choice, work involvement, and satisfaction come about?
2. Why do most people have orderly careers when the individual jobs in their work histories are categorized using an occupational-classification scheme?
3. Why do people change jobs? What influences their search for new jobs?
4. Why do some people make vocational choices that are congruent with assessment data, others do not, and still others are "undecided"?

In this chapter, Holland and Gottfredson provide an extension of previous formulations and give their current thinking on the answers to each of the above questions.

In an important section of the chapter, they demonstrate how a typology can be used to reinterpret vocational developmental constructs. In Holland's view, critics are incorrect when they state that the typological model cannot adequately consider career decisions and problems from a developmental perspective. He demonstrates how degree of consistency of career choices, realism of career choices, career-choice competencies, career-choice attitudes, degree of career development, personal integration, identity, crystallization of interests, and vocational adjustment are all translatable into typological terms, with the added benefit of directly tying data to theory. Holland and Gottfredson's intentions in this section are to clarify vocational developmental constructs and to illustrate the versatility of the Holland typology.

Developmental approaches are presented as frequently ignoring significant strengths of the typological approach. Cited as examples of this lack of attention are interaction of people with environments, forecasts of achievement and satisfaction, and organization of occupational data, including work histories, in a practical way. How the typology can be used to consider career problems throughout the lifespan is explored on the basis of not making assumptions about characteristic vocational crises or problems at different stages of life. The typological approach involves assessing a person and the career situation at any age with an explicit structure that asks what type of person and environment is involved and what environmental alternatives are possible.

Holland and Gottfredson amplify the above notions. Vocational coping is seen as a function of the interaction of type of personality and environment, in addition to differentiation and consistency of each, with type and personality pattern especially important. Life-stage speculations have value in suggesting additional hypotheses about the nature of the individual's current difficulties, but the person/environment model is applicable from adolescence through retirement. Career-development measures may assist in providing suggestions about the origins of career problems, but they are unlikely to lead to ideas on remedial actions or to reassure clients about the wisdom of a proposed choice.

Holland and Gottfredson argue that a single theory is applicable for all client groups, including women and minorities. They cite three reasons. First, the psychological principles underlying vocational behavior are the same for all groups, since they are members of the same species. Second, empirical research, upon examination, does not support the claim that different psychological processes exist for different groups. Third, the use of the same typology and assessments with all client groups has important practical benefits: it allows the assessment of the cumulative effects of heredity and socialization, it facilitates the visualization of desirable areas of vocational development, and it makes possible the design of job-seeking strategies by specifying promising alternatives.

The authors extend the practical implications of the typology for vocational guidance in the areas of personal and group counseling and close with a discussion of the strengths and weaknesses of the Holland typology. As they present them, the weaknesses of the Holland typology are five: (1) Important personal and environmental contingencies lie outside the scope of the typology. (2) Different devices used to assess types may yield slightly different occupational classifications. (3) A more comprehensive examination is needed of the formulations about personal development. (4) More testing is needed of the hypotheses about person/environment interactions. (5) Vocational-environment hypotheses are as yet only partially tested.

The strengths of Holland's approach, as they see it, are easy to summarize: (1) The typology is easy to understand. (2) The definitions are clear. (3) The structure is internally consistent. (4) The scope is broad and has formulations for dealing with both personal development and change. (5) A broad base of research support has been developed using diverse populations. And (6) the theory is quite simply applied to practical problems such as developing assessment devices, classifying and interpreting personal environmental data, and conducting vocational counseling.

In Chapter 8, Carl Thoresen and Craig Ewart provide a new conceptual framework for considering career development and career counseling—namely, behavioral self-control. Behavioral self-control is defined as "learnable cognitive processes that a person uses to develop controlling actions which, in turn, function to alter factors influencing behavior."

Their new approach, which is within the social-learning framework, can be viewed with perspective by considering (1) what they believe people need, (2) the counselor's role as they see it, and (3) the critique they offer of existing vocational theory and research. They believe people need "specific help in learning how to self-manage their actions so that change is made and sustained." Criteria for how to make a decision are already known; the authors identify "specifying the task, gathering relevant information, identifying alternatives, selecting an alternative, taking action toward a tentative decision." In addition, clarifying the problem, identifying options, and selecting an alternative for future action are important career decision-making activities.

The role of counselors in career decision making involves teaching clients to approach life in a way that is "new, demanding, and possibly threatening," the counselor's job being one of helping clients to "engineer" their own decisions. To implement this role, counselors need to have practical knowledge of how to help clients accomplish the following: clarify needed decisions and goals; commit themselves to exploring; understand their own needs, interests, and abilities; change beliefs and misconceptions; restructure the environment to help engage in desirable behaviors and to evaluate and maintain progress in the direction of personal goals.

This is quite a different perception of what clients need and of the role of the counselor than those usually offered by counselors. Thoresen and Ewart also differ from most counselors in their assessment of existing vocational theories and of the research approach that will make the greatest contribution to future knowledge. They critique the approaches by Holland and Super, as these are the two that have had the most empirical investigation.

Holland's typology is seen as constituting an important contribution to career counseling "as an intelligible and empirically sound system for organizing vocational information and instruction." The limitation of the research based on the typology, however, is that "it has not been directed at some major needs of the career counselor." By this remark they mean several different things. First, the practical applications based on the results from research are limited by the fact that two thirds of the research studies have used high school or college populations. Second, the large sample-population designs used by researchers on the Holland theory yield results that have limited applicability to problems of individual clients. A more powerful design, in Thoresen and Ewart's view, would be an intensive, as opposed to extensive, design. The extensive designs have been useful in the past, however, as they have served to verify the validity of the model as a whole. Third, the "over-dependence" on correlational techniques that establish associational relationships between elements involved in career counseling has been at the expense of determining cause-and-effect relationships based on experimental investigations. In Thoresen and Ewart's view, experimental investigations must be employed, "if we are to further our understanding of the processes and conditions of vocational development and changes." They identify for future experimental investigation such important questions as "What are the origins of career orientations?" "What is the difficulty of altering them?" and "What experiences have the greatest impact on career choice and enjoyment?" They believe that counseling effectiveness is severely limited by the counseling profession's inability to answer such questions.

A basic issue in the Holland system is whether the typology can predict career choices and satisfactions in the future. This issue is the key to how useful the typology will be to clients on a practical basis. Thoresen and Ewart explore how the typology can be researched in such a manner as to make it more useful in future applications. The career-decision research activity on self-concept theory has been largely based on the work of Donald Super and his associates. It is the contention of Thoresen and Ewart that the self-concept approach would be even more useful to clients if research designs were implemented that would develop an understanding of the nature of the causal link, if any, between self-descriptions and job choices. Previous research has shown that statistically significant associations exist between how people view themselves and what kind of work they do. As Thoresen and Ewart note, the causal issue is not resolved by demonstrating that a sense of personal identity is associated with the work a person does. A different type of research design would help answer important practical questions such as whether people select careers in which they will do well because they have positive self-concepts or whether positive self-concepts reflect their having chosen careers in which they succeeded.

Current research on the self-concept model also does not take into account factors such as how self-concepts can be modified by specific training or how specific situations affect self-concept. In concluding their section on other approaches, Thoresen and Ewart single out four needed changes in research focus. First, a wider range of clients (than high school and college students) needs to be studied. They specifically identify women, minorities, and adult career changers. Second, there should be more emphasis on experimental control and immediacy of observation, with less attention to statistical-significance testing. This approach will hopefully result in a gain in the type of knowledge that helps people make major self-changes. They specifically suggest single case studies that can give important insights "about how cognitive and emotional behaviors influence career aspirations, decisions, and satisfactions." Third, more attention must be given to the situations in which individuals live, work, and make choices. This will hopefully result in knowledge of how self-attitudes and occupational decisions are affected by situational factors in order that counselors may help clients restructure their environments with a view toward developing life styles of their choice. Fourth, an experimental approach that seeks to find causal factors would aid counselors in helping clients make real-life decisions.

After a brief review and summarization of Krumboltz's social-learning model of career selection, Thoresen and Ewart proceed to the presentation of their own work in the application of self-control or self-management psychology to the problem of career counseling. Self-control is not a personality trait but becomes a matter of what behaviors, viewed as self-controlling, a person can exercise in different situations. Involved in self-control are behaviors such as analyzing the environment, committing oneself to action (both initiating and maintaining it), identifying and altering faulty perceptions, trying new actions, and fostering encouragement and promoting change by restructuring the environment.

The tentative framework for presenting and acquiring self-control skills stresses four areas: commitment, awareness, restructuring of environments, and evaluation of consequences and standards. Commitment in the sense of motivation is viewed not as static but as "developing and building commitment behaviors slowly over time." Awareness, while related to commitment, refers to learned self-observation through self-recording and self-monitoring and sets the stage for deciding what to alter in the environment. Restructuring environments builds on the first two and focuses on modifying aspects of the environment from hindering to helping client efforts to change. The intent is to shape the environment to be more supportive of the client's moving in the direction he or she wishes to move. The final component of the framework is evaluating consequences and standards for self-evaluations. Here the emphasis is on scrutinizing how the environment helps support behavior the client wishes to change, assessing short- and long-term goals, and using self-rewarding and self-punishing experiences as consequences of desired and undesired actions, respectively. Clients are taught how to encourage and support long-term efforts by arranging consequences appropriately.

Since this chapter represents an original application of self-control theory to career counseling, much research is necessary. Further, another very useful avenue for future work would be to directly apply self-control theory to career-counseling problems in the same detail as Thoresen and Ewart did with the self-control weight-reduction program for children and adolescents, which constitutes Table 3 of their chapter.

Chapter 9, by G. Brian Jones and Steven Jung, focuses on research priorities in the area of career decision making. The basis of this chapter was the extensive investigation of the topic conducted by the American Institutes for Research (AIR) under a contract from the National Institute for Education (NIE). The work was very thorough, consisting of an extensive literature review, four regional workshops, a national conference to consider key career decision-making issues, and the collection and review of data bases for the Careers Research Data Set Index, which is an on-line computer-based index containing 95 data sets. Career decision making is an important component of career counseling. The NIE-supported work is an intensive investigation of research priorities in the area. The Jones and Jung chapter is essentially a brief summary of the project.

The reasons for including the Jones and Jung chapter are two. First, career decision making is a central area within career counseling, and the focusing of research priorities is very useful to advancing the field. Second, the AIR-NIE endeavor is a useful model for other researchers to follow in focusing research priorities in other areas within career counseling.

Chapter 10, by Robert Wise, Ivan Charner, and Mary Lou Randour, develops a conceptual framework for considering the career-awareness component of career decision making. As with the article by Jones and Jung, the focus here is on research. Career awareness is seen as "the basis for making choices that affect the direction of a person's career." The intent of the conceptual framework is to clarify the important aspects of career awareness and to establish how these aspects relate to each other and to their antecedents and consequences.

Wise, Charner, and Randour have developed a four-part framework. Institutional influences including the family, the school, the mass media, and community groups constitute one part. A second part is the concept of career awareness itself—the "inventory of knowledge, values, preferences, and self-concepts which an individual draws on in the course of making career-related choices." A third part encompasses the various skills involved in self-assessment and decision making. The fourth part considers the actual decision making itself.

The final chapter of the book, by L. Lee Knefelkamp and Ron Slepitza, consists of the application of cognitive-developmental theory to career development. This is a new application of cognitive-developmental theory and opens up an entirely new area for research inquiry and practical application for career counselors.

Cognitive-developmental theory integrates the developmental processes over the life span, with special reference to stages of growth in cognitive processes, including organizing and integrating functions. Cognitive-developmental theory has previously been applied to the growth of cognitive processes in children and the ways they make moral judgments (Piaget, 1932, 1952), the stages of moral reasoning (Kohlberg, 1969), and the intellectual and ethical growth of college students (Perry, 1970).

Knefelkamp and Slepitza present nine variables that are the subject of qualitative changes making up a developmental sequence. First, students progress from control based on others to control based on their own internal reference. Second, as analytical ability develops, it becomes possible to see cause-and-effect relationships. Third, after analytical ability reaches a certain level of complexity, the ability develops to synthesize—to integrate diverse components into a complex whole. Fourth, the use of absolutes in semantic structures changes in a direction allowing for greater alternatives through the use of qualifiers and modifiers. Fifth, closely paralleling the growth of analysis is the development of the ability to examine oneself and to be cognizant of "one's defining factors." Sixth, there is growth of the ability to understand and scrutinize other people's points of view. Seventh, there is a progression in the willingness to accept the consequences of personal actions or decisions. Eighth, there is an increased capacity to take on new roles, to seek and master them, and to expand and integrate old and new roles. Ninth, and closely related to role taking, there is the ability to take risks with the self in the area of self-esteem, particularly as this allows a focus on new learning and experiences.

The nine variables are applied to create a nine-stage career-development model organized under four headings. The first heading is dualism, which is characterized by dichotomous thinking. External events or people control the person's environment. Others are seen as the source for identifying that one "right" career. Authority provides the "answer," as individuals with dualistic thinking lack the capacity to analyze and synthesize career material. The second heading is multiplicity, which is characterized by more cognitive complexity but with a remaining external locus of control. Cause-and-effect relationships are perceived, but the person still does not accept full responsibility for himself or herself. The third heading, relativism, includes a shift from external to internal reference points, a more complex use of analysis, an examination of a variety of options, and the beginning of the ability to synthesize. At this stage of development, individuals begin to accept responsibility for their career decisions. The final heading is commitment with relativism, wherein synthesis is a major mode of thinking, there is an integration of who an individual is with how he or she interacts with the environment, and consistency becomes a personal defining characteristic. There is an awareness of the potential positive and negative effects of their actions on both themselves and on others.

The final part of the chapter is very important, as Knefelkamp and Slepitza discuss the problem of moving from a "descriptive model of student career development," which they have outlined earlier in the chapter, to "prescriptive interventions." One of the important discoveries in the cognitive-developmental approach has been that carefully designed educational programs will accelerate individuals along the stages of development. While this has yet to be demonstrated with the cognitive-developmental approach to careers, the task is one of great potential benefit and merits early and intensive investigation.

REFERENCES

Bordin, E. S. *Psychological counseling* (2nd ed.). New York: Appleton-Century-Crofts, 1968.

Campbell, D. P. Have hexagon—will travel. *Contemporary Psychology*, 1974, *19*, 585-587.

Corsini, R. *Current psychotherapies*. Itasca, Ill.: Peacock, 1973.

Darley, J. G. Conduct of the interview. In A. H. Brayfield (Ed.), *Readings in modern methods of counseling*. New York: Appleton-Century-Crofts, 1950. Pp. 265-272.

Ford, D. H., & Urban, H. B. *Systems of psychotherapy*. New York: Wiley, 1963.

Goodstein, L. D. Behavioral views of counseling. In B. Steffire & W. H. Grant (Eds.), *Theories of counseling*. New York: McGraw-Hill, 1972. Pp. 243-286.

Harmon, L. W. Review of making vocational choices: A theory of careers. *Measurement and Evaluation in Guidance*, 1974, *7*, 198-199.

Holland, J. L. *Making vocational choices: A theory of careers*. Englewood Cliffs, N.J.: Prentice-Hall, 1973.

Kiesler, D. J. Some myths of psychotherapy research and the search for a paradigm. *Psychological Bulletin*, 1966, *65*, 110-136.

King, P. T., & Bennington, K. F. Psychoanalysis and counseling. In B. Steffire & W. H. Grant (Eds.), *Theories of counseling*. New York: McGraw-Hill, 1972. Pp. 177-242.

Kohlberg, L. Stage and sequence: The cognitive-developmental approach to socialization. In D. Goslin (Ed.), *Handbook of socialization theory and research*. New York: Rand McNally, 1969.

Krumboltz, J. D., & Baker, R. D. Behavioral counseling for vocational decision. In H. Borow (Ed.), *Career guidance for a new age*. Boston: Houghton Mifflin, 1973. Pp. 235-283.

Krumboltz, J. D., & Thoresen, C. E. (Eds.). *Behavioral counseling: Cases and techniques*. New York: Holt, Rinehart & Winston, 1969.

Osipow, S. H. *Theories of career development*. New York: Appleton-Century-Crofts, 1973.

Paterson, D. J., & Darley, J. G. *Men, women, and jobs*. Minneapolis: University of Minnesota Press, 1936.

Patterson, C. H. Counseling: Self-clarification and the helping relationship. In H. Borow (Ed.), *Man in a world at work*. Boston: Houghton Mifflin, 1964. Pp. 434-459.

Perry, W., Jr. *Intellectual and ethical development in the college years*. New York: Holt, Rinehart & Winston, 1970.

Piaget, J. *The moral judgment of the child*. New York: Harcourt, Brace & World, 1932.

Piaget, J. *The language and thought of the child*. London: Routledge & Kegan Paul, 1952.

Super, D. E. *The dynamics of vocational adjustment*. New York: Harper, 1942.

Super, D. E. Career patterns as a basis for vocational counseling. *Journal of Counseling Psychology*, 1954, *1*, 12-20.

Super, D. E. The dimensions and measurement of vocational maturity. *Teachers College Record*, 1955, *57*, 151-163.

Super, D. E. The preliminary appraisal in vocational counseling. *Personnel and Guidance Journal*, 1957, *36*, 154-161. (a)

Super, D. E. *The psychology of careers*. New York: Harper, 1957. (b)

Super, D. E., & Overstreet, P. L. *The vocational maturity of ninth grade boys*. New York: Teachers College Bureau of Publications, 1960.

Walsh, W. B. *Theories of person-environment interaction: Implications for the college student* (Monograph 10). Iowa City: American College Testing Program, 1973.

Warnath, C. F. Review of making vocational choices: A theory of careers. *Personnel and Guidance Journal,* 1974, *52,* 337-338.

Williamson, E. G. *How to counsel students.* New York: McGraw-Hill, 1939. (a)

Williamson, E. G. The clinical method of guidance. *Review of Educational Research,* 1939, *9,* 214-217. (b)

CAREER COUNSELING: A REVIEW OF MAJOR APPROACHES

2

JOHN O. CRITES
University of Maryland

Concurrent with the development of vocational psychology as a scientific discipline (Crites, 1969), there has emerged during the past half century the related yet distinct practice earlier known as vocational guidance and more widely called *career counseling*. More precisely, a historical survey of vocational guidance and career counseling reveals not one but several different approaches to assisting individuals with their choice of a life's work.[1] Dating from Parsons' (1909) tripartite model for "choosing a vocation," the trait-and-factor approach to career counseling dominated the field during the 1930's and 1940's. In the latter decade, however, its tenets were seriously questioned by Rogers' (1942) system of nondirective or client-centered counseling as applied to career decision-making (Covner, 1947; Combs, 1947). By the 1950's still another orientation to career counseling was being articulated within the conceptual framework of psychoanalytic theory (Bordin, 1955) and exemplified by case studies (Cautela, 1959). Embracing elements from each of these but embellishing them with concepts and principles drawn from developmental psychology, Super (1957b) proposed a broadly based developmental approach to career counseling in which decision making is viewed as an ongoing, life-long process. Most recently in the history of career counseling, the focus has been upon the application of behavioral principles to the analysis and modification of information-seeking and other decisional behaviors (Krumboltz and Thoresen, 1969).

Substantive statements of each of these approaches are available to the career counselor, but nowhere are they collectively compared and contrasted.

This article is condensed from a book in process entitled *Career Counseling: Models, Methods, and Materials.*

[1]Only the major approaches are discussed here. Others, such as the sociological (Sanderson, 1954), rehabilitative (Lofquist, 1957), and computer-assisted (Super, 1970), are more specialized in applicability.

18

Nor have they been critically analyzed across common dimensions of theory and technique to identify their relative strengths and weaknesses, so that their strengths might be synthesized to provide a conceptual and experiential basis for formulating a comprehensive approach to career counseling. Indeed it would appear that now, possibly more than ever before, there is a need for comprehensive counseling maximally applicable to idiosyncratic combinations of counselors and clients in a great variety of settings. Given the contemporary emphasis upon career education, with one of its principal objectives being the facilitation of career development, career counseling appropriate to students at any and all grade levels in the elementary and secondary schools assumes critical proportions. At the same time, in many colleges and universities across the nation, recent surveys have established that, in this period of job scarcity and hard money, the psychological service students request more than any other is career counseling. The Army and Air Force, too, have felt the need to institute transitional career counseling programs for returning and retiring servicemen to aid them in readjustment to civilian life, and the Veterans Administration continues to offer career counseling through many of its hospitals and other services. Industry also has found a new role for career counseling with the hard-core unemployed, the work-alienated and the executive in mid-career crisis.

That any one approach to career counseling is applicable to these diverse populations and situations is unlikely, just as there appears to be no one type of psychotherapy which is universally effective (Kiesler, 1966). What is needed is a system of career counseling sufficiently comprehensive so that it approximates as closely as possible the uniqueness of each client/counselor dyad. To facilitate such a formulation, the taxonomy shown in Figure 1 was conceived. Along the horizontal axis are listed the major approaches to career counseling which have evolved over the years, in their approximate order of historical development from left to right. On the vertical axis are enumerated the principal dimensions of theory and technique which the various approaches have in common and which provide a framework for comparing and contrasting their *models* and *methods*. These dimensions are neither exclusive nor exhaustive, but they *are* central to all kinds of career counseling. In this article, each approach will be descriptively reviewed on each dimension (proceeding down columns). Then, in a later article, the several approaches will be critically analyzed dimension by dimension (reading across rows), and an attempt will be made to synthesize them into a comprehensive approach to career counseling which is maximally applicable to various combinations of client/counselor parameters.

APPROACHES TO CAREER COUNSELING

The term *approach* as applied to career counseling refers to a relatively well-articulated model and method of assisting individuals in making decisions about their lifelong roles in the world of work and in solving

		Trait-and-Factor	Client-Centered	Psychodynamic	Developmental	Behavioral
M O D E L S	Diagnosis					
	Process					
	Outcomes					
M E T H O D S	Interview Techniques					
	Test Interpretation					
	Use of Occupational Information					

Figure 1. Taxonomy of approaches to career counseling.

problems which arise in the course of the choice process (Crites, 1969). The *model* of an approach is defined along the temporal continuum which career counseling spans, beginning with the *diagnosis* of a client's problem, proceeding through the *process* of client/counselor interviews or interactions, and culminating in certain *outcomes*. The model, then, is a theoretical explication of the assumptions and propositions which are made about the principal components of any approach to career counseling. In contrast, the *methods* of an approach are the specific procedures used to implement the model of career counseling and include *interview techniques, test interpretations* and *use of occupational information*. The models and methods of career counseling vary widely from one approach to another, as an analysis of each of these dimensions makes clear. Following the schema outlined in Figure 1, the various approaches to career counseling are briefly reviewed in this order: (1) Trait-and-Factor; (2) Client-Centered; (3) Psychodynamic; (4) Developmental; and (5) Behavioral. Limitations of space preclude an extensive discussion of the models and methods; therefore, only the central concepts and practices have been selected for the summary which follows.

Trait-and-Factor Career Counseling

The *model* of this approach was fashioned from the pragmatics of assisting men and women dislocated from their jobs during the era of the Great Depression to retrain and find new employment (Paterson and Darley, 1936).

Stemming from the interdisciplinary work of the Twin Cities Occupational Analysis Clinic, early trait-and-factor career counseling reflected the rudiments of Parsons' (1909) "matching men and jobs" conceptualization, but it went beyond his pioneer paradigm to incorporate the sophistication of the newly developing psychometrics, which produced the fabled "Minnesota" tests of clerical aptitude, manual dexterity, spatial perception, etc., and the fund of occupational information compiled by the U. S. Employment Service for the first edition (1939) of the Dictionary of Occupational Titles (DOT). Philosophically, trait-and-factor career counseling has always had a strong commitment to the uniqueness of the individual; psychologically, this value has meant a long-time predilection for the tenets of differential psychology. As a consequence, there have been two significant implications for the model upon which this approach is based. First, it is largely *atheoretical*; other than that, it subscribes to the proposition that individuals differ. It does not posit organizing concepts or hypothetical constructs, such as are characteristic of the client-centered and psychodynamic approaches. Second, it is analytical and atomistic in its orientation. It adheres closely to the schemata of scientific problem-solving, as exemplified by a nosological concept of diagnosis, a rationalistic process of counseling and a specific set of decisional outcomes.

 1. Diagnosis. As the hallmark of trait-and-factor career counseling, diagnosis is defined by Williamson (1939a) as

> a process in logical thinking or the "teasing out," from a mass of relevant and irrelevant facts, of a consistent pattern of meaning and an understanding of the [client's] assets and liabilities together with a prognosis or judgment of significance of this pattern for future adjustments to be made by the [client] (pp. 102-103).[2]

To aid in diagnosing problems in career decision-making, Williamson (1939b) has proposed these four categories: (1) no choice, (2) uncertain choice, (3) unwise choice, and (4) discrepancy between interests and aptitudes. Contingent upon which problem a client is judged to have, an appropriate process of career counseling would be formulated. Thus, the role of diagnosis in trait-and-factor career counseling is much as it is in the "medical model": differential courses of treatment stem from a determination of what is "wrong" with the client.

 2. Process. Williamson (1939b) delineates six steps which comprise trait-and-factor career counseling:

> *Analysis*—collecting data from many sources about attitudes, interests, family background, knowledge, educational progress, aptitudes, etc., by means of both subjective and objective techniques.

---

[2]From *How to Counsel Students*, by E. G. Williamson. Copyright 1939 by McGraw-Hill, Inc. This and all other quotations from this source are used by permission of McGraw-Hill Book Company.

Synthesis—collating and summarizing the data by means of case-study techniques and test profiles to "highlight" the [client's] uniqueness or individuality.

Diagnosis—describing the outstanding characteristics and problems of the [client], comparing the individual's profile with educational and occupational ability profiles, and ferreting out the causes of the problems.

Prognosis—judging the probable consequences of problems, the probabilities for adjustments, and thereby indicating the alternative actions and adjustments for the [client's] consideration.

Counseling, or *treatment*—cooperatively advising with the client concerning what to do to effect a desired adjustment now or in the future.

Follow-up—repeating the above steps as new problems arise and further assisting the [client] to carry out a desirable program of action (p. 214).

The first four steps of this process are exclusively engaged in by the counselor; only in the last two does the client actively participate. Most of the process, then, involves the mental activity of the counselor in gathering, processing and interpreting data on the client.

   3. *Outcomes.* The immediate goal of trait-and-factor career counseling is to resolve the presenting problem of the client. If his/her choice was unwise, for example, then counseling should eventuate in a more realistic career decision. The longer-term objective has been stated by Williamson (1965) as follows: "The task of the trait-factor type of counseling is to aid the individual in successive approximations of self-understanding and self-management by means of helping him to assess his assets and liabilities in relation to the requirements of progressively changing life goals and his vocational career" (p. 198). Stated somewhat differently, Thompson (1954) has pointed out that this approach not only should assist the client to make a specific decision but should also "result in the individual's being better able to solve future problems" (p. 535).

   The *methods* used by trait-and-factor career counselors reflect the rationalistic, cognitive model of this approach. Interview techniques, test-interpretation procedures, uses of occupational information—taken together, they constitute a logical "attack" upon the client's decision-making problem. They are what the "thinking man" would do when confronted with a choice among alternative courses of action. They are largely action-oriented, and the counselor is highly active in using these methods. Not only is most of the processing of data on the client a counselor activity, as outlined in the process of trait-and-factor career counseling, but the lead in the interviews is typically taken by the counselor. This role should not be construed to mean, however, that the counselor is insensitive or unresponsive to the client's feelings and emotions and attitudes. Quite the contrary, as Darley (1950) notes in discussing acceptance of the client: "The interviewer must indicate to the client that he has accepted but not passed judgment on these [the client's] feelings and attitudes" (p. 268). Whether dealing with feeling or content, the trait-and-factor career counselor nevertheless appears to be "in charge." The counselor role in this approach is probably best characterized as assertive, dominant and participative (as contrasted with reactive and reflective), all of which earned the trait-and-factor counselor the appellation of "directive" during the heyday of Rogerian "nondirective" counseling in the 1950's. To use these methods effectively presumes that they are compatible with the counselor's personality:

1. Interview techniques. Williamson (1939a) has identified five general techniques which he recommends for trait-and-factor career counseling: "(1) establishing rapport, (2) cultivating self-understanding, (3) advising or planning a program of action, (4) carrying out the plan, and (5) referring the [client] to another personnel worker for additional assistance" (p. 130). More specifically, Darley (1950) enunciates four principles of interviewing which the counselor should follow:

1. Do not lecture or talk down to the client.
2. Use simple words and confine the information that you give the client to a relatively few ideas.
3. Make very sure that you know what it is he really wants to talk about before giving any information or answers.
4. Make very sure that you sense or feel the attitudes that he holds, because these will either block the discussion or keep the main problems out of it (p. 266).

He then discusses several different aspects of the interview which are too numerous to recount here but which cover such functions as opening the interview, phrasing questions, handling silences and maintaining control of the interaction. If these methods were to be described and summarized by one rubric, it would be *pragmatic*. Their essence is technological, not teleological.

2. Test interpretation. This phase of trait-and-factor career counseling is subsumed by those interview techniques which Williamson (1939a) calls "advising or planning a program of action" (p.139), and they include the following:

a. Direct advising, in which the counselor frankly states his opinion as to what the client should do.

b. Persuasion, in which the counselor "marshals the evidence in such a reasonable and logical manner that the [client] is able to anticipate clearly the probable outcomes of alternative actions."

c. Explanation, in which the counselor extrapolates "the implications of the diagnoses and the probable outcome of each choice considered by the [client]" (p. 139).

In Williamson's (1939a) opinion, the last method is "by all odds the most complete and satisfactory method of counseling" (p. 139). He illustrates this type of test interpretation in this excerpt from a counselor explanation:

As far as I can tell from this evidence of aptitude, your chances of getting into medical school are poor; but your possiblities in business seem to be much more promising. These are the reasons for my conclusions: You do not have the pattern of interests characteristic of successful doctors which probably indicates you would not find the practice of medicine congenial. On the other hand you do have an excellent grasp of mathematics, good general ability, and the interests of an accountant. These facts seem to me to argue for your selection of accountancy as an occupation (p. 139).

Thus, the counselor relies upon his/her expertise to make authoritative interpretations of the test results and to draw conclusions and recommendations from them for the client's deliberation.

3. *Occupational information.* Probably the most widely cited statement of the use of occupational information in trait-and-factor career counseling is that of Brayfield (1950), who has distinguished among three different functions of this material:

a. *Informational.* The counselor provides a client with information about occupations in order to confirm a choice which has already been made, to resolve indecision between two equally attractive and appropriate options, or to simply increase the client's knowledge about a choice which otherwise is realistic.

b. *Readjustive.* The counselor introduces occupational information, so that the client has a basis for reality testing an inappropriate choice, the process unfolding something like this:

> The counselor first uses leading questions regarding the nature of the occupation or field which the counselee has chosen. In turn, the counselor provides accurate information which may enable the client to gain insight into the illusory nature of his thinking when he finds that his conception of the occupation or field does not fit the objective facts. At this point the counselor usually is able to turn the interview to a consideration of the realistic bases upon which sound occupational choices are founded (Brayfield, 1950, p. 218).

c. *Motivational.* The counselor uses occupational information to involve the client actively in the decision-making process, to "hold" or maintain contact with dependent clients until they assume greater responsibility for their choice, and to maintain motivation for choice when a client's current activities seem irrelevant to long-term career goals. Other delineations of essentially the same strategies in presenting occupational information to clients have been made by Baer and Roeber (1951) and Christensen (1949). If there is any significant difference among them, it is Brayfield's (1950) insistence that "any use of occupational information should be preceded by individual diagnosis" (p. 220), which stems directly from the process sequence in the model of trait-and-factor career counseling.

Comment. For many years, trait-and-factor career counseling held sway as the only approach to assisting clients engaged in the process of deciding upon their life's work, and in the hands of its highly competent and enlightened originators it is probably as viable today as it was in the past (Williamson, 1972). But as practiced by too many journeyman trait-and-factor counselors who have not updated the model (Super and Bachrach, 1957) and methods (Williamson, 1972), this approach has gone into an incipient decline. It has devolved into what has been caricatured as "three interviews and a cloud of dust." The first interview is typically conducted to gather some background data on the client and for the counselor to assign tests. The client takes the tests—usually a lengthy battery administered in "shotgun" style (Super, 1950)—and then returns for the second interview, at which time the results are interpreted. Not atypically, this session amounts to the counselor "teaching" the client certain necessary psychometric concepts—e.g., the meaning of percentile ranks or standard scores—in order to engage in a lengthy discussion of the tests, one by one, scale by scale. The third interview is usually devoted to reviewing the client's career choice in light of the test results and to briefing the client on the use of the occupational information file for possible further exploration of the world of work. And then the client leaves ("cloud of dust"), often without using these materials on his own, because of the lack of initiative which produced the problems that brought him to career counseling in the first place. At best, this widespread oversimplification of trait-and-factor career counseling provides the client with a mass of test information, which is frequently forgotten or distorted (Froehlich and Moser, 1954). At worst, it completely ignores the psychological realities of decision-making which lead to indecision and unrealism in career choice (Crites, 1969), and it fails to foster those more general competencies—e.g., self-management—which are the essence of true trait-and-factor career counseling (Williamson, 1972).

Client-Centered Career Counseling

The *model* for this approach to career counseling stems only indirectly and by inference from the more general system of psychotherapy proposed by Rogers (1942, 1951). In the latter, Rogers had little to say about career decision-making processes, his concern being primarily with the emotional-social adjustment and functioning of the person. Some client-centered counselors (e.g., Arbuckle, 1961; Doleys, 1961) have contended that, if a client becomes well adjusted psychologically, then he/she will be able to solve whatever career problems are encountered without specifically attending to them in career counseling. Other counselors of a client-centered bent, however, have recognized that, although general and vocational adjustment are related, the correlation is less than perfect (Crites, 1969), and thus a separate focus upon career choices can be justified. During the early years of client-centered counseling (the 1940's), when trait-and-factor counselors were attempting to reconcile and synthesize its principles and procedures with established techniques, several extrapolations from the newer approach to traditional career counseling were made (e.g., Bixler and Bixler, 1945; Covner, 1947; Combs, 1947; Bown, 1947; Seeman, 1948). There ensued a heated controversy in which the relative merits of the "directive" and "nondirective" orientations were debated loud and long, with seemingly no immediate resolution other than a contrived and tenuous eclecticism awkwardly known as "nondirective" career counseling (Hahn and Kendall, 1947). Not until almost two decades later was an articulate and comprehensive statement of client-centered career counseling formulated by Patterson (1964), although it had been presaged by Super's (1950, 1951, 1957b) writings on the self-concept and career development. It is primarily Patterson's conceptualization which is drawn upon in explicating the client-centered position on diagnosis, process and outcomes.

1. *Diagnosis.* Of all the concepts on which directive and nondirective counselors differed, the divergence in their viewpoints was probably greatest on diagnosis. Whereas diagnosis was the fulcrum of the trait-and-factor approach, it was eschewed by Rogers (1942) as potentially disruptive of the client-counselor relationship: "When the counselor assumes the information-getting attitude which is necessary for the assembling of a good case history, the client cannot help feeling that the responsibility for the solution of his problems is being taken over by the counselor" (p. 81).

Similarly, although he does not discuss diagnosis directly, Patterson (1964) subscribes to this point of view when he states that "the client-centered counselor does not deal differently with a client who has a vocational problem and one who has any other kind of problem" (p. 435). Yet, he argues that career counseling can be distinguished from other types of counseling because it focuses "upon a particular area—or problem—in an individual's life" (Patterson, 1964, p. 435) and facilitates the "handling" of it. Thus, he implies that some determination is made whether a client has a "vocational" problem, but he does not consider this a diagnosis.

2. *Process.* Patterson (1964) refers generally to the "process" of client-centered career counseling but neglects to analyze it into distinct stages or phases as does Rogers (1961) for psychotherapy. Extrapolating from the latter, however, as well as from empirical research, it can be inferred that vocational clients enter career counseling at a stage of "experiencing" roughly equivalent to that at which personal clients leave psychotherapy. This is the sixth stage in experiencing, during which a higher level of congruence is achieved by the client, so that he/she "owns" feelings and problems rather than externalizing them: "The client is living, subjectively, a phase of his problem. It is not an object" (Rogers, 1961, p. 150). Clinical impressions of vocational clients, in addition to findings on their general adjustment status (Gaudet and Kulick, 1954; Goodstein, Crites, Heilbrun and Rempel, 1961), suggest that they have reached this stage, on the average, before they start career counseling. Corroboration also comes from a study by Williams (1962), in which he obtained Q-adjustment scores on vocational-educational clients and compared them with [personal] clients from Dymond's (1954) research on client-centered psychotherapy, the *pre*counseling mean of the former being 50.53 and the *post*counseling mean of the latter being 49.30. From these

findings, Williams (1962) concluded that "the adjustment level of personal clients *following* counseling is approximately that of [vocational-educational] clients *before* counseling" (italics in original) (p. 26). Since the vocational-educational clients' *post*counseling mean was 58.76, indicating a still higher level of adjustment, it would appear that career counseling largely encompasses the seventh (and highest) stage in Rogers' (1961) schema of counseling process. Patterson (1973) describes this stage thusly: "The client experiences new feelings with immediacy and richness and uses them as referents for knowing who he is, what he wants, and what his attitudes are. . . . Since all the elements of experience are available to awareness, there is the experiencing of real and effective choice" (p.394).

3. Outcomes. Implicit in this conceptualization of process are the assumed outcomes of client-centered career counseling. Grummon (1972) notes:

> It is difficult to distinguish clearly between process and outcomes. When we study outcomes directly, we examine the differences between two sets of observations made at the beginning and end of the interview series. Many process studies make successive observations over a series of counseling interviews and, in a sense, are miniature outcome measures which establish a trend line for the case (p. 110).

At each point along this line and as the overall outcome, the goal in client-centered psychotherapy is *reorganization of the self:* the client is more congruent, more open to his experience, less defensive (Rogers, 1959). In client-centered career counseling, however, the "successful resolution of many educational and vocational problems (as well as other presenting problems) does not require a reorganization of self" (Grummon, 1972, p. 119). Rather, the goal is to facilitate the clarification and implementation of the self-concept in a compatible occupational role, at whatever point on the continuum of career development the client is. Patterson (1964) cites Super's (1957) revision of the NVGA definition of "vocational guidance" as delineating the desired outcomes of client-centered career counseling: "[It] is the process of helping a person to develop and accept an integrated picture of himself and of his role in the world of work, to test this concept against reality, and to convert it into reality, with satisfaction to himself and benefit to society" (p. 442).[3]

The *methods* by which these outcomes are attained presume certain basic attitudes on the part of the counselor. Much as Rogers (1957) emphasized such conative dispositions as necessary for successful client-centered psychotherapy, so Patterson (1964) has observed that the client-centered approach to career counseling is "essentially an *attitude* rather than a technique" (p. 442). More specifically, there are three attitudes which

[3]From *The Psychology of Careers*, by D. E. Super. Copyright © 1957 by Harper & Row, Publishers, Inc. This and all other quotations from this source are reprinted by permission.

characterize the ideally functioning client-centered counselor (Rogers, 1957, 1961):

a. Congruence—being genuine and open; not playing a role or presenting a facade; the counselor "is aware of and accepts his own feelings, with a willingness to be and express these feelings and attitudes, in words or behavior" (Patterson, 1973, p. 396).

b. Understanding—perceiving the client's phenomenal field; sensing the client's inner world "as if" it were the counselor's; not diagnostic or evaluative; empathy.

c. Acceptance—"unconditional positive regard"; the counselor accepts the client "as an individual, as he is, with his conflicts and inconsistencies, his good and bad points" (Patterson, 1973, p. 396).

Given these counselor attitudes and their communication to a client, who must be experiencing at least a minimal degree of incongruence as a source of motivation for treatment, there results a relationship in which change—i.e., increased client congruence—can occur. These counselor attitudes are communicated in client-centered career counseling via distinctive techniques of interviewing, test interpretation, and use of occupational information.

1. Interview techniques. Once stereotyped as "un-huh" counseling in its early days of development, owing to Rogers' (1942) emphasis upon nondirective interview techniques, the client-centered approach has evolved into a much more sophisticated repertoire of counselor interview behaviors in recent years. In tracing this evolution, Hart and Tomlinson (1970) have delineated three periods during which different interview techniques predominated:

a. Nondirective period (1940-1950). Counselor used verbal responses with a minimal degree of "lead" (Robinson, 1950), such as simple acceptance, clarification and restatement, to achieve client insight.

b. Reflective period (1950-1957). Counselor concentrated almost exclusively upon reflection of feelings, which was substituted for clarification from the preceding period, the goal being to "mirror the client's phenomenological world to him" (Hart and Tomlinson, 1970, p. 8).

c. Experiental period (1957-present). Counselor engages in a wide range of interview behaviors to express basic attitudes and, in contrast to previous roles, relates relevant personal experiences to the client, in order to facilitate the latter's experiencing.

Thus, in contemporary client-centered psychotherapy, the counselor is much more active than ever before, as indexed, for example, by client/counselor "talk ratios." Presumably the same would be true of client-centered career counseling, although neither Patterson nor others have made this application as yet. Assuming that the extrapolation is justified, it would mean that the client-centered career counselor would make responses during the interview with a higher degree of "lead," such as approval, open-ended questions and tentative interpretations, the purpose of which would be to foster and enrich client experiencing as it relates to implementing the self-concept in an occupational role.

2. *Test interpretation.* One of the central issues with which client-centered career counselors have had to contend has been how to reconcile the use of tests with the tenets of the Rogerian approach. To resolve what appears to be a basic incompatibility between the nonevaluative counselor attitudes of acceptance, congruence and understanding on the one hand, and the evaluative information derived from tests on the other, client-centered career counselors have proposed that tests be used primarily for the *client's* edification, not the counselor's. Patterson (1964) argues that "the essential basis for the use of tests in [client-centered] career counseling is that *they provide information which the client needs and wants,* information concerning questions raised by the client in counseling" (italics in original) (p. 449). Similarly, Grummon (1972) concludes that "tests can be useful in [client-centered career counseling], provided that the information they supply is integrated into the self-concept" (p. 126). To achieve this "client-centeredness" in using tests, several innovative procedures have been proposed. First, tests are introduced as *needed* and *requested* by the client—what Super (1950) has termed "precision" testing, as opposed to "saturation" testing. In other words, the client can take tests whenever appropriate throughout the course of career counseling, rather than as a battery before it starts. Second, the client participates in the test selection process (Bordin and Bixler, 1946). The counselor describes the kind of information the client can gain from the various tests available, and the client decides which behaviors he/she wants to assess. The counselor then usually designates the most appropriate measures with respect to their psychometric characteristics (applicability, norms, reliability, validity). Finally, when the tests have been taken and scored, the counselor reports the results to the client in as objective, nonjudgmental a way as possible and responds to the latter's reactions within a client-centered atmosphere (see Bixler and Bixler, 1946, for interview excerpts which illustrate this type of test interpretation).

3. *Occupational information.* The principles underlying the use of occupational information in client-centered career counseling are much the same as those governing test interpretation. Patterson (1964) enumerates four of them:

1. Occupational information is introduced into the counseling process when there is a recognized need for it on the part of the client . . . .
2. Occupational information is not used to influence or manipulate the client . . . .
3. The most objective way to provide occupational information, and a way which maximizes client initiative and .responsibility, is to encourage the client to obtain the information from original sources,

that is, publications, employers, and persons engaged in occupations . . . .
4. The client's attitudes and feelings about occupations and jobs must be
allowed expression and be dealt with therapeutically (pp. 453-455).

Grummon (1972) adds the observation that, in the process of presenting
occupational information, the career counselor should not lose sight of the
Rogerian dictum, stemming from phenomenological theory, that "reality for
the individual is his perception of that reality" (p. 122). Thus, Rusalem (1954)
proposes that "the presentation of occupational information must assume that
for the client it becomes a process of selective perception" (pp. 85-86).
Likewise, Samler (1964) states that "the process of occupational exploration is
psychological in the sense that the client's perceptions are taken into account"
(p. 426). The client-centered career counselor recognizes, then, that
occupational information has personal meanings to the client which must be
understood and explored within the context of needs and values as well as
objective reality.

Comment. The model and methods of client-centered career counseling
not only represent an application of Rogerian principles to decision-making
but also synthesize this approach with core concepts from trait-and-factor and
developmental theory. Patterson (1964) incorporates a refined "matching men
and jobs" concept of career choice when he states that it "may still be broadly
conceived as the matching of the individual and a career, but in a manner much
more complex than was originally thought" (p. 441), and he draws heavily
upon Super's (1957) self-theory of career development to introduce this
dimension into the otherwise historical, "right now" focus of client-centered
psychotherapy. It is problematical, however, whether even this comprehensive
a synthesis, which might also include the contemporary client-centered
emphasis upon greater counselor activity, meets some of the criticisms which
have been leveled at client-centered career counseling. Theoretically,
Grummon (1972) has expressed concern over the almost exclusively
phenomenological orientation of the client-centered approach, which ignores
the effect of stimulus variables upon the acquisition and processing of
information about self and the world of work. He observes that "the theory's
failure to elaborate how the environment influences perception and behavior
is for the writer [Grummon] a significant omission which has special relevance
for many counseling situations" (p. 123). Pragmatically, the principal pitfall
also concerns the potential disjunction and disruption that the introduction of
information into the interview process by the counselor often creates. It is still
not clear from Patterson's formulation how the counselor informs the client
about occupations without shifting from a client-centered role to a didactic
one, thereby compromising the very attitudes which supposedly promote self-
clarification and actualization. His suggestion that the counselor *read*

occupational information aloud to the client does not appear to be the panacea.

Psychodynamic Career Counseling

The *model* underlying this approach to career counseling has been constructed primarily by Bordin (1968) and his associates, although others (e.g., King and Bennington, 1972) have also applied the principles of psychoanalytic theory and therapy to counseling phenomena. It has been Bordin, however, who has had an enduring interest and involvement in conceptualizing career counseling, as well as career development (Bordin, Nachmann and Segal, 1963), within the psychoanalytic tradition. The term *psychodynamic* has been chosen to characterize his orientation, not only because it more accurately portrays the broader scope of Bordin's model than does the scholastic meaning of psychoanalytic, but also because it more precisely connotes the essence of his theoretical commitment, which is twofold: career choice involves the client's needs, and it is a developmental process. Bordin (1968) asserts:

> Our pivotal assumption is that insofar as he has freedom of choice an individual tends to gravitate toward those occupations whose activities permit him to express his preferred ways of seeking gratification and of protecting himself from anxiety . . . . Psychoanalytic theory suggests that a developmental approach to vocation should examine the full sweep of influences shaping personality from birth, even from conception (p. 427).

To "prevent crippling psychological conflicts" in the course of personality-vocational development, the psychodynamically oriented career counselor intervenes at the "transitional points in the life cycle," utilizing the following concepts of diagnosis, process, and outcomes.

1. Diagnosis. On the issue of whether to diagnose or not, Bordin (1968) is unequivocal: "We are convinced that counselors should not undertake counseling responsibility without at least a rudimentary knowledge of diagnosis and diagnostic techniques" (p. 296). But his view of diagnosis is not the traditional, nosological one of trait-and-factor career counseling. In fact, Bordin (1946) was the first to seriously question such nondynamic taxonomies of client problems and proposed instead more psychologically based constructs, such as choice anxiety, dependence and self-conflict. Just recently, he (Bordin and Kopplin, 1973) has reiterated the value of dynamic diagnosis in asserting "we must reject a false dichotomy between classification and dynamic understanding. It is true that classifications have been used in static ways; neither as tools in an ongoing process of understanding nor as guides in an interaction process" (p. 155). Analyzing the sources of motivational conflict experienced by college students seeking career counseling, Bordin and Kopplin (1973) have proposed a new diagnostic system consisting of seven major categories, with some further subdivisions into more specific problems. These categories are as follows:

a. *Synthetic difficulties*—A limiting case of minimum pathology and conflict, in which the major problem is to be found in the difficulty of synthesizing or achieving cognitive clarity. The client is able to work productively in counseling.

b. *Identity problems*—These are assumed to be associated with the formation of a viable self and self-percept (not necessarily fully conscious).

c. *Gratification conflicts*—This classification takes its inspiration from the point of view that examines occupations in terms of the opportunities each offers for finding particular forms of psychosocial gratification in the work activities.

d. *Change orientation*—The client is dissatisfied with himself and struggles via vocational choice to change himself.

e. *Overt pathology*—Even though the contact was initiated around vocational choice, it becomes evident that the disturbance makes it impossible for the student to do any kind of work on this question.

f. *Unclassifiable*—Except that it is a problem involving [sic] motivational conflict.

g. *Unclassifiable*—Except that it is a problem involving no motivational conflict (pp. 156-159).

To assess the reliability of this system, two judges classified the career motivational conflicts of 82 former clients. On the first 47 cases, they reconciled disagreements through consultation, but still attained only 51 percent exact agreement, with partial agreement in a remaining 28 percent. From these results, Bordin and Kopplin (1973) concluded:

In general, we must concede that, though tolerable, our level of agreement was not satisfying. However, we do not find it discouraging because we take into account the sparseness of the case notes in so many instances that forced us into the guessing situation that the reliability figures document. A further factor in unreliability is that the counselors were not oriented to the issues raised by our categories (p. 159).

Even granting that the reliability of this new system might be increased to a satisfactory level, however, of what use is it to the career counselor? It is wholly *post hoc:* the diagnosis is made from reading the notes and summaries of cases which have already been closed out! Such a procedure may have some value for research purposes, but it does not provide the career counselor with the requisite data for diagnosis *before* a course of career counseling is formulated. As Bordin (1946) stipulated many years ago, "the most vital characteristic of a set of diagnostic classifications is that they form the basis for the choice of treatment" (p. 172).

2. *Process.* Bordin (1968) breaks the process of career counseling down into three stages, which are a microcosm for the overall process of career development. In the first stage, *exploration and contract setting*, the critical task of the psychodynamic career counselor is to avoid a superficial rationalistic examination of the client's choice problem as well as a seductive attempt to engage him/her in nonvocationally oriented therapy. Rather, as the name of this approach implies, the focus should be upon the *psychodynamics* of career decision making, the interface between the personal and the vocational in the client's life. The counselor strives to articulate the relationship between these two—to extrapolate the implications, for example, of a fearful, defensive identification of a failing engineering student, who wants to change majors, with an overdemanding and stern father. The second stage is that of *critical decision*, not necessarily of career but between the alternatives of counseling limited to choice or broadened to encompass personality change. In other words, the psychodynamic counselor offers the client the option of becoming engaged in counseling focused upon facets of personal development other than just the vocational. The last stage in the process of psychodynamic career counseling is *working for change*. It is presumed that the client will opt for at least some change in personality, even if it is circumscribed to vocational identity—hence the thrust of this final stage toward increased awareness and understanding of self.

3. *Outcomes.* Although not explicitly stated, the expected outcomes of psychodynamic career counseling are apparent from an analysis of the stages in the process. One objective is to assist the client in career decision-making. The problems which clients may present run the gamut of those enumerated previously in the discussion of "diagnosis"—e.g., synthetic difficulties, gratification conflicts, etc. A broader goal is to effect some positive change in the client's personality, which can be accomplished in two principal ways. Even though the client may choose more narrowly defined career counseling, it may well have salubrious effects upon personal development. Thus, a juxtaposition of a pervasive indecisiveness in decision-making with submission to an authoritarian father may motivate a dependent client to assume greater personal responsibility without the counselor directly dealing with the latter. If the client is willing to undertake personal counseling relatively distinct from a career emphasis, then the avowed outcome is some kind of personality change, albeit only symptomatic anxiety reduction. Both career decision and personality change, achieved through whatever modes, are the desired end states of the client following successful psychodynamic career counseling.

The *methods* of psychodynamic career counseling, as espoused primarily by Bordin (1968), are an amalgam of techniques derived not only from psychoanalytic practices but also from the trait-and-factor and client-centered approaches. More than a mere eclectic gathering together of disparate counseling procedures, they are a true synthesis of theories and methods, leavened by Bordin's many years of experience as an active counselor. As the ensuing descriptions of psychodynamic interview techniques, test-interpretation processes, and uses of occupational information bring out, they constitute sophisticated and refined methods for assisting clients in career decision-making.

  1. Interview techniques. Drawing upon the work of Colby (1951), a psychoanalytically disposed psychotherapist, Bordin (1968) enumerates three "interpretive" counselor response categories which can be used to conduct the interview. The first of these, *clarifications*, are intended to focus the client's thinking and verbalization upon material relevant to the presenting problem. They also serve to open up new areas of discourse and summarize others. Typically, clarifications take the grammatical form of questions, mild imperatives or simplified restatements—what Colby calls "interpositions"—and, because of their form and content, their highest incidence is usually during the beginning stage of counseling. A second type of counselor response is *comparison*, in which two or more topics are juxtaposed to present in sharper relief the similarities or differences among dynamic phenomena. This technique is central to explicating the interrelationship of personal and career development. To illustrate, a counselor might respond to an indecisive client's unconscious rebellion against imposed parental occupational aspirations by saying "On the one hand, your parents want you to be something you don't want to be; yet, on the other, you cannot decide what you want to be. Do you see any connection between the two?" Comparisons are probably most characteristic of the middle stage of counseling. The third technique, which is more pointedly therapeutic in purpose than the other two, is the interpretation of *wish-defense* systems, as exemplified in a case study cited by Cautela (1959). A client who was well suited for medicine by virtue of both abilities and interests, and who was doing well in his pre-med course, expressed a desire in career counseling to change his major to architecture, for which he had no apparent talent. In subsequent interviews, he reported that, shortly before his decision to consider architecture, his mother was almost completely paralyzed because of a cerebral hemorrhage and that his father had intimated he was partially responsible because she waited on him continually. On the psychodynamic hypothesis that "buildings symbolically represent the female figure," the counselor interpreted the client's contemplated shift to architecture as a way of "*re*building his mother" and hence reducing his guilt over having originally precipitated her paralysis. Pursuing the implications of this wish-defense interpretation over a span of twenty interviews, which psychodynamic career counseling not infrequently runs, the client finally decided that architecture was an unrealistic, reactive choice and that he would pursue his studies in pre-med.

  2. Test interpretation. Bordin has made three major contributions to using tests in psychodynamic career counseling. First, in collaboration with a colleague (Bordin and Bixler, 1946), he proposed, in the spirit of the client-centered approach, that the client be an active participant in selecting the tests which he/she would take. A description of different types of tests (e.g., aptitude, interest, personality) is given to the client, who then determines which kind of self-appraisal information might be most useful in terms of the career problem. But the counselor selects the specific tests (e.g., the Strong Vocational Interest Blank) to be administered, since he/she knows what their psychometric characteristics are.

Second, once the client has taken the tests, Bordin (1968) delineates four ways in which they may be used: (1) to provide diagnostic information for the counselor, (2) to aid the client in developing more realistic expectations about counseling, (3) to make appraisal data available to the client, and (4) to stimulate the client in self-exploration. In communicating test results to clients, Bordin subscribes to the procedure developed by Bixler and Bixler (1946), in which scores are reported in as nonevaluative a way as possible. The counselor simply gives the client a statistical prediction, such as "The chances are about 3½ to 1 that if you go into this occupation you will stay in it for 20 years or more," and then discusses the client's reaction to the factual statement.

Third, Bordin (1968) has suggested that this method of test interpretation not only lends itself but is enhanced by the counselor *verbally* relating the client's scores rather than presenting them visually on profile sheets or psychographs. Several advantages accrue from this approach: (1) the counselor can maintain a consistent role as a "collaborator" with the client, rather than shifting to one of "expert" or teacher who explains the psychometric meaning of test scores; (2) the test results can be introduced into the client/counselor interaction as needed, rather than all at once as is routinely done in trait-and-factor career counseling; and (3) the client has a greater likelihood of remembering the implications of the testing, because they have been expressed and integrated into his/her vernacular and thinking about career choice. There is compelling research evidence that clients either forget or distort test information disseminated by the traditional method (Froehlich and Moser, 1954; Kamm and Wrenn, 1950), a problem which can be largely circumvented by the counselor's verbal presentation of test results as part of the ongoing dialogue with the client.

3. Occupational information. The type of information about occupations which is integral to psychodynamic career counseling is that which might best be described as based upon "need analysis" of job duties and tasks. A series of such studies has been conducted under Bordin's general sponsorship at the University of Michigan on accountants and creative writers (Segal, 1961); dentists, lawyers, and social workers (Nachmann, 1960); clinical psychologists and physicists (Galinsky, 1962); and engineers (Beall and Bordin, 1964). In addition, Bordin, Nachmann and Segal (1963) have delineated several dimensions of psychosexual development along which occupational groups can be characterized in terms of need-gratifying activities and instrumental modes of adjustment to work. Knowledge of how and why members of specific occupations engage psychodynamically in their jobs as they do can be used to assist clients in choosing careers in which they may have the greatest probability of satisfying their needs. Thus, although this is clearly the trait-and-factor paradigm of "matching men and jobs," the variables are personality dynamics (needs) and gratifying work conditions (satisfiers) rather than the static characteristics of the individual and occupation.

Comment. As has been true of psychoanalytic theory in general, the model of psychodynamic career counseling suffers from the limitation that it disproportionately emphasizes "internal" factors as the most salient ones in career choice and minimizes external ones (Ginzberg, Ginsburg, Axelrad and Herman, 1951). The assumption is that "insofar as the client has freedom of choice," career choice is a function of individual psychodynamics, but scant attention is given to the conditions and variables which impose constraints upon the decision-making process (Crites, 1969, Ch. 3). Moreover, from a behavioristic point of view, the excessive concern of the psychodynamic career counselor with motivational (nonobservable) constructs introduces unnecessary complexity into the conceptualization of career determination, and rests upon the tenuous assumption that overt decision-making behaviors are somehow mediated by internal "needs." This criticism might be less telling were it not that Bordin has not yet devised an *a priori* diagnostic system which is linked to differentially effective career counseling methods. He is acutely aware, however, of the need for such a conceptualization when he and Kopplin (1973) observe that "it would be useful to make more explicit the differential treatment implications of this classification of motivational conflicts related to vocational development" (p. 160). They then propose some general considerations which the psychodynamic career counselor should make in treating clients with different problems, but these recommendations—e.g., "the counselor must explore the family constellation and client's experience of it so as to understand how identity formation is influencing his learning" (Bordin and Kopplin, 1973, p. 160)—are hardly specific enough to guide interview behavior. Their value lies not on this tactical level but on the strategic one of fashioning career counseling to the psychodynamics of each client, a flexibility and perspicacity in approach which is too often missing from the pedestrian practice of trait-and-factor and client-centered career counseling.

Developmental Career Counseling

A confluence of several streams of conceptualization in career counseling has contributed the theoretical foundation upon which the developmental approach to assisting clients engaged in decision-making has been built. Foremost among the architects of this frame of reference, and its recognized progenitor, is Donald E. Super, who has articulated the precepts and principles of developmental career counseling since the early 1940's. At that time, when the trait-and-factor orientation was predominant, he adapted Buehler's (1933) life-stage schema to the analysis of career behavior in his book *The Dynamics of Vocational Adjustment* (Super, 1942). However, he did not neglect the demonstrated value of the "actuarial method," as he referred to it later (Super, 1954), which he considered to be the "cornerstone of vocational guidance." Indeed, his monumental volume on *Appraising Vocational Fitness* (Super, 1949) represents the traditional approach at its best, but throughout his treatment of vocational appraisal by means of psychological tests there is interwoven his long-standing commitment to developmental psychology and his nascent self-concept theory, as evidenced particularly in his summary of "The Nature of Interests" (Super, 1949). His synthesis of these diverse, and often manifestly contradictory, substantive areas evolved through a series of landmark papers (Super, 1951, 1954, 1955, 1957a, 1960), a book on the *Psychology of Careers* (Super, 1957b), and a Career Pattern Study monograph (Super and Overstreet, 1960) during the 1950's and early 1960's. Implicit in these writings is a model of developmental career counseling based upon distinctive concepts of diagnosis, process and outcomes.

1. Diagnosis. Super (1957a) uses the term *appraisal* instead of diagnosis but considers them to be essentially synonymous, although it is apparent from his discussion of appraisal that this concept is not only broader in scope than diagnosis but that it has a more positive connotation and portent. He delineates three kinds of appraisal, which focus upon the client's potentialities as well as problems (cf., Witryol and Boly, 1954):

a. Problem appraisal. The client's experienced difficulty and expectations of career counseling are assessed, much as in the psychodynamic approach, presumably using some classification system such as Bordin's (1946), although Super (1957a) does not discuss the diagnostic constructs he would use.

b. Personal appraisal. A psychological "picture" of the client is obtained from a variety of demographic, psychometric and social data, the analogue being the clinical case study (Darley, 1940); both vocational assets and liabilities are assessed and expressed in normative terms (e.g., "The client is above average in fine finger dexterity but below average in clerical speed and accuracy.").

c. Prognostic appraisal. Based largely upon the personal appraisal, predictions of the client's probable success and satisfaction—the two principal components of career adjustment (Crites, 1969)—are made. More specifically, appraisal data can be collected and organized according to the format shown in Table 1, which has been devised by the writer from Super's (1957a) formulation.

This outline (Table 1) can be used for both cross-sectional and developmental appraisals, although Super (1942, 1954) clearly opts for the latter if the appropriate data are available. What he terms the "thematic-expolative" method of appraisal, as contrasted with a more narrowly conceived actuarial model, strives to provide an impression of the client's behavior within a developmental context. "The assumption underlying this approach is that one way to understand what an individual will do in the future is to understand what he did in the past. It postulates that one way to

Table 1. Outline for a vocational appraisal

This outline is applicable to either a counseling or a personnel situation. Also, it might be used for research purposes. It is designed to summarize background, interview, and test data on an individual in a systematic fashion. Changes in the outline may be necessary, however, to adapt it to special problems or situations.

Title ("Vocational Appraisal of _____")

Person Appraisal

(Description of the individual in terms of his status on psychological, sociological and physical dimensions)

Present Status and Functioning. (1) How does the individual "stand" on the various pertinent dimensions? What are his general and special attitudes? Interests? Personality characteristics? Attitudes? Educational background and achievement? Socioeconomic status? (2) How is the individual adjusting to the various aspects or areas of his physical and psychological environment, including himself? What is his "self-concept?" Daily pattern of living (sleeping, eating, personal hygiene, study, work and recreational habits)? What are the nature and quality of his relationships with peers? Family? Teachers? Superiors and subordinates? General authorities (administrative officers, police)? What is his general level of adjustment? Personality integration? What are his predominant adjustment mechanisms?

Developmental History. (1) Has the individual had any significant physical illness which either affected his psycho-social development or left him with special disabilities and handicaps? (2) What is the family background of the individual? Intact or broken home? Number and order of siblings? Parents? Parental attitudes (acceptance, concentration, avoidance)? Parental identification? What were the individual's relationships to peers (accepted as equal, leader, follower, isolate, etc.)? (3) Early interests and abilities (hobbies, sports, organizations, etc.)? (4) Early vocational choices and plans (preferred occupations, age of first choice, motives for choices, indecision, etc.)? (5) School achievement and adjustment (grades, attitudes toward school, best and least liked subjects, favorite teachers, etc.)?

Problem Appraisal

(Identification of the individual's problem; assessment of his strengths as well as his weaknesses—e.g., motivation to change self or assume responsibility for problem solution, adaptability and flexibility, equanimity and sense of humor, constructive and integrative behavior)

Vocational Problem. (1) Classify according to one of the currently available diagnostic systems. (2) Assess the individual's vocational thinking. How involved is he in the decision-making process? How does he perceive occupations—as ends in themselves or means to other ends? Does he think in "either/or" terms about occupations? How does he "reason through" the problem of vocational choice? Is his thinking logical or does it have "psychological" fallacies in it—e.g., parataxic distortions? (3) Evaluate whether the individual's vocational problem arises because of immaturity or maladjustment. Does he simply not know how to choose an occupation, or is he conflicted to the extent that he cannot make the appropriate response?

Factors Related to Vocational Problem. (1) What part is played by the individual's family in his choice problem? (2) What is the relationship of his personality to his choice problem? (3) What other factors, such as financial resources, military obligations, marriage plans, academic achievement, etc., are relevant?

Prognostic Appraisal
(Predictions about the individual's future behavior in counseling or on the job)

Vocational Counseling. (1) Motivation: How well will the individual respond to counseling? Will he "work" on his problem, or will he want the counselor to solve it for him? Why did he apply for counseling? What are his expectations? (2) Interview behavior: How will the client respond verbally? Will he talk readily or not? Will he be verbally hostile or not? How will he relate to the counselor? Will he be dependent, aggressive, aloof, etc.? (3) Counseling goals and plans: What can be achieved with this individual? Should the counselor simply give him test and occupational information, or should he try to "think through" the vocational problem with the individual? Should the counselor focus only upon the specific choice problem of the individual, or should he help him learn how to solve other vocational problems which he may encounter in the future? Can the counseling be primarily vocational in nature, or should personal-adjustment counseling precede a consideration of the individual's vocational problem? How can the counseling best be implemented? What techniques should be used?

Vocational Adjustment. (1) Success: Which occupations are within the limits of the individual's capabilities? (2) Satisfaction: In which occupation is the client most likely to find satisfaction? What problems might his personality create for him on the job with respect to doing the work itself, getting along with others, adjusting to the physical conditions of the work, and in realizing his aspirations and goals (material rewards, recognition, prestige, etc.)? (3) Contingencies: What factors which are known might either facilitate or adversely affect the individual's future vocational adjustment if they should occur (for example, military service, marriage, change of job duties, transfer to another region of the country, slow or fast promotion, incompatible social life and obligations, etc.)?

Summary
(A "thumb-nail" sketch of the individual which pulls together the various parts of the vocational appraisal)

Based on information from "The Preliminary Appraisal in Vocational Counseling," by D. E. Super. In *Personnel and Guidance Journal,* 1957, *36,* 154-161.

---

understand what he did in the past is to analyze the sequence of events and the development of characteristics in order to ascertain the recurring themes and underlying trends" (Super, 1954, p. 13). From data on the patterning of the client's educational and vocational experiences, from knowledge of the subsequent careers of others like the client at the same life stage, and from assessment of the client's personal resources and competence to use them (Super, 1957b), the counselor derives what Pepinsky and Pepinsky (1954) have called a "hypothetical client," which serves as a basis for making predictions about future career development. That is, from this personal appraisal, and with cognizance of the problem appraisal, extrapolations are made as to the client's future career behavior and the effect which interventive career counseling may have upon it.

Throughout this process of accumulating data and making appraisals, the client is an active participant in extrapolating thema concerning his/her career choice and development. Super (1957b) states that "the best appraisals are made collectively" (p. 307) and that the counselor's "sharing the results of his appraisal with the client" constitutes a safeguard against faulty inferences (Super, 1957a, p. 158.) He has further stated that "the client's reactions to the data and to the counselor's tentative interpretations (often put in the form of a question beginning with 'could that mean . . . ') provide a healthy corrective for the counselor's own possible biases" (Super, 1959, pp. 536-540). By including the client in the appraisal process, Super largely resolves the dilemma, posed by the opposition of client-centered theory to the counselor's assuming an evaluative attitude, of whether to diagnose or not. No longer is the counselor solely responsible for the appraisal process. Endorsing and elaborating upon a similar viewpoint proposed by Tyler (1953/1961), Super (1957a) observes that "it will be instead a course of action for which the client is completely willing to take the consequences, *leading to a goal which is based on a cooperative realistic appraisal of the factors involved*" (italics are Super's addendum to Tyler) (p. 156). Thus, in developmental career counseling, as formulated primarily by Super but widely received and refined by others, appraisal (or diagnosis) plays a central role in "getting to know" the client, both hypothetically from life-history data and personally from his/her active engagement in the appraisal process.

2. Process. The course of developmental career counseling follows closely the broader spectrum of career development. What takes place in the contacts between client and counselor depends upon the point the client has reached on the continuum of career development. The counselor must first determine the career life stage of the client and assess his/her degree of career maturity (Super, 1955). If the client is relatively immature in career behavior, as compared with his/her age or peers (Super and Overstreet, 1960), then developmental career counseling concentrates upon orientation and explora-tion, which precede decision-making and reality-testing in the macrocosm of career development. With the career-immature client, Super and Overstreet (1960) observe that "it is not so much counseling concerning choice, as counseling to develop readiness for choice, to develop planfulness. It involves helping [the client] to understand the personal, social, and other factors which have a bearing on the making of educational and vocational decisions, and how they may operate in his own vocational development" (p. 157). In contrast, if the client is more career mature—i.e., has a more fully developed awareness of the need to choose a career—then the counselor proceeds differently. "Working with a client who is vocationally mature is essentially the familiar process of vocational counseling. It involves helping him to assemble, review, and assimilate relevant information about himself and about his situation, which will enable him to draw immediately called-for conclusions as to the implications of these choices for future decisions" (Super and Overstreet, 1960, p. 150). In sum, the overall process of career development progresses from orientation and readiness for career choice to decision-making and reality-testing, and the developmental career counselor initiates counseling at that point in the process which the client has reached.

3. Outcomes. The immediate, and more circumscribed, objective of developmental career counseling is to facilitate and enhance the client's career development, whether this means fostering increased awareness of the world of work or mastering the career developmental tasks of choosing and implementing a career goal. The maturation of the client toward these desiderata of career development can be charted on a career-maturity profile, which encompasses several dimensions of career behavior (Super, 1955; Crites, 1973). The latter include Consistency of Career Choice, Realism of Career Choice, Career Choice Competencies and Career Choice Attitudes (Crites, 1974). The more a client develops ("gains") along these dimensions, the more efficacious the career counseling is. But there is a broader, more inclusive goal of developmental career counseling which Super (1955) would propose:

> One underlying hypothesis has been that, by relieving tensions, clarifying feelings, giving insight, helping attain success, and developing a feeling of competence in one important area of adjustment, it is possible to release the individual's ability to cope more adequately with other aspects of living, thus bringing about improvements in his general adjustment. A second hypothesis underlying the approach used is that this is best done by building on the individual's assets, by working with his strengths rather than with his weaknesses (p. 217).

That these hypotheses are viable ones is evidenced not only by the demonstrated empirical relationship (moderate positive) between general and career adjustment (Super, 1957a; Crites, 1969) but also by the studies of Williams (1962) and Williams and Hills (1962), in which it was found that self-ideal congruence, as an index of personal-adjustment status, significantly increases as a by-product of career counseling *without* direct treatment of the client's personality functioning. In short, career counseling can further both career *and* personal development.

Much as the model of developmental career counseling reflects an integration of different conceptual and substantive emphases, so too the *methods* of this approach constitute a synthesis of diverse counseling procedures. They have been drawn by Super and others primarily from the trait-and-factor and client-centered orientations, although the influence of developmental principles is also apparent. That the synthesis is more than a superficial eclecticism follows from Super's (1951) imaginative and meaningful interweaving of career counseling conceived as information-giving and as personal therapy. His basic premise is that people are both rational *and* emotional and that, therefore, "the best vocational counseling is a combination of the two, somewhere between the theoretical extremes" (Super, 1951, p. 91). He (Super, 1951) then describes such a *via media* in terms of the kinds of questions the counselor may assist the client in answering:

"What sort of person do I *think* I am? How do I feel about myself as I think I am? What sort of person would I *like* to be? What are my values and needs? What are my aptitudes and interests? What can I do to reconcile my self-ideal with my real self? What outlets are there for me with my needs, values, interests and aptitudes? How can I make use of these outlets?" (p. 91). Consonant with the foci of these questions, upon both the objective and subjective facets of the client's personality and environment, are the *modi operandi* of developmental career counseling: its interview techniques, test interpretation procedures, and uses of occupational information.

1. Interview techniques. Because Super (1957a) sees career counseling as dealing with both the rational and the emotional aspects of self-exploration, decision-making, and reality-testing, he contends that, if the techniques of interviewing are appropriate and consistent, they should occur in approximately the following cycle:

a. Nondirective problem exploration and self-concept portrayal.
b. Directive topic setting, for further exploration.
c. Nondirective reflection and clarification of feeling for self-acceptance and insight.
d. Directive exploration of factual data from tests, occupational pamphlets, extracurricular experiences, grades, etc., for reality testing.
e. Nondirective exploration and working through of attitudes and feelings aroused by reality testing.
f. Nondirective consideration of possible lines of action, for· help in decision making (p. 308).

Kilby (1949) has outlined a similar sequence of the cyclical use of directive and nondirective interviewing techniques in career counseling, and both he and Super give examples of how they can be used by the counselor to interact with the client, which are too extensive to cite here. Suffice it to say that the essence of the "cyclical" approach is to respond directively to content statements by the client and nondirectively to expressions of feeling. Thus, the counselor ranges back and forth among such response categories as restatement, reflection, clarification, summary, interpretation and confrontation.

2. Test interpretation. The philosophy and pragmatics of using tests in developmental career counseling which Super has evolved, as is true of his entire approach, synthesizes the best of other orientations into a coherent method for disseminating psychometrics to the client, so that they will be maximally useful. The rationale for his use of tests stems from the distinction between *saturation* and *precision* testing, the former referring to a battery of tests administered to the client usually after a short, preliminary interview (as in trait-and-factor career counseling), and the latter designating individual test administration throughout the course of career counseling. With reference to precision testing, Super (1950) describes it as: "testing which is done as part of the counseling process, to get needed facts as these facts are needed and as the individual is ready to use them. It is *testing-in-counseling*" (p. 96). As such, the client is intimately involved in selecting, taking and interpreting the tests, and, as a consequence, the likelihood increases that "the test results will be accepted and used intelligently by the client" (p. 96). This is particularly the case if the counselor orients the client with respect to the precision use of tests in career counseling. Structuring how the process will unfold, both verbally and nonverbally, gives the client an explicit expectation of what is going to happen and counteracts the stereotype of saturation testing which many clients bring to the initial interview (Super and Crites, 1962, pp. 613-620). The thrust of using tests in developmental career counseling, then, is to maximize their value in decision making (1) by administering them in a discriminating way, and (2) by involving the client in every phase of the process.

3. Occupational information. To inform the client about the structure of the world of work, occupational trends and forecasts, job duties and tasks, and employment opportunities, traditional types of occupational information can be presented by brochures, pamphlets or volumes like the *Occupational Outlook Handbook*. The most appropriate information for developmental career counseling, however, is the description of career patterns in different occupational pursuits. There have been some studies of career patterns, notably those of Davidson and Anderson (1937) and Miller and Form (1951), but they are out of date and dealt only with occupational level, not field. Super (1954) observes that there are at least six kinds of descriptive data on career patterns which are needed for developmental career counseling:

a. What are the typical entry, intermediate, and regular adult occupations of persons from different socio-economic levels?

b. To what extent do "regular adult occupations" exist, and what is the relationship between parental socio-economic level and having a regular adult occupation?

c. What are the lines and rates of movement from entry toward regular adult occupation?

d. What factors are related to the direction and rate of movement from one job or occupation to another?

e. What is the relationship between occupational field and factors, such as accessibility of the occupation or industry, and the possession of various aptitudes, values, and personality characteristics?

f. What is the relationship of differences between actual and parental occupational levels to possible causal factors, such as accessibility of the occupation or industry, and the possession of aptitudes, interests, values, personality characteristics? (pp. 17-18).

Unfortunately, both private publishers and governmental agencies, as well as professional organizations, continue to proliferate occupational information which is largely irrelevant for developmental career counseling. In lieu of career-pattern data, the career counselor must rely upon his/her knowledge of career psychology, leavened with astute observation and personal experience.

Comment. The hallmark of developmental career counseling is its synthesis of several theoretical and procedural strains, particularly the trait-and-factor and client-centered. But it goes beyond these and casts them into the context of the client's ongoing career development, which Super (1957b) aptly characterizes as "coterminal" with career counseling. Some may contend, however, that even as comprehensive an approach as this suffers from conceptual lacunae which make it less than optimally effective. Psychodynamically oriented career counselors might question the basically descriptive or normative, rather than explanatory, nature of developmental concepts and principles, whereas certain behavioristically inclined career counselors might contend that the historical focus of developmental career counseling is unnecessary, since career behavior is largely conditioned by its consequences, not its antecedents. Perhaps these are less short-comings of commission than they are of omission. Only recently have measures of career maturity (Super, 1974) been constructed and related to other aspects of personality functioning (Crites, 1973). Likewise, conceptualization of learning models of career development has just begun (Crites, 1971), but research designed to test them has been initiated (Oliver, 1973). All of which leads to the conclusion that, although developmental career counseling may still be incomplete in certain respects, it is the most comprehensive and coherent system of assisting clients with career problems which has as yet been formulated, and it may be refined even further by articulating its relationship to learning phenomena and processes.

Behavioral Career Counseling

It is more accurate to refer to the *model* for this approach in the plural than the singular. Goodstein (1972) observes that, although they share common antecedents in the experimental psychology of learning, there are two distinct orientations in behavioral counseling: one which he terms the *indirect*, which focuses upon the linguistic mediational variables which precede and elicit overt responses, and the other the *direct*, which concentrates upon the consequences of responses—whether they are followed by a rewarding or punishing state of affairs. A further differentiation might also be made between two emphases within direct behavioral counseling, which might be labeled behavioral-*theoretic* and behavioral-*pragmatic*. As these designations connote, the former draws upon concepts and principles from learning theory to explain career behaviors and to deduce counseling methods for changing them, whereas the latter proceeds more inductively and empirically to identify those techniques which "work" in bringing about behavioral changes. The recognized spokesmen of the two viewpoints are Goodstein (1972) for the theoretic and Krumboltz and Thoresen (1969) for the pragmatic. These relative theoretical dispositions are juxtaposed to each other, when they differ pointedly, in the discussion of diagnosis, process, and outcome which follows as well as with indirect behavioral counseling.

   1. Diagnosis. Goodstein (1972) attributes a central role to anxiety in the etiology of behavioral problems in general and career-choice problems in particular. He makes a detailed analysis of the part which anxiety can play, both as an antecedent and a consequent, in career indecision. He distinguishes between what might be called simple *indecision* and pervasive *indecisiveness* (Tyler, 1961). These two types of client choice problems can be conceptualized as shown in Figure 2 (Crites, 1969), where it can be seen that they develop sequentially from different origins. The principal etiological factor in simple indecision, according to Goodstein, is lack of information about self and work due to a limitation of experience, much as is assumed in the classical trait-and-factor approach. The client cannot make a choice, or possibly makes an unrealistic one, and as a consequence feels anxious about not having mastered the career developmental task (often expressed socially as "What are you going to do when you grow up?") of declaring an appropriate vocation. Note that in this process the anxiety is a *consequent*, not an antecedent, of the indecision. In contrast, indecisiveness arises from long-standing anxiety associated with decision-making, which precedes the task of career choice. It is not infrequently attributed by clients to domineering or over-demanding parents. For this individual, who is often paralyzed in making *any* kind of choice, anxiety also follows failure to decide upon a career; i.e., it is both an antecedent *and* a consequent, thereby compounding the client's feelings of discomfort and inadequacy. Goodstein (1972) concludes: "One of the goals of diagnosis in counseling and therapy with such cases is the identification of the cues that arouse this anxiety so that the anxiety can be eliminated or reduced, permitting the client to now learn appropriate skills" (p. 261).

   Krumboltz and Thoresen (1969) and their associates seldom mention either anxiety or diagnosis in their pragmatically oriented version of behavioral career counseling. Rather, they prefer the rubrics *behavioral analysis* or *problem identification*, and they closely relate these to the specification of goals for counseling. That is, the client's difficulties are complementary to the goals ("outcomes") which client and counselor strive to achieve through their interactions with each other. Thus, if the client's presenting problem is that he/she has "no career choice," then the goal of the career counseling is to make a career choice. Krumboltz and Thoresen (1969) enumerate seven general categories of problems ("difficulties in formulating goals") which may beset clients in counseling:

	Limitation of Experience (Insufficient opportunity to acquire or learn adaptive or adequate responses)	Inadequate or Non-adaptive Behavior (No vocational choice; unrealistic vocational choice)	Failure (Unable to solve choice problem)	Anxiety (Consequent) (Conflict between inability to solve choice problem and social pressure to do so)
(INDECISION)				
	Availability of Experience (Sufficient opportunity to acquire or learn adaptive or adequate responses)	Anxiety (Antecedent) (Making a choice is anxiety-arousing, because it may mean defying parents, becoming independent, etc., all of which "cue" anxiety)	Nonuse of Learning Opportunities (May have appropriate information for making a choice, but anxiety prevents him from utilizing it, or anxiety may interfere with acquisition of information, even though opportunity to learn is available)	Inadequate or Non-adaptive Behavior (No vocational choice or unrealistic choice)
(INDECISIVENESS)				

Figure 2. The role of anxiety in indecision and indecisiveness. (Adapted from "Behavioral Views of Counseling," by L. D. Goodstein. In B. Stefflre & W. H. Grant (Eds.), *Theories of Counseling.* Copyright 1972 by McGraw-Hill, Inc. Used with permission of McGraw-Hill Book Company.)

a. The problem is someone else's behavior.
b. The problem is expressed as a feeling.
c. The problem is the absence of a goal.
d. The problem is that the desired behavior is undesirable.
e. The problem is that the client does not know his behavior is inappropriate.
f. The problem is a choice conflict.
g. The problem is a vested interest in not identifying any problem (pp. 9-18).

Of these problems, those which bear upon career counseling are indecision ("absence of a goal"), unrealism ("expressed feeling" about overly high aspirations), and multipotentiality ("choice conflict" among equally desirable alternatives). Within each of these problem types, specific behaviors can be delineated as the goals of career counseling (see "Outcomes").

2. *Process.* In the behavioral-*theoretic* view of career counseling, if it is determined diagnostically that a client's decision-making problems are a function of antecedent anxiety, then it is assumed that this anxiety must be eliminated *before* effective cognitive consideration of career choice can be undertaken. In other words, the elimination of anxiety is a *sine qua non* for subsequent career decision-making. In this case, then, the process of career counseling has two stages, much as Shoben (1949) has proposed for psychotherapy: during the first, the counselor attempts to eliminate the anxiety associated with decision-making, whether career or otherwise, primarily through counterconditioning it; and in the second, after the client has been freed of the interfering effects of anxiety, instrumental learning can occur, in which the client can acquire those responses—e.g., information-seeking—needed to choose a career. If the client's problem is one of simple indecision, however, with no evidence of debilitating previous anxiety, then career counseling would begin with stage two, instrumental learning. What this client needs to learn is *how* to make a career choice, *which* options are available to him/her, *what* the consequences of each are, etc.—in short, to be exposed to the experiences which have not been available in his/her prior career development. Thus, the process of career counseling, as deduced from behavior theory primarily by Goodstein (1972), varies with the etiology of the client's problem: if it involves antecedent anxiety, there are the two stages of counterconditioning and instrumental learning, but if it stems from limited decision-making experiences, it consists only of instrumental learning.

Juxtaposed to this model is that of Krumboltz, Thoresen and others, the most recent exposition of which has been summarized by Krumboltz and Baker (1973), who outline eight steps taken by the counselor and client in the course of career counseling:

a. Defining the problem and the client's goals.
b. Agreeing mutually to achieve counseling goals.
c. Generating alternative problem solutions.

    d. Collecting information about the alternatives.
    e. Examining the consequences of the alternatives.
    f. Revaluing goals, alternatives and consequences.
    g. Making the decision or tentatively selecting an alternative contingent upon new developments and new opportunities.
    h. Generalizing the decision-making process to new problems (p. 240).

This series of mutual actions on the part of the counselor and client generally follows informed opinion on how career decisions can best be made (Gelatt, 1962; Yabroff, 1969), but it is not necessarily invariant: "The sequence may vary, but the priorities remain" (Krumboltz and Baker, 1973, p. 240). Conspicuous by its absence in this process is any mention of anxiety or its reduction. Rather, the focus is upon "the eternal environment" (Krumboltz and Baker, 1973, p. 262). Behavioral-pragmatic career counseling, therefore, appears to be closely aligned with the view expressed by Eysenck (1960) and others that "anxiety elimination should not be the counselor's primary concern but rather that therapy should be directed at the elimination of nonadjustive behavior pattern (sic) and/or providing conditions for learning more adjustive responses" (Goodstein, 1972, p. 274).

    3. Outcomes. The two hypothesized outcomes of behavioral-*theoretic* career counseling are (1) elimination or reduction of both antecedent and consequent anxiety and/or (2) acquisition of decision-making skills. Whether both outcomes are expected depends upon the extent to which anxiety preceded the emergence of the client's problem, as mentioned previously. An experimental paradigm for evaluating the effectiveness of this variety of behavioral counseling has been designed (Crites, 1969) but not yet utilized in research. The goals of behavioral-*pragmatic* career counseling are akin to the general one of skill acquisition but are more idiosyncratic. Krumboltz (1966a) states that any set of goals for counseling should satisfy three criteria:

    a. *The goals of counseling should be capable of being stated differently for each individual client. . . .*
    b. *The goals of counseling for each client should be compatible with, though not necessarily identical to, the values of the counselor. . . .*
    c. *The degree to which the goals of counseling are attained by each client should be observable. . .* (italics in original) (pp. 154-155).

Given these constraints, he then identifies three counseling goals which are consistent with them: (1) altering maladaptive behavior, (2) learning the decision-making process and (3) preventing problems. Ultimately, however, Krumboltz (1966a) contends that any "type of behavior change desired by a client and agreed to by his counselor" (p. 155), regardless of the above criteria, is an acceptable goal (outcome) of counseling, whether it deals with career or some other aspect of functioning.

    The methods of behavioral career counseling, of whichever subspecies, sometimes strike counselors of other persuasions as "cookbookish" and unduly specific, and they question their expediency in terms of broader goals and values (Patterson, 1964)—e.g., the "self-actualization" of the client. The behaviorists are quick to reply that they subscribe fully to such ideals as "self-actualization," but "as a counseling goal, the abstract and ambiguous terminology makes it difficult for clients or counselors to know what they are trying to do and when they have succeeded" (Krumboltz and Thoresen, 1969, p. 2). Hence the emphasis upon, and commitment to, whatever counseling technique "works." What may seem like blatant pragmatism to some, however, is tempered by the behavioral career counselor's recognition of his/her relationship to the client as a basic dimension of their interaction, along with communication. Goodstein (1972) notes:

> Several writers in this area, especially Wolpe (1958, 1969), point out the need for establishing a good interpersonal relationship as an integral part of the treatment process. Indeed, it has been noted that an essential role for the counselor to play is that of a reinforcing agent, a role that depends upon the developing counseling relationship (p. 281).

It should be understood, therefore, that the interview techniques, methods of test interpretation and uses of occupational information described below are sketched in relief against a background of the relationship which develops between counselor and client.

 1. Interview techniques. For the alleviation of anxiety, particularly that which is etiologically significant in aberrant career decision-making processes, Goodstein (1972) proposed three procedures, which are widely used in behaviorally-oriented psychotherapy and which are applicable to career counseling: (1) desensitization, (2) inhibitory conditioning and (3) counterconditioning. He notes that these techniques are theoretically distinguishable but that most "real-life attempts to eliminate or reduce anxiety would seem to involve some combination of these methods, and it is difficult to find pure procedures" (p. 264). The most general, and hence most potent, of them is counterconditioning, which involves desensitization as well. For the acquisition of skills—e.g., information-seeking, deliberation and decision behaviors—Goodstein recommends (1) counselor reinforcement of desired client responses, (2) social modeling and vicarious learning and (3) discrimination learning. He discusses these techniques generally and cites some examples, but he does not explicate them in nearly the detail provided by Krumboltz and Thoresen (1969) in their "casebook" for behavioral counseling. No attempt will be made here to review and summarize these procedures, except to note that none of them which are designed to reduce "self-defeating fears and anxiety" are also suggested by Krumboltz and .Thoresen (1969) for improving "deficient decision-making skills." Again the fundamental variance between the behavioral-*theoretic* and behavioral-*pragmatic* conceptualizations of career counseling is highlighted, the role of anxiety in career problems being the differentia.

2. Test interpretation. Allusions to the use of tests in career counseling, much less extended discussions, by either those of a theoretical or a pragmatic behavioral bent are difficult to find. The reason is, of course, that they subscribe to an S-R model of behavior, with or without intervening variables like anxiety, whereas most tests are constructed within an R-R model, with S (items) standardized across individuals (Underwood, 1957; Crites, 1961). In other words, test scores measure individual differences in behavior, but they seldom reflect individual/environment interactions, which are of primary concern to the behavioral career counselor. Consequently, traditional tests (aptitude, interest, personality) are typically eschewed, and objective indices of behavior *in situ* are gathered, although some effort is being expended to assess S-R situations with paper-and-pencil instruments (Goldfried and D'Zurilla, 1969). Krumboltz and Baker (1973) do allow that "objective empirical data can be useful to counselor and client in their study of outcome probabilities" (p. 255) as part of "examining the consequences of alternatives" (see "Process" above). In addition, they present a counselor/client dialogue, in which the counselor reports entrance test scores as expectancy data much as a client-centered career counselor would—viz., as simple statistical predictions. But they otherwise ignore tests, although they conclude from Thorndike's (1935) early study that interests "are assumed to be learned; they are acquired by experience" (p. 274). They reason further that "if interests are learned, then it should be possible to alter, shape, promote, or diminish them by means of experimental intervention" (p. 274), and they cite studies by Krumboltz, Sheppard, Jones, Johnson and Baker (1967) and by Krumboltz, Baker and Johnson (1968) which they interpret as confirmatory of this hypothesis.

3. Occupational information. Some of the most creative and imaginative contributions which have been made by behavioral career counselors are in the area of occupational information. Krumboltz and his associates (Krumboltz and Bergland, 1969; Bergland and Krumboltz, 1969; Hamilton and Krumboltz, 1969; Krumboltz and Sheppard, 1969) have systematically devised a set of problem-solving career kits which simulate selected activities from 20 different occupations, including accountant, electronics technician, police officer, X-ray technologist, etc. The specifications for these kits were as follows:

> (1) the problem should be realistic and representative of the type of problems faced by members of the occupation; (2) 95 percent of the target population (high school students) should have no difficulty in reading the problem; (3) the problem should be considered intrinsically interesting by the majority of the target population; (4) at least 75 percent of the target population should be able to read the material and solve the problem successfully within 50 minutes; (5) the problem should be completely self-contained and self-administered (Krumboltz and Sheppard, 1969).

Evidence from try-outs and evaluations by experts indicates that the kits largely fulfill these criteria. Results are also available from several studies (Krumboltz, Sheppard, Jones, Johnson and Baker, 1967; Krumboltz, Baker and Johnson, 1968) which establish that the kits are useful in stimulating further career exploration and decision-making. Career counselors can use them with the expectation that clients will learn at least as much, if not considerably more, about different careers than they will from printed occupational information.

Comment. Krumboltz (1966b) has heralded the behavioral approach as no less than a "revolution in counseling," and the temptation to agree unreservedly would be great, were it not that several disquieting issues are yet to be resolved. Foremost among these concerns is the role of anxiety in the etiology of problems in career decision-making. If a counselor follows the current formulation of behavioral-*pragmatic* career counseling, he/she would take the client's presenting problem of "no choice," for example, at face value and most likely agree to work toward the goal of "deciding upon a career," using reinforcement and modeling and simulation in the process. For insufficient prior learning experiences, this would probably be effective career counseling, but for the client with pervasive indecisiveness the outcome would be problematical. How many of these clients have career counselors expended their best information-giving and decision-making efforts on, only to have them terminate counseling with the epitaph "Well, I still don't really know what I want to do." It is not long before the mounting frustration of the counselor prompts him/her to wonder whether there is some competing response tendency which inhibits the client from making a career decision, given the relevant information about self and work or not. The behavioral-*theoretic* point of view would posit that it is the anxiety associated with decision-making, occasioned by punishing past experiences, which prevents the indecisive client from declaring a career choice. Once this anxiety has been sufficiently reduced, information-seeking and decisional responses can be learned, or made if they were already in the client's behavioral repertoire, and the instrumental phase of career counseling can proceed. A resolution of this issue, both theoretically and pragmatically, appears critical, if a coherent system of behavioral career counseling is to be formulated.

SUMMARY

Each of the approaches to career counseling which has been reviewed makes a unique contribution to the ways in which clients can be assisted in their career decision-making. From the trait-and-factor orientation, the model of "matching men and jobs" is as viable today as it was in yesteryear, and it finds expression, in one form or another, in most of the other approaches. The client-centered point of view has heightened the career counselor's sensitivity to the role which the client should play throughout the decision-making process and has highlighted the implementation of the self-concept in an occupational role. The psychodynamic framework broadens even more the scope of career counseling to encompass motivational constructs and conflicts within the context of interacting aspects of personal and career development, incorporating procedures from both the trait-and-factor and client-centered approaches for its implementation. Equally systematic, but with greater emphasis upon maturational than motivational factors in decision-making, developmental career counseling accepts the client at whatever vocational life stage he/she has reached and attempts to increase the career maturity of the client by providing relevant conative and cognitive learning experiences. And, behavioral career counseling, whether direct or indirect, theoretic or pragmatic, has made counselors aware, as they have never been before, of the actual behaviors which they and their clients are striving to change. The task is now to synthesize these several theoretical and procedural contributions, each of which has its unique value but none of which is sufficient, into a comprehensive approach to career counseling that has both generality and specificity in its applicability. In a later article, a "provisional try" will be made to accomplish this task.

REFERENCES

Arbuckle, D. S. *Counseling: An introduction.* Boston: Allyn & Bacon, 1961.

Baer, M. F., & Roeber, E. C. *Occupational information: Its nature and use.* Chicago: Science Research Associates, 1951.

Beall, L., & Bordin, E. S. The development and personality of engineers. *Personnel and Guidance Journal,* 1964, *43,* 23-32.

Bergland, B. W., & Krumboltz, J. D. An optimal grade level for career exploration. *Vocational Guidance Quarterly,* 1969, *18,* 29-33.

Bixler, R. H., & Bixler, V. H. Clinical counseling in vocational guidance. *Journal of Clinical Psychology,* 1945, *1,* 186-190.

Bixler, R. H., & Bixler, V. H. Test interpretation in vocational counseling. *Educational and Psychological Measurement,* 1946, *6,* 145-156.

Bordin, E. S. Diagnosis in counseling and psychotherapy. *Educational and Psychological Measurement,* 1946, *6,* 169-184.

Bordin, E. S. *Psychological counseling.* New York: Appleton-Century-Crofts, 1955.

Bordin, E. S. *Psychological counseling* (2nd ed.). New York: Appleton-Century-Crofts, 1968.

Bordin, E. S., & Bixler, R. H. Test selection: A process of counseling. *Educational and Psychological Measurement,* 1946, *6,* 361-373.

Bordin, E. S., & Kopplin, D. A. Motivational conflict and vocational development. *Journal of Counseling Psychology,* 1973, *20,* 154-161.

Bordin, E. S., Nachmann, B., & Segal, S. J. An articulated framework for vocational development. *Journal of Counseling Psychology,* 1963, *10,* 107-116.

Bown, O. H. The client-centered approach to educational and vocational guidance. *The Personal Counselor,* 1947, *2,* 1-5.

Brayfield, A. H. Putting occupational information across. In A. H. Brayfield (Ed.), *Readings in modern methods of counseling.* New York: Appleton-Century-Crofts, 1950. Pp. 212-220.

Buehler, C. *Der menschliche Lebensauf als psychologisches Problem.* Leipzig: Hirzel, 1933.

Cautela, J. R. The factor of psychological need in occupational choice. *Personnel and Guidance Journal,* 1959, *38,* 46-48.

Christensen, T. E. Functions of occupational information in counseling. *Occupations,* 1949, *28,* 11-14.

Colby, K. M. *A primer for psychotherapists.* New York: Ronald, 1951.

Combs, A. Nondirective techniques and vocational counseling. *Occupations,* 1947, *25,* 261-267.

Covner, B. J. Nondirective interviewing techniques in vocational counseling. *Journal of Consulting Psychology,* 1947, *11,* 70-73.

Crites, J. O. A model for the measurement of vocational maturity. *Journal of Counseling Psychology,* 1961, *8,* 255-259.

Crites, J. O. *Vocational psychology.* New York: McGraw-Hill, 1969.

Crites, J. O. The maturity of vocational attitudes and learning processes in adolescence. Paper presented at the 17th Annual Convention of the International Congress of Applied Psychology, Liege, Belgium, 1971.

Crites, J. O. *Theory and research handbook for the Career Maturity Inventory.* Monterey, Calif.: CTB/McGraw-Hill, 1973.

Crites, J. O. Career development processes: A model of vocational maturity. In E. L. Herr (Ed.), *Vocational guidance and human development.* Boston: Houghton Mifflin, 1974.

Darley, J. G. The structure of the systematic case study in individual diagnosis and counseling. *Journal of Consulting Psychology,* 1940, *4,* 215-220.

Darley, J. G. Conduct of the interview. In A. H. Brayfield (Ed.), *Readings in modern methods of counseling.* New York: Appleton-Century-Crofts, 1950. Pp. 265-272.

Davidson, P. E., & Anderson, H. B. *Occupational mobility in an American community.* Palo Alto: Stanford University Press, 1937.

Doleys, E. J. Are there "kinds" of counselors? *Counseling News and Views,* 1961, *13,* 5-9.

Dymond, R. F. Adjustment changes over therapy from self-sorts. In C. R. Rogers & R. F. Dymond (Eds.), *Psychotherapy and personality change.* Chicago: University of Chicago Press, 1954. Pp. 76-84.

Eysenck, J. H. (ed.). *Behavioral therapy and the neuroses.* New York: Macmillan, 1960.

Froehlich, C. P., & Moser, W. E. Do counselees remember test scores? *Journal of Counseling Psychology,* 1954, *1,* 149-152.

Galinsky, M. D. Personality development and vocational choice of clinical psychologists and physicists. *Journal of Counseling Psychology,* 1962, *9,* 299-305.

Gaudet, F. J., & Kulick, W. Who comes to a vocational guidance center? *Personnel and Guidance Journal,* 1954, *33,* 211-215.

Gelatt, A. B. Decision-making: A conceptual frame of reference for counseling. *Journal of Counseling Psychology,* 1962, *9,* 240-245.

Ginzberg, E., Ginsburg, S. W., Axelrad, S., & Herman, J. L. *Occupational choice.* New York: Columbia University Press, 1951.

Goldfried, M. R., & D'Zurilla, T. J. A behavioral-analytic model for assessing competence. In C. D. Spielberger (Ed.), *Current topics in clinical and community psychology.* Vol. 1. New York: Academic Press, 1969. Pp. 151-196.

Goodstein, L. D. Behavioral views of counseling. In B. Stefflre & W. H. Grant (Eds.), *Theories of counseling.* New York: McGraw-Hill, 1972. Pp. 243-286.

Goodstein, L. D., Crites, J. O., Heilbrun, A. B., Jr., & Rempel, P. P. The use of the California Psychological Inventory in a university counseling service. *Journal of Counseling Psychology,* 1961, *8,* 147-153.

Grummon, D. L. Client-centered theory. In B. Stefflre & W. H. Grant (Eds.), *Theories of counseling* (2nd ed.). New York: McGraw-Hill, 1972. Pp. 73-135.

Hahn, M. E., & Kendall, W. E. Some comments in defense of non-directive counseling. *Journal of Consulting Psychology,* 1947, *11,* 74-81.

Hamilton, J. A., & Krumboltz, J. D. Simulated work experience: How realistic should it be? *Personnel and Guidance Journal,* 1969, *48,* 39-44.

Hart, J. T., & Tomlinson, T. M. (Eds.). *New directions in client-centered therapy.* Boston: Houghton Mifflin, 1970.

Kamm, R. B., & Wrenn, C. G. Client acceptance of self-information in counseling. *Educational and Psychological Measurement,* 1950, *10,* 32-42.

Kiesler, D. J. Some myths of psychotherapy research and the search for a paradigm. *Psychological Bulletin,* 1966, *65,* 110-136.

Kilby, R. W. Some vocational counseling methods. *Educational and Psychological Measurement,* 1949, *19,* 173-192.

King, P. T., & Bennington, K. F. Psychoanalysis and counseling. In B. Stefflre & W. H. Grant (Eds.), *Theories of counseling.* New York: McGraw-Hill, 1972. Pp. 177-242.

Krumboltz, J. D. Behavioral goals for counseling. *Journal of Counseling Psychology,* 1966, *13,* 153-159. (a)

Krumboltz, J. D. (Ed.). *Revolution in counseling: Implications of behavioral science.* Boston: Houghton Mifflin, 1966..(b)

Krumboltz, J. D., & Baker, R. D. Behavioral counseling for vocational decision. In H. Borow (Ed.), *Career guidance for a new age.* Boston: Houghton Mifflin, 1973. Pp. 235-283.

Krumboltz, J. D., Baker, R. D., & Johnson, R. G. Vocational problem-solving experiences for stimulating career exploration and interest: Phase II. Final Report, Office of Education Grant 4-7-070111-2890. School of Education, Stanford University, 1968.

Krumboltz, J. D., & Bergland, B. W. Experiencing work almost like it is. *Educational Technology,* 1969, *9,* 47-49.

Krumboltz, J. D., & Sheppard, L. E. Vocational problem-solving experiences. In J. D. Krumboltz & C. E. Thoresen (Eds.), *Behavioral counseling: Cases and techniques.* New York: Holt, Rinehart & Winston, 1969. Pp. 293-306.

Krumboltz, J. D., Sheppard, L. E., Jones, G. B., Johnson, R. G., & Baker, R. D. Vocational problem-solving experiences for stimulating career exploration and interest. Final Report, Office of Education, Stanford University, 1967.

Krumboltz, J. D., & Thoresen, C. E. (Eds.), *Behavioral counseling: Cases and techniques.* New York: Holt, Rinehart & Winston, 1969.

Lofquist, L. H. *Vocational counseling with the physically handicapped.* New York: Appleton-Century-Crofts, 1957.

Miller, D. C., & Form, W. H. *Industrial sociology.* New York: Harper & Row, 1951.

Nachmann, B. Childhood experience and vocational choice in law, dentistry, and social work. *Journal of Counseling Psychology,* 1960, *7,* 243-250.

Oliver, L. Verbal reinforcement of career choice realism in relation to career attitude maturity. Unpublished manuscript, Department of Psychology, University of Maryland, 1973.

Parsons, F. *Choosing a vocation*. Boston: Houghton Mifflin, 1909.

Paterson, D. G., & Darley, J. G. *Men, women, and jobs*. Minneapolis: University of Minnesota Press, 1936.

Patterson, C. H. Counseling: Self-clarification and the helping relationship. In H. Borow (Ed.), *Man in a world at work*. Boston: Houghton Mifflin, 1964. Pp. 434-459.

Patterson, C. H. *Theories of counseling and psychotherapy* (2nd ed.). New York: Harper & Row, 1973.

Pepinsky, H. B., & Pepinsky, P. N. *Counseling theory and practice*. New York: Ronald, 1954.

Robinson, F. P. *Principles and procedures in student counseling*. New York: Harper, 1950.

Rogers, C. R. *Counseling and psychotherapy*. Boston: Houghton Mifflin, 1942.

Rogers, C. R. *Client-centered therapy*. Boston: Houghton Mifflin, 1951.

Rogers, C. R. The necessary and sufficient conditions of therapeutic personality change. *Journal of Consulting Psychology*, 1957, *21*, 95-103.

Rogers, C. R. A theory of therapy, personality, and interpersonal relationships, as developed in the client-centered framework. In S. Koch (Ed.), *Psychology: A study of a science*. Study I. *Conceptual and systematic*. Vol. 3. *Formulations of the person and the social context*. New York: McGraw-Hill, 1959. Pp. 184-256.

Rogers, C. R. *On becoming a person*. Boston: Houghton Mifflin, 1961.

Rusalem, H. New insights on the role of occupational information in counseling. *Journal of Counseling Psychology*, 1954, *1*, 84-88.

Samler, J. Occupational exploration in counseling: A proposed reorientation. In H. Borow (Ed.), *Man in a world at work*. Boston: Houghton Mifflin, 1964. Pp. 411-433.

Sanderson, H. *Basic concepts in vocational guidance*. New York: McGraw-Hill, 1954.

Seeman, J. A study of client self-selection of tests in vocational counseling. *Educational and Psychological Measurement*, 1948, *8*, 327-346.

Segal, S. J. A psychoanalytic analysis of personality factors in vocational choice. *Journal of Counseling Psychology*, 1961, *8*, 202-210.

Shoben, E. J., Jr. Psychotherapy as a problem in learning theory. *Psychological Bulletin, 1949, 46*, 366-392.

Super, D. E. *The dynamics of vocational adjustment*. New York: Harper, 1942.

Super, D. E. *Appraising vocational fitness*. New York: Harper, 1949.

Super, D. E. Testing and using test results in counseling. *Occupations*, 1950, *29*, 95-97.

Super, D. E. Vocational adjustment: Implementing a self-concept. *Occupations*, 1951, *30*, 88-92.

Super, D. E. Career patterns as a basis for vocational counseling. *Journal of Counseling Psychology*, 1954, *1*, 12-20.

Super, D. E. The dimensions and measurement of vocational maturity. *Teachers College Record*, 1955, *57*, 151-163.

Super, D. E. The preliminary appraisal in vocational counseling. *Personnel and Guidance Journal*, 1957, *36*, 154-161. (a)

Super, D. E. *The psychology of careers*. New York: Harper, 1957. (b)

Super, D. E. The critical ninth grade: Vocational choice or vocational exploration? *Personnel and Guidance Journal*, 1960, *39*, 106-109.

Super, D. E. (Ed.). *Computer-assisted counseling.* New York: Teachers College Press, 1970.

Super, D. E. (Ed.). *Measuring vocational maturity for counseling and evaluation.* Washington, D. C.: National Vocational Guidance Association, 1974.

Super, D. E., & Bachrach, P. B. *Scientific careers and vocational development theory.* New York: Teachers College Bureau of Publications, 1957.

Super, D. E., & Crites, J. O. *Appraising vocational fitness* (Rev. ed.). New York: Harper & Row, 1962.

Super, D. E., & Overstreet, P. L. *The vocational maturity of ninth grade boys.* New York: Teachers College Bureau of Publications, 1960.

Thompson, A. S. A rationale for vocational guidance. *Personnel and Guidance Journal,* 1954, *32,* 533-535.

Thorndike, E. L. *Adult interests.* New York: Macmillan, 1935.

Tyler, L. E. *The work of the counselor* (2nd ed.). New York: Appleton-Century-Crofts, 1961. (Originally published, 1953.)

Underwood, B. J. *Psychological research.* New York: Appleton-Century-Crofts, 1957.

Williams, J. E. Changes in self and other perceptions following brief educational-vocational counseling. *Journal of Counseling Psychology,* 1962, *9,* 18-30.

Williams, J. E., & Hills, D. A. More on brief educational-vocational counseling. *Journal of Counseling Psychology,* 1962, *9,* 366-368.

Williamson, E. G. *How to counsel students.* New York: McGraw-Hill, 1939. (a)

Williamson, E. G. The clinical method of guidance. *Review of Educational Research,* 1939, *9,* 214-217. (b)

Williamson, E. G. Vocational counseling: Trait-factor theory. In B. Stefflre (Ed.), *Theories of counseling.* New York: McGraw-Hill, 1965. Pp. 193-214.

Williamson, E. G. Trait-factor theory and individual differences. In B. Stefflre & W. H. Grant (Eds.), *Theories of counseling* (2nd ed.). New York: McGraw-Hill, 1972. Pp. 136-176.

Witryol, S. L., & Boly, L. F. Positive diagnosis in personality counseling of college students. *Journal of Counseling Psychology,* 1954, *1,* 63-69.

Wolpe, J. *Psychotherapy by reciprocal inhibition.* Stanford, Calif.: Stanford University Press, 1958.

Wolpe, J. *The practice of behavior therapy.* New York: Pergamon, 1969.

Yabroff, W. Learning decision making. In J. D. Krumboltz & C. E. Thoresen (Eds.), *Behavioral counseling: Cases and techniques.* New York: Holt, Rinehart & Winston, 1969. Pp. 329-343.

RESPONSES TO THE CRITES ANALYSIS 3

Career Counseling: Then, Now, and What's Next?

JOHN L. HOLLAND
The Johns Hopkins University

I had mixed reactions to John Crites' review. I admire his skill and tenacity for coping with the history of vocational counseling (alias "career counseling"). At the same time, his taxonomy of approaches to career counseling was discouraging, for it is a vivid reminder of where vocational counseling has been and largely still is: we continue to devote much effort to the most expensive method of assistance (interviewing) and to intellectual wars about the best approach.

I cannot resist engaging in this endless and pleasurable activity. For example, Crites beats up the trait-and-factor approach one more time by calling it "atheoretical . . . analytical . . . atomistic," but he defends the high priests of that approach by referring to them as "highly competent and enlightened originators." As an adherent of a modified trait-and-factor view, it is easy to reply that we are not all alike; we can also be theoretical, synthetic, and even developmental. Adherents of other orientations can provide similar defenses, revisionistic statements, corrections, or "Who me?" disclaimers.

It seems more helpful to review some promising approaches that are just now getting underway rather than to score Crites' review for its historical accuracy. My avoidance of this internecine activity should not be interpreted as a sign of mellowing or even of a midcareer crisis, but rather as an assumption that these activities have had a low rate of intellectual return. In addition, it appears more useful to anticipate a portion of Crites' next article— "a comprehensive approach" to vocational counseling. In short, I have used Crites' review as a stimulus to report some encouraging developments and trends in vocational assistance, to indicate some goals and yardsticks for improving vocational service, and to indicate some common deficiencies in vocational counseling approaches.

COMMON WEAKNESSES

Aside from their intellectual and scientific problems, the major vocational counseling approaches share a common core of societal, financial, organizational, and practical weaknesses. First, and perhaps most important, these interview-oriented methods have not met the societal need for service. It is unlikely that our society will ever have the resources to provide one-to-one vocational counseling. Second, despite some protestation about diagnosis, most people receive the same treatment whether they need it or not. Differential treatment or levels of treatment from superficial to reconstruction usually depend upon a professional's predilections rather than upon a person's special needs. Third, vocational counseling is one of many services in an asystematic group of services which often work independently rather than cooperatively. Formal services usually have only fortuitous relations with other environmental influences related to student or employee vocational decision-making. Fourth, vocational professionals often suffer from psychological sentimentality and professional ambition which prevent them from seeking solutions for their clients outside the realms of listening or talking carefully. These difficulties have been compounded by the yearly selection of people who, in turn, prefer to sit a lot, talk or listen, although we need more people interested in creating systems of efficient service and managing or evaluating such services. Other professionals wail about the complexity of human motivation, the sheer amount of occupational information, the difficulty of planning in a changing society, and the need for meaning, as if the only road to peace of mind lay on the lips or ears of a sophisticated counselor (Warnath, 1971). This intellectual trash has to be counteracted so counseling people can see that there are many roads to effective service and that roads with superficial surfaces (workbooks and tests, etc.) can be just as useful as roads paved with hearts of gold (psychological counseling).

NEW DEVELOPMENTS AND TRENDS

There are several encouraging trends in research, thought, and service. Recent studies of actual job descriptions reveal that there are only four to eight different kinds of occupations (Jeanneret and McCormick, 1972). Other studies of old and new vocational-interest inventories also indicate that four to eight categories of interest account for most interest inventory scales and, equally important, these interest factors parallel the job factors. Consequently, we have some useful ways for organizing that infinite appearing set of occupational labels. In addition, the usefulness of seeing vocational problems in a developmental context has received increasing support (Super et al., 1967).

Along with more useful information for organizing vocational information for understanding how people get to a particular group of jobs, there are some signs of more constructive attitudes and beliefs about vocational counseling and vocational problems. They include:

1. A frank admission, by a few, that the old methods will never allow us to reach everyone who needs vocational assistance.

2. A realization that we must organize vocational assistance to give maximum benefit.

3. A belief in levels of treatment—everyone does not need every treatment at every age level—and a corollary belief that superficial-appearing treatment may be as important to a person as "fundamental" treatments offered by a professional.

4. An acceptance of the possibility that the provision of information about self and careers in comprehensive, accessible, and inexpensive ways may do for vocational counseling what penicillin has done for medicine.

5. A begrudging understanding of the cost/benefit ratio.

I have outlined some of these ideas in more detail elsewhere (Holland, 1973a, 1973b), but here I would like to review some of the developments which I think flow from these new realizations, the older approaches, and some new research.

For example, the cutting of budgets has been a powerful stimulus for both demoralization and creative activity. Some counseling psychologists have simply cried; others have developed some more efficient approaches for reaching large numbers. Career and curricular information services have been developed to deliver vocational assessment and information in dormitories, counseling centers, or special facilities (Johnston, 1973; Reardon et al., 1973; Helms, 1973; and others). These centers use self-administered vocational assessment experience, workbooks, and occupational information by organizing materials in single occupational classification schemes, so that a user's initiative is encouraged, the cost of service is reduced, and more people get help.

Another group has been developing group activities—seminars, workshops, etc.—which capitalize on the techniques of the encounter movement and new therapies. In so doing they may have rejuvenated vocational group counseling (Garfield and Nelson, 1973; Magoon, 1969; Pappas et al., 1972). Informal and experiential reports suggest that this form of treatment may be unusually helpful for people who find individual and self-administered help ineffective. At any rate, it is responsive to the need to make more efficient use of limited resources and appears to be at least as helpful as traditional counseling.

Special adult services for poor people and for women have also been increasing. Likewise, career education remains a major movement because of its strong federal support. It is unlikely that career education will survive once its financial support diminishes, because it entails many major administrative, substantive, and theoretical weaknesses: (1) a hyper-extension of what we know about vocational development (many applications without substantive support), (2) an atheoretical and *a priori* classification scheme, and (3) an excessive comprehensiveness and complexity, so that it is especially vulnerable to breakdown, uncoordination, and misdirection. Many women's services sponsored by the women's movement have a similar group of difficulties. Their forte appears to be motivating older women to re-enter the labor force. If this skill can be linked to a more rational use of traditional tools, these services may survive.

These current approaches capitalize on many old as well as relatively recent points of view. The new approaches (1) assume that a person can do more for himself than has usually been assumed; (2) capitalize on a person's knowledge of his competencies and interests (White, 1973); (3) emphasize information, experience, and immediate reinforcement rather than insight, talking, and remote reinforcement; (4) encourage experience and exploration; (5) accept a person's goals or definition of the problem; (6) emphasize levels and varieties of treatment (If this doesn't help, how about this module?); and (7) make use of structural theories and classifications.

In short, many of the new approaches incorporate the main strengths inherent in most of the older approaches to vocational counseling—especially the trait-and-factor, client-centered, and behavioral points of view.

GOALS AND YARDSTICKS

The continued renovation of vocational counseling and related forms of vocational assistance can be accelerated and improved by a more explicit allegiance to the following goals. (I don't think these goals are inhumane, insensitive, oversimplified, impossible, or neglectful of values, although some will think so.)

1. Focus on the vocational problems in society, not on the problems and worries of practitioners, teachers, or researchers. There are many ways to orient research and development, but a return to fundamentals is rarely all bad, and it is certainly better than an orientation to professional concerns.

2. Emphasize those services which help the most people at the lowest average cost. In this regard, make one-to-one vocational counseling the treatment of last resort and as an experience for learning about human personality for practitioners, teachers, developers, and researchers.

3. Get organized. Although some disenchanted soul has characterized

systems theory as "a method for getting organized at greater than normal expense," systematic examination of all the vocational influences and treatments in an institution encourages the development of a more rational and effective set of services. A review of current services may help to identify missing services, duplication, levels of service, problems of coordination, and so on.

4. Make more comprehensive but circumspect use of research and theory. Vocational theory is often used more to bless desired practices than to sustain them in an explicit manner. Groups with new notions of practice sometimes avoid previous research so they will remain uncontaminated by either data or thought. The "right to read" program should be superceded by "the responsibility to know your field" program.

5. Perform evaluation and monitoring activities more regularly and listen to the data. These activities do not have to be Hollywood productions. They can be a valuable source of information for revising services or creating new ones.

6. Regroup so that the effort devoted to individual vocational counseling is reduced and the development of other kinds of service is increased.

If all goes well, vocational counseling will eventually be used only for a few unusual clients, and a variety of printed and audio-visual materials, workbooks, books, and a few group activities arranged in some systematic way will dominate. Somewhat later, computers may be helpful. A few psychologists will give demonstrations at conventions to illustrate how vocational counseling used to be done, but eventually they will be shunted off to hobby fairs along with bookbinding and calligraphy.

REFERENCES

Garfield, N. J., & Nelson, R. E. Vocational exploration groups. Career Information Center, University Testing and Counseling Service, University of Missouri, Columbia, 1973.

Helms, S. T. Practical applications of the Holland occupational classification in counseling. Paper read at APGA Convention, San Diego, February 1973.

Holland, J. L. *Making vocational choices: A theory of careers.* Englewood Cliffs, N.J.: Prentice-Hall, 1973. (a)

Holland, J. L. Some practical remedies for providing vocational guidance for everyone. Research Report No. 160. Center for Social Organization of Schools, Johns Hopkins University, Baltimore, Maryland, 1973. (b)

Jeanneret, P. R., & McCormick, E. J. The dimensions of human work. *Personnel Psychology*, 1972, in press.

Johnston, J. The Career Information Center. University Testing and Counseling Service, University of Missouri, Columbia, 1973.

Magoon, T. A. Developing skills for solving educational and vocational problems. In J. D. Krumboltz & C. E. Thoresen (Eds.), *Behavioral counseling.* New York: Holt, Rinehart & Winston, 1969.

Pappas, J. P., Fuhriman, A., Packard, T., Warshaw, P., Stoddard, K. B., & Carney, C. G. Career development symposium. R & D Report No. 43. University of Utah, Counseling and Psychological Services, 1972.

Reardon, R. C., Burkhard, M. Q., Domkowski, D., Minor, C. W., & Smith, J. D. Curricular-career information service. Office of Undergraduate Advising and Counseling, Florida State University, Tallahassee, 1973.

Super, D. E., Kowalski, R. S., & Gotkin, E. H. *Floundering and trial after high school.* Career Pattern Study, Monograph IV. Cooperative Research Project No. 1393. New York: Teachers College, Columbia University, 1967.

Warnath, C. F. *New myths and old realities.* San Francisco: Jossey-Bass, 1971.

White, R. W. The concept of healthy personality: What do we really mean? *The Counseling Psychologist,* 1973, *4*(2), 3-12.

Reactions to Crites' Review
of the Major Approaches
to Career Counseling

LOUISE VETTER
Ohio State University

As Crites (and counseling psychology) moves toward "a comprehensive approach to career counseling which is maximally applicable to combinations of client/counselor parameters," I would hope that due consideration will be given to the following points:

1. One important parameter which must be considered is gender. There are male and female counselors, and there are male and female clients. It would help to refer to "matching people and jobs" rather than "matching men and jobs," if that type of terminology is retained. Much of our terminology stems from earlier times when such concerns may not have been paramount, but in today's world, where nearly 40 percent of the labor force is female (Women's Bureau, 1972) and legislation provides for equal opportunity, we need to think in terms of people.

Recent studies (Pietrofesa and Schlossberg, 1970; Broverman, Broverman, Clarkson, Rosenkrantz, and Vogel, 1970; Naffziger, 1972; Thomas and Stewart, 1971; Hawley, 1972; Bingham and House, 1973a, 1973b) have documented the kinds of biases held by counselors, both men and women, which lead them to ascribe differing roles to men and women. Some of these biases may stem from the counselor's lack of information about the realities of women's careers. Counselor behavior in interviews often reflects these biases and lack of information, with counselors indicating to women clients that some careers are not to be considered because the careers are for men. At other times, counselors may indicate that women do not need to consider career planning seriously, while men need to give this serious consideration. Bingham and House (1973b) indicate that their evidence suggests that high-school women might anticipate greater support on important dimensions of vocational behavior from female counselors than from male counselors. Perhaps we need to be concerned with "matching clients and counselors."

2. Use of some forms of career information can be more of a problem than a solution, given the current status of the materials available. According to Samler (1964), the realities of work, the work force, and the labor structure

are not really considered in occupational materials. The major emphasis is on the economics of working, while psycho-social factors are neglected. In 1968, a national sample of high-school counselors and vocational instructors indicated that career information for high-school students not planning college education was inadequate (Perrone, 1968).

In a study of racial and sex role stereotyping in career information illustrations, Birk, Cooper, and Tanney (1973) examined over 2000 illustrations which appeared in the *Occupational Outlook Handbook* (1972), the *Encyclopedia of Careers and Vocational Guidance, Volumes I and II* (Hopke, 1972), the *Science Research Associates Occupational Briefs* (1972), and a selected array of career information pamphlets and brochures. Very few women, very few blacks, even fewer Orientals, and no Mexican Americans or American Indians appeared in any of the over 2000 illustrations examined. The authors observed that "the American world of work seems to be almost exclusively populated by white men" (p. 4).

As Borow (1966) has pointed out, there is always selective perception of information in ways that fit with the person's concept of self. The problem is further compounded when it is indicated that women and minority-group persons do not work (even if only by omission), when in fact they do work. Similarly, when women or minority-group persons are not shown in some of the occupations in which they do work, career planning of these people may be affected. Kaufman, Schaefer, Lewis, Stevens, and House (1967) have pointed out that many of the expressed attitudes and plans of high-school senior women are based on a very restricted view of the possibilities open to them as adult women. Other studies (Lee, Ray, Vetter, Murphy, and Sethney, 1971; Vetter and Sethney, 1972) have documented the lack of information which high-school women have about women in the labor force and how this affects the attitudes they hold and the plans they make. Thus, the use of inaccurate career information risks the distortion of the reality of the work world and, in consequence, distorted career planning on the part of youth.

To accurately reflect the reality existent in today's world may not be enough, however. Career information, at its best, would present emerging patterns existing within today's society as students are preparing for tomorrow's world, not today's. The career options available for both men and women, for both majority and minority groups, should be open-ended, not limiting.

Perhaps this is a problem for publishers, not counselors, but as long as counselors buy and make use of biased occupational information in their career counseling, clients will be handicapped in their career planning and self-development.

3. Counselors must be alert to and open to career information which is available through the other social-science disciplines. For example, information which would be useful in providing the kinds of career-pattern data for career counseling is available in the sociological and economic literature.

From sociology, Blau and Duncan's (1967) work on the American occupational structure provides information on the patterns of occupational movement, historical trends, ascribed and achieved occupational status, the process of occupational stratification, and geographical and social mobility for the 60 percent of the labor force which is male.

From economics, a five-year longitudinal study of the labor-market experience of four groups of the United States population is being conducted by the Center for Human Resource Research at Ohio State University. The four groups include: men 45-59 years of age, women 30-44, and young men and women 14-24. There were approximately 5000 subjects in each of the four groups at the time of the first data collection.

The studies of the young men, entitled *Career Thresholds*, include information on patterns of labor force and employment status, occupational change, and changes in educational and occupational goals of students. The first four volumes of this series are now available. Two of the volumes in the series on young women, entitled *Years for Decision*, are now available and include information on employment patterns, educational aspirations and changes, geographic movement, and knowledge of the world of work.

The Pre-Retirement Years studies provide longitudinal measures of the labor-force participation and unemployment of men aged 45-59. The three volumes now available also provide information on changes in personal and family characteristics of the subjects. The studies of women aged 30-44, entitled *Dual Careers*, provide information on labor force and employment status, marital and family status, changes in job status, and changes in job satisfaction. Two volumes of this series are available.

The studies cited above are examples of what is available but certainly do not exhaust the helpful informational possibilities from other social sciences. In addition, I would like to see consideration of the career-patterns studies of women (e.g., Mulvey, 1963; Astin and Myint, 1971; Wolfson, 1972) which are available in the psychology literature.

4. Finally, and I hope I speak for many of my colleagues, I am grateful to John Crites for providing this review of approaches to career counseling, and I am eagerly awaiting a future article on the subject.

REFERENCES

Astin, H. S., & Myint, T. Career development of young women during the post-high school years. *Journal of Counseling Psychology*, 1971, *18*, 369-393.

Bingham, W. C., & House, E. W. Counselors view women and work: Accuracy of information. *Vocational Guidance Quarterly*, 1973, *21*, 262-268. (a)

Bingham, W. C., & House, E. W. Counselors' attitudes toward women and work. *Vocational Guidance Quarterly*, 1973, *22*, 16-23. (b)

Birk, J. M., Cooper, J., & Tanney, M. F. Racial and sex role stereotyping in career information illustration. Paper presented at the American Psychological Association Annual Meeting, Montreal, August 1973.

Blau, P. M., & Duncan, O. D. *The American occupational structure*. New York: Wiley, 1967.

Borow, H. Occupational information in guidance practice viewed in the perspective of vocational development theory and research. Paper presented at the Conference on Occupational Information and Vocational Guidance, Pittsburgh, Pennsylvania, March 1966.

Broverman, I. K., Broverman, D. M., Clarkson, F. E., Rosenkrantz, P. S., & Vogel, S. R. Sex-role stereotypes and clinical judgments of mental health. *Journal of Consulting and Clinical Psychology*, 1970, *34*, 1-7.

Hawley, P. Perceptions of male models of femininity related to career choice. *Journal of Counseling Psychology*, 1972, *19*, 308-313.

Hopke, W. (Ed.). *Encyclopedia of careers and vocational guidance* (Vols. 1 and 2). Chicago: J. G. Ferguson, 1972.

Kaufman, J. J., Schaefer, C. J., Lewis, M. V., Stevens, D. W., & House, E. W. *The role of the secondary schools in the preparation of youth for employment.* University Park, Pennsylvania: Institute for Research of Human Resources, 1967.

Lee, S. L., Ray, E. M., Vetter, L., Murphy, L., & Sethney, B. J. *High school senior girls and the world of work: Occupational knowledge, attitudes and plans.* Columbus, Ohio: The Center for Vocational and Technical Education, The Ohio State University, January 1971. (Research and Development Series No. 42)

Mulvey, M. C. Psychological and sociological factors in prediction of career patterns of women. *Genetic Psychology Monographs*, 1963, *68*, 309-386.

Naffziger, K. G. A survey of counselor-educators' and other selected professionals' attitudes toward women's roles. (Doctoral dissertation, University of Oregon) Ann Arbor, Michigan: University Microfilms, 1972, No. 72-956.

Occupational outlook handbook. Washington, D. C.: U. S. Government Printing Office, 1972.

Perrone, P. A. *A national school counselor evaluation of occupational information.* Madison, Wisconsin: Center for Studies in Vocational and Technical Education, Industrial Relations Research Institute, University of Wisconsin, April 1968.

Pietrofesa, J. J., & Schlossberg, N. K. Counselor bias and the female occupational role. Detroit: Wayne State University, 1970. (ERIC Document, CG 006 056)

Samler, J. Occupational exploration in counseling: A proposed reorientation. In Borow, H. (Ed.), *Man in a world at work.* Boston: Houghton Mifflin, 1964. Pp. 411-433.

Science Research Associates occupational briefs. Chicago: Science Research Associates, 1972.

Thomas, H., & Stewart, N. R. Counselor response to female clients with deviate and conforming career goals. *Journal of Counseling Psychology*, 1971, *18*, 352-357.

Vetter, L., & Sethney, B. J. *Women in the work force: Development and field testing of curriculum materials.* Columbus, Ohio: The Center for Vocational and Technical Education, Ohio State University, December 1972. (Research and Development Series No. 81)

Wolfson, K. T. P. Career development of college women. (Doctoral dissertation, University of Minnesota) Ann Arbor, Michigan: University Microfilms, 1972. No. 72-20, 160.

Women's Bureau, U. S. Department of Labor. *Twenty facts on women workers.* Washington, D. C.: Women's Bureau, 1972.

After Reading Crites' Article . . .

LENORE W. HARMON
LORRAINE JACOBS
JOHN L. KAPELLUSCH
THOMAS J. MEYER
YVONNE R. PORTER
University of Wisconsin—Milwaukee

This collection of four responses to Crites are by graduate students in a master's-level program in counseling at the University of Wisconsin—Milwaukee. They appear here as a result of two recent experiences of mine.

At the 1973 convention of the American Personnel and Guidance Association in San Diego, I chaired a fairly controversial symposium. There was time for questions, but dozens of people wanted to talk. I called upon people who had made significant contributions in the area under discussion because I believed that others would like to see and hear them. After the meeting, some members of the audience challenged my selection procedure as being biased against anyone "under 30." When I explained my rationale one person replied "We can read what they have to say in the journals, but no one listens to us." I have become sensitive to situations in which we may be professionally isolating ourselves from challenging new opinions.

During the fall semester of 1973, I asked the students in my Career Development class to discuss what they always wanted to know about career development—and were not learning from the theories currently available. As I read some of their answers, I felt definitely challenged and pretty defensive as a counseling psychologist. My first reaction was "They are practitioners who will need to use the theories and procedures they have been learning, which gives them a right if not a responsibility to criticize."

As a result, I realized that we all might profit from what these young people have to say. John Whiteley agreed, and I invited four of them to respond briefly to Crites' paper. They are all under 30 and aspire to be practicing counselors.

Lenore W. Harmon

Finding the appropriate approach or technique to use in vocational counseling is a task well worth undertaking. Indeed, trying to ascertain just what will be effective in any given situation is a real problem. It is a concern not only because there are a myriad of techniques to choose from but also because the client and counselor bring different values and attitudes to the counseling situation.

In order to get to the problem and solve it, yet keep from alienating the client (or reducing the effect of the counseling), the counselor needs to quickly approximate not only what technique is empirically the best to use in this type of case but also which one will succeed with this particular client and counselor. Finding an approach which is simultaneously best for the situation and best for the client/counselor relationship is difficult. This, of course, is why Rogers, Ellis, and others often refuse to handle certain cases; even though they believe in their theories, they are aware of their shortcomings and cognizant of cases where their theories are just not appropriate. Moreover, they are aware that there are instances when they, themselves, are not the best counselor choice available for that particular client and/or situation.

Because there are so many problems and so many different types of people, no one has arrived at a comprehensive and conclusive technique as yet. In fact, there is no approach which all counselors can successfully employ to solve all of the problems all of the time.

Every technique to date has had its shortcomings. Crites, in his "Review of Major Approaches," brings many of these limitations to light, and it appears that what Crites further intends to do, now that he has reviewed the existing approaches, is to take the best of each, add something of his own, and then weld it all into a coherent whole. This "new" approach, rid of the shortcomings of the past, will conceivably be the new "panacea" for career counseling.

Yet this approach, too, will have shortcomings. Most probably, it will, by its very nature as a composite, be too unwieldy and too general and will require a super counselor to handle all aspects competently.

What this synthesized approach may offer, however, is a more stable base or starting point for new counselors. That may be important in that it may encourage new counselors to use a varied approach to begin with and, from this composite, to eventually select the parts which are applicable to that particular counselor's style, the clients he deals with, and the problems presented by his clients. However, in this day of specialization, we may be asking too much of this composite theory, for each vocational problem can be very unique and each counselor is an individual whose traits enable him to handle certain approaches better than others. In light of these specialized needs and abilities, can a composite theory provide enough direction?

As much as there is a need for a good general theory, at least as a starting point, one hopes that Crites' contribution will be more than just a taxonomy where one plugs in the problem and pulls out an approach or technique. The problem here would be that a counselor may select and use one of these special approaches without the benefit of the specialized theory behind it, relying instead on Crites' value-laden review of the approaches (an adequate review, even though the conceptualization of it is impeded by some unfortunate word choices).

If Crites can, in his later article, direct himself to solving some specific counseling problems or if he can introduce something really unique, then his "provisional try" may be well worth the effort. If not, Crites may end up producing a mildly eclectic approach—eclectic in the sense that it is composed of, and reliant upon, many theories. In this case, Crites may be wasting his time (or ours), since the relative "weight" he would assign (or even infer) to each theory incorporated into the composite would invariably be different from that some other counselor would assign. Crites' assignments would be in relation to his values and what he perceives most counseling sessions and problems to be like, and, inherently, his values and perceptions would be quite different from every other counselor's. Moreover, counselor abilities vary, so, if an eclectic or composite approach is desired, each individual counselor should construct the composite according to all the variables associated with his particular situation and/or abilities. If built-in adjustments to handle each individual situation are available in the Crites approach, the model may be generally useful. If not, the composite will be useful to but Crites himself.

John Kapellusch

The major approaches to career counseling all assume that there is such a thing as a good vocational choice, possibly several good vocational choices, for any particular individual to make. Nevertheless, the theorists all hesitate to commit themselves by recommending a concrete course of action. We are told which factors are pertinent to making a good vocational choice but not which are, or ought to be, given the most weight. Super, for example, is particularly frustrating because he seems to ask all the right questions but stops short of tackling the business of what should be done with the answers to those questions.

Perhaps this is because we still do not know enough about the meaning of work in people's lives. If career counseling is to be a science, we must be able to predict with assurance which decisions will probably be more beneficial to our clients. Holland and others have made good progress in that area but we need a wider research base in order to feel more confident in using materials such as Holland's "The Occupations Finder."

This is not to say that career counseling should be mechanized to an extent where it would suffice to give our clients a battery of tests which would automatically categorize them into certain occupations, but this writer is uncomfortable, for instance, with the client-centered approach to vocational counseling. This approach leaves the impression that the client ought to receive a lot of understanding at a time when he is chiefly seeking guidance. It is not enough to classify people solely according to the facts, but neither is it sufficient to empathize with the client. Empathy and understanding of the client's situation and his perception of it are, of course, essential. To say, however, that by understanding these things you will come to a reliable decision is not sensible. As counselors we must be able to depend on something which transcends our limited personal experiences.

It would be exceedingly useful to know more about the role of work in people's lives. The role of work is the root issue from which the different approaches stem. Whether one believes that work satisfies certain unconscious needs that people have or that vocational choice is largely a function of environmental inputs will greatly influence which factors one will give uppermost consideration. If this issue were resolved, we would have a solid base from which we could expand. Even if our investigations indicated that there is no single role that work plays in all our lives, our position would be improved.

Yvonne R. Porter

If I were a writer, reading this article would dismay me. It is understood that the problems of writing an overview of the literature in a field are considerable, but it should still be done in as readable a manner as possible. Readable writing does not unnecessarily use archaic word forms (technics), nor does it use rare words (lacunae) where a common one (gaps) will do. Finally, readable writing avoids such inscrutable grammatical constructions as "These relative theoretical dispositions are juxtaposed to each other, when they differ pointedly, in the discussion of diagnosis, process, and outcome which follows as well as with indirect behavioral counseling" (page 45).

The style in which an article is written helps determine its readership. This article will be read by those whose business it is to read it. It will not be read by those whose business it is written about.

In my role as a student of vocational counseling I value Mr. Crites' review. He has done what seems to me an exemplary job of outlining the various theories. I am looking forward to his next article wherein "Figure I. Taxonomy of approaches to career counseling" will be completed. With such a side-by-side chart comparisons can be made more accurately. That is, I suppose, the reason such charts are included in textbooks.

From my viewpoint as a potential vocational counselor I find this review, in intent, to be beside the point. It is headed in the right direction but falls short of usefulness and lands instead in an area labeled academic. It is meant to be read and to be criticized and perhaps even to spawn other articles which in turn are read and criticized. Such an article is not directed at the people in the profession.

I am willing to admit that the strands of vocational counseling theory can be interwoven. I can understand that by pointing out similarities and recognizing the evolution of one theory into another our knowledge will be increased. This sort of thing has happened in other fields which have doubtless served as models here.

It also seems to me that, if a vocational counselor had unlimited time and resources available to a client, the trend of the literature in the field would provide him with a consensus on "models" and "methods."

No one would agree more than I with Crites' statement that the need for career counseling "assumes critical proportions" and that schools, colleges, the Armed Forces, the Veterans Administration, and industry all have use for the vocational counselor. One way to fulfill these needs would be to "formulate a comprehensive approach to career counseling."

Such a formulation could, over the years, be generally agreed upon. It could be taught as the one true way in the universities, always, of course, with the reminder that the technics enumerated, although falling in total under the rubric "comprehensive approach," must in part be extrapolated to facilitate the confluence of the counselor/client interaction process (my apologies to Dr. Crites). In short, now that you have learned the one true way, go out and do a good job.

This has been the traditional approach.

My education was based on such an approach. I have a liberal-arts background tempered by five years of teaching in an inner-city junior high school. My undergraduate background in education was sufficient to convince me that I knew more than I did know while preparing me for a job situation I never found. I was taught the one true way.

My years as a teacher have convinced me that there are, in fact, certain educational principles relevant to widely divergent teaching situations but that the way in which they are used (and reached) varies according to the job situation. Teaching with the same goals will require different methods and materials of teachers in suburban and inner-city situations. Schools of Education tend to teach their students as though they were all going to teach in the same school (the one true way). Teachers who do not end up in a white suburban school have to adapt. They have lost the benefit of their education and the interest of educational publishers.

The result of massive on-the-job adaption is erratic. Some individuals do brilliantly as long as they can keep up the pace of doing their job and adapting texts, methods, and curriculums. Others only go through the motions. The results in the end are the same—low-quality service to the client.

Coming from this background, one can imagine my disappointment in reading Crites' article. Just as others in my past training have done, he is suggesting that there is one true way ("a comprehensive approach").

An improvement on this traditional approach would recognize the existence of a range of job situations, each type requiring a different job strategy. Vocational counselors will, regardless of their job situation, find a way of coping with the demands of their job. My thesis is that higher-quality service to the client would result from theory matched in methods and resources to each type of job situation.

Such a system could be developed along with "a comprehensive approach to career counseling." Indeed, at some points Crites seems to be thinking along these lines, and some of Super's statements would also tend to support such an idea. I maintain, however, that it is not enough to hint at or suggest the need for the development of job strategies which include the adaptation of methods and models. Hinting at or suggesting adaptations will, in the long run, leave the responsibility for them once again on the beleaguered person on the job, and low-quality service would be the result.

No radical innovations would be necessary to incorporate the need for job strategies into a "comprehensive approach to career counseling." I am not naive enough to propose a Cultural Revolution in academia, whereby all professors (Webster: "any person claiming or presumed to be especially skilled or experienced . . .") must serve several weeks yearly doing manual labor in remote (underpaid, time-pressed) vocational-counseling situations. Neither am I proposing that anyone follow the example of the Florida professor in police administration who took leave for two years from the university to serve as a "beat" policeman and who has continued to serve part time on the police force since his return to the university.

I do humbly suggest that a person who underwent a corresponding set of experiences would write with a different purpose than Dr. Crites did in this article and that the difference in purpose would increase the job satisfaction of vocational counselors and the quality of their service to their clients and would change the relationship between counselors and educators of counselors.

Thomas J. Meyer

In choosing among the many theories of career development available, the counselor should keep in mind two important considerations. First, the specific problem to be dealt with and, second, the amount of time he will be able to spend with the client.

Some problems which are not handled adequately by the existing theories are those of:

1. The many highly-trained and skilled workers who are forced into the job market at middle age because of layoffs and firings;

2. The young women and girls who need encouragement and education to prompt them to begin thinking about careers which were previously described as "masculine" but which satisfy needs that are human rather than sexually categorized;

3. The women who are now re-entering the world of work after years of developing skills related to the home and motherhood but who are without the skills and motivations most adaptive in today's job market; and

4. Those high-school-age clients who are not inclined, due to ability or motivation, toward college.

Each theory must be analyzed in terms of its usefulness in counseling with clients with these problems.

The other important consideration is the amount of time available for each client. It is governed by the situation in which the counselor is employed. In a private agency, where the client pays fees, the most time-consuming method is justified if it is the most effective. However, less time per client is available to the counselor on a college campus, and even less time per client is allowed to the high school counselor. A counseling approach which takes a long time may not be feasible for a high-school counselor, no matter how effective it could be.

One of the most helpful aspects of Crites' article on Career Counseling was his development of a taxonomy of approaches to career counseling. The subdivision of theories into models related to particular interview techniques is very helpful in analyzing and comparing the theories described. The use of such a chart would be beneficial in a preliminary analysis of available theories, when trying to develop the most personally workable combination. Once the theories are categorized and subdivided for comparison on this chart, it is necessary for the counselor to consider the factors and needs already discussed above and, in examining the dissected elements of each theory, find a combination best suited to a specific counselor situation.

Personally, I am looking for a theory which takes account of the effect of external factors which influence career choice. In examining the desired outcomes of career-counseling theories, the client-centered and developmental approaches seem most likely to recognize external factors. One estimate of the extent to which a theory considers socioeconomic factors is the manner in which occupational information is gathered and used by the client and counselor. Again, the client-centered and developmental approaches encourage the client to explore external factors, while the trait-factor and psychodynamic approaches minimize the client's exploration of external factors and how they influence career development and decisions. The behavioral approach to occupational information, occupational simulation, seems like an excellent way to encourage the individual to consider factors external to himself in making career choices.

The developmental and client-centered approaches, along with the occupational kits developed in the behavioral approach, seem to have most to offer in counseling with the specific kinds of clients discussed earlier. It is disappointing that none of the approaches take account of the time constraints under which most counselors work. Super's theory seems likely to facilitate the most career development, but it may also take the most time. Perhaps the only way to increase the quality of career counseling is to hire more counselors.

Lorraine Jacobs

CAREER COUNSELING: A COMPREHENSIVE APPROACH 4

JOHN O. CRITES
University of Maryland

In Chapter 2 of this text, I presented a review of the major approaches to assisting clients engaged in career decision making, along with limited critical analysis of each. More specifically, the five approaches to career counseling listed across the horizontal dimension of Figure 1 were respectively considered

		Trait-and-Factor	Client-Centered	Psychodynamic	Developmental	Behavioral
M O D E L S	Diagnosis					
	Process					
	Outcomes					
M E T H O D S	Interview Techniques					
	Test Interpretation					
	Use of Occupational Information					

Figure 1. Taxonomy of approaches to career counseling.

and summarized down the vertical axis, which enumerates the more salient and presumably universal continua along which they can be described and differentiated. The *model* of an approach to career counseling explicates its theoretical framework, its conceptual outline, its *raison d'être*. It encompasses the three principal chronological stages of any career-counseling encounter, regardless of temporal span: the beginning, during which a *diagnosis* of the client's problem is typically made; the middle, in which the *process* of intervention with the client is implemented; and the end, during which the *outcomes* of the experience are enumerated and evaluated by the client and counselor. In contrast, the *methods* of career counseling are pragmatic rather than theoretic, their purpose being to translate the model into operational terms. In career counseling, they include the interview techniques used by the counselor, the test-interpretation procedures engaged in by client and counselor, and the acquisition/use of occupational information by the client. Together, the model and methods of career counseling serve to define the unique parameters of a given approach, and they provide a schema for synthesizing the several approaches into a comprehensive one which has maximal applicability.

That none of the major approaches to career counseling was sufficient with respect to its model and methods emerged from the previous review. But each has its contribution to make to a comprehensive approach. To extrapolate what these are and to integrate them into a cogent and coherent system of career counseling, a synthesis of the approaches for each aspect of model and method has been attempted. That is, reading *across* the row of Figure 1 a "provisional try" has been made to synthesize the best theory and practice, buttressed by confirmatory experiential and empirical evidence, on diagnosis, process, outcomes, interview techniques, test interpretation, and occupational information. What has resulted is, hopefully, more than an eclectic grafting together of disparate parts. The objective was to articulate a comprehensive approach to career counseling based upon an explicit rationale for the interrelationship of its elements. In the discussion which follows, the latter are delineated first (across the rows of Figure 1), and then they are interrelated within the context of the client/counselor interaction. Thus, this outline of a comprehensive approach to career counseling is divided into one section on Model (or theory), a second on Methods (or techniques), and a concluding one on Materials (or case studies), which illustrates its principles and procedures with an account and analysis of a recent career-counseling case.

A MODEL OF COMPREHENSIVE CAREER COUNSELING

In formulating a model of comprehensive career counseling, concepts and principles have been utilized which come not only from the major approaches already reviewed (Chapter 2 of this text) but also from more general systems of counseling and psychotherapy (Ford & Urban, 1963; Corsini, 1973). Moreover, the model reflects experience gained from many case conference presentations and supervisory sessions which leaven and authenticate its formal characteristics. The concepts of diagnosis, process, and outcomes which it embraces, therefore, have been derived experientially as well as logically, the purpose being to blend the theoretical and pragmatic as meaningfully as possible.

Diagnosis

The central issue in synthesizing this facet of the model for comprehensive career counseling is whether to diagnose or not. All but the client-centered approach would affirm the value of diagnosis in identifying and solving the client's problems, although viewpoints vary on the type of diagnosis which should be made (see below). The client-centered position is that diagnosis shifts the locus of responsibility for decision making to the counselor and fosters critical or evaluative attitudes which interfere with "unconditional positive regard" for the client. Yet client-centered career counselors (e.g., Patterson, 1964, 1973) actually make two kinds of diagnoses but nevertheless assume that they have not usurped the client's decision-making prerogatives. First, they assume that *all* clients have the *same* problem—namely, a lack of congruence between perceptions of self and perceptions of reality (Rogers, 1951). In other words, they diagnose but not *differentially*. But, second, they distinguish among the life areas in which a lack of congruence may arise, thus allowing for career counseling as a treatment modality peculiarly suited to "vocational" problems (Patterson, 1964). This inconsistency in client-centered views of diagnosis is not only conceptual; it is also empirical. Findings from both the Chicago (Kirtner & Cartwright, 1958) and the Wisconsin (Rogers, Gendlin, Kiesler, & Traux, 1967) studies have revealed that client-centered counseling is not uniformly effective with all types of psychological disorders. It works better with some clients—more intelligent, less disturbed ones—than it does with others. Thus, diagnosis appears necessary for client-centered as well as other approaches to career counseling.

Given this precept as an integral part of the model for comprehensive career counseling, several questions immediately arise: What is meant by "diagnosis"? How are diagnoses made, and can they be made reliably? And, what is the relationship of diagnosis to process in career counseling? From the trait-and-factor approaches comes the well-known concept of diagnosis as the *differential* classification of clients according to the distinguishing characteristics of their career problems. For example, individuals who cannot state which occupation they intend to enter upon completion of their training (Crites, 1969) are designated as having "no choice" or being "undecided" (Williamson, 1939). Several systems for the differential diagnosis of vocational problems have been developed, but they have foundered primarily upon the unreliability of counselors in using them. Interjudge agreement seldom exceeds 25-30 percent (Crites, 1969, Ch. 7). Moreover, the categories in these systems are neither mutually exclusive nor exhaustive. Thus, some clients can be classified into more than one problem category, and others cannot be classified into any category. To rectify these shortcomings, Crites (1969, pp. 292-303) has proposed a system which eliminates subjective judgments and hence is perfectly reliable and which consists of exclusive and exhaustive categories—at least for the diagnostic criteria used. In brief, it defines differential career problems by identifying the discrepancies which exist between career choice, on the one hand, and aptitudes and interests, on the other. To illustrate, if a client chooses an occupation which requires greater aptitude than s/he has, then the client is diagnosed as "unrealistic." Without further elaboration, suffice it to say that the system can be used reliably and validly by counselors for the differential diagnosis of client career problems.

Differential diagnosis addresses the question: *What* is the client's career decisional problem? *Dynamic* diagnosis asks the question: *Why* does the client have the problem? The answer has been formulated largely within the psychodynamic approach to career counseling. Bordin (1946) early criticized differential diagnostic systems (e.g., Williamson, 1939) because they failed to identify the causes of psychological problems. As noted in the review of this approach (Chapter 2 of this text), he then proposed diagnostic constructs, such as choice anxiety and dependence, which focused upon the etiology of the client's problem rather than simply its symptomatology (Bordin, 1946). More recently, Bordin and Kopplin (1973) have formulated another set of problem categories, based upon an analysis of "motivational conflicts," but both have been plagued with low interjudge agreement which has limited their usefulness. As with differential diagnosis, what is needed are explicit operational criteria for the definition of etiological factors in career problems which clearly distinguish their dynamics. One such analysis has been made by Crites (1969, Chapter 2 of this text) to explicate the role of anxiety in indecision as contrasted with indecisiveness. Given only the differential diagnosis of "no choice" (Williamson, 1939), it is difficult, if not impossible, for a career counselor to know whether the client's problem is one of simple indecision or pervasive indecisiveness, unless a dynamic diagnosis of how anxiety has affected antecedent decisional experiences is made. Recent research (Schrader, 1970) as well as current studies, following an experimental paradigm suggested by Crites (1969, pp. 599-604), have indicated that indecision and indecisiveness can be dynamically differentiated early in career counseling by administering standardized measures of manifest anxiety and career maturity. There is emerging evidence, based upon reliable test scores rather than unreliable judgments, that indecisive clients are more anxious and less mature than those with simple indecision.

To make differential and dynamic diagnoses is necessary but *not* sufficient to identify a client's problem(s). These types of diagnosis attend primarily to the *content* of career choice; they do not directly deal with the *process* of career choice. The distinction between the content and process of career choice has not been generally recognized (Crites, 1974b), although it is implicit in both the developmental and behavioral approaches to career counseling. Career-choice content pertains to *which* occupation the client intends to enter. In contrast, career-choice process refers to *how* the decision was made. Knowing only that a client has "no choice" (differential diagnosis) and that s/he is "indecisive" (dynamic diagnosis) in most decision-making situations does not identify whatever problems arise in the client's approach to career choice. To determine deviations or disjunctions in how career choices are made necessitates a *decisional diagnosis.* A conceptual framework and assessment methodology for this kind of diagnosis can be extrapolated from an integration of behavioral and developmental career counseling. From the former comes a schema for optimal career decision making (Gelatt, 1962; Gelatt, Varenhorst, & Carey, 1972; Krumboltz & Baker, 1973) which delineates the sequence which a client might follow to arrive at a realistic career choice, and from the latter is derived a model of career maturity (Crites, 1974c) which casts this process into a development context, so that a client's career maturity at any given point in time can be assessed and diagnosed. For example, a client's scores on the *Career Maturity Inventory (CMI)*, which was constructed to measure maturity in optimal career decision making (Crites, 1973), may indicate above-average competencies in self-appraisal and occupational information but below-average goal selection for the client's stage of career development. The decisional diagnosis might be that the client's problem lies in the process of relating self to work, not in gathering information, and consequently career counseling would focus upon this facet of decision making rather than others.

Synthesis. When a client requests career counseling, a twofold conceptual and pragmatic issue is posed: *What* is the client's problem and *why* does s/he experience it? If it is granted that diagnosis is necessary to address this issue and to ultimately choose an appropriate course of treatment, irrespective of the interventive orientation, then a comprehensive approach to career counseling would involve this synthesis of what is known about diagnosis. First, a differential diagnosis of the client's career problem would be made, using a system such as that proposed by Crites (1969), in which the principal categories are (1) indecision and (2) unrealism. Second, once the nosological classification of the client's problem has been made, a dynamic diagnosis is undertaken to identify the antecedents and contingencies which have generated the problem. Here, although research findings are suggestive (Schrader, 1970), the basic procedure is inferential, using constructs such as those formulated by Bordin (1946; Bordin & Kopplin, 1973). The most reliable and valid reasoning starts on the data-language level (demographic and psychometric information, interview impressions), moves to the theory-language level with the formulation of hypotheses, and returns to the data-language level for hypothesis testing (Goldman, 1964; McArthur, 1954). Thus, the dynamics of the client's career problem are extrapolated from an ongoing interaction between the empirical and the conceptual, the purpose being to understand the so-called "causes" of the client's felt difficulty. And, third, against this background of the what and the why of the client's problem, a decisional diagnosis of disjunctions in the process of career choice is attempted. How career-mature in choice attitudes and competencies, as assessed by an instrument like the *Career Maturity Inventory*, is the client, and how are these attitudes and competencies related to the choice content problem? Taken together, the differential, dynamic, and decisional diagnoses of the client's career problem allow the counselor to draw better-than-chance conclusions about what the problem is, why it has occurred, and how it is being dealt with. They also have import for deciding upon which career counseling processes may be most appropriate for assisting the client to resolve the problems.

Process

The basic unit of process in career counseling is the interview interaction between client and counselor (cf., Kiesler, 1973). Career counseling may consist of only one interview, but typically the overall process is comprised of a series of interviews. Whether one interview or many, however, the process corresponds to an opening interview, in which the counselor collects data on the client, a second interview, during which tests are interpreted, and a third interview, when occupational information is presented. The client-centered approach varies from this schema somewhat, depending upon the inclinations of the counselor, but the broad outlines are the same: opening self-exploration of difficulties in career decision making, intermediate internalizing or "owning" of these problems, and eventual resolution of them through "the experiencing of real and effective choice" (Patterson, 1973, p. 394). Similarly, psychodynamic career counseling, as largely formulated by Bordin (1968), proceeds through three stages: exploration and contract setting, critical decision, and working for change. In the developmental approach, much the same phasing is apparent—the process beginning with orientation to and readiness for decision making, progressing through exploration of self and work, and culminating in planning for the future. And, behavioral career counseling, whether theoretic or pragmatic, follows much the same three-phased cycle of problem identification, intervention (e.g., counterconditioning, modeling, etc.), and generalization.

The lead-in to the first stage of the process of career counseling is diagnosis. Both test and nontest data are gathered by the counselor, not only to identify the parameters of the client's problem but also to "get to know" the client. What are the antecedents of the client's current decision making? How career-mature are the client's choice attitudes and competencies? And, have the client's experiences with career and other choices been positive or negative? The focus is upon a wide-ranging exploration of the client's presenting problem and the background factors which have possibly occasioned it. Using a conceptual framework such as that proposed by Ginzberg, Ginsburg, Axelrad, and Herma (1951) and a measure of career maturity like the CMI, the counselor can locate the place the client has reached on the continuum of career development (Super, 1955) and then collaborate with the client in establishing goals for the career counseling which, if achieved, will further the client's growth along that continuum toward greater career maturity in both choice content and process (see "Outcomes" below). Equally important during this first stage of career counseling, however, are the counselor's perceptions of the relationship which the client is establishing with her/him. Often it becomes readily apparent that a central facet of the client's career-choice problem is avoiding personal responsibility for resolving it. Rather, in any one of a number of ways, most notably passive dependence, the client attempts to shift the locus of this responsibility to the counselor. The content of the client problem thus becomes inextricably interwoven with the dynamics of the client's relationship with the counselor, and the task of the opening gambit of career counseling emerges as the complex one of clarifying the client's responsibility in decision making while concomitantly dealing with its substance.

The middle stage in the career-counseling process occupies most of the time which the client and counselor spend together. It is a time of problem clarification and specification. The client and counselor *collaboratively* identify the attitudes and behaviors of the career problem which are interfering with the decision-making process, and together they survey the range of possible solutions. The counselor emphasizes collaboration in the relationship to counteract the typical dependence of the undecided client and the defensiveness of the unrealistic client. Moreover, a collaborative client/counselor interaction achieves an optimal balance between the characteristic "paternalism" of traditional trait-and-factor career counseling and the "laissez faire" orientation of the early client-centered approach. These extremes are moderated by the counselor's willingness to accept the client's perception of reality as valid, on the one hand, and to disclose his/her personal experiences as meaningful and facilitative to the client, on the other. What evolves is a higher-order relational experience in which client and counselor share responsibility for problem solution. If a collaborative relationship can be fashioned as the career counseling moves through this intermediate phase, it not only increases the involvement of the client in the decisional process but also may have salutary effects upon his/her self-esteem. For many clients, it may be the first time in their lives that a "significant other" (usually an adult) has taken an active interest in their problems, and it may be the first time that they realize they *are* competent to cope effectively with their lives. This stage of career counseling is critical, then, to both the explication of the client's career problems and the client's assumption of responsibility for solutions to the problems.

The process of career counseling culminates in a stage which can best be characterized as problem resolution. If the client has become aware of the nature of her/his problem and has become actively engaged in its solution, then the career counseling turns to a consideration of what the client must do—what behaviors are now necessary? The focus is upon instrumental learning: How can information about self and work be gathered? What negative decisions need to be made in career-goal selection in order to narrow the range of options? What are the steps to be followed in reaching the goal (means-end cognizance), and how are they ordered along the temporal dimension (planning)? And, how are unforeseen contingencies dealt with when they interfere with goal attainment? Through modeling and shaping and reinforcement (see "Interview Techniques" below), the counselor sets the learning conditions for the client to acquire those career-mature behaviors which are problem-resolving. But probably more important, the counselor encourages the generalization of these behaviors to the solution of other life problems. If the career counseling is efficacious, the client learns an approach to problem solving and decision making which can be used not only in future career adjustments but also in personal, marital, and social adjustments. Furthermore, the client gains confidence in his/her competence to solve problems and make decisions independently of others. The client becomes a responsible individual, personally as well as vocationally.

Synthesis. That stages occur in the process of career counseling is posited by all approaches at least in broad outline if not also in detail. The stages are delineated essentially in terms which correspond to generally recognized steps in problem solving: background of the problem, statement of the problem, and resolution of the problem. Superimposed upon the stages are the complementary dimensions of any client/counselor interaction: communication and relationship. The content of the communication between client and counselor defines the parameters of the problem: its etiology, its symptomatology, and its possible solutions. The dynamics of the relationship set the conditions for the extent to which the client learns to assume personal responsibility for career decision making, both in the present and in the future. Together, communication and relationship are universal dimensions of career counseling to which all approaches contribute. The trait-and-factor and behavioral have emphasized communication concerning the substantive aspects of the problem and the formulation of solutions to it. The client-centered has contributed an understanding of the conditions which facilitate such communication, and the psychodynamic has identified the dynamics of the relationships which can be formed between client and counselor. And the developmental has sketched the background against which client growth can be calibrated in moving toward greater career maturity.

Outcomes

The expected outcomes of career counseling are largely implied by diagnosis of a client's problem—i.e., its differential, dynamic, and decisional diagnosis. It is anticipated that the type of career-counseling intervention which the client and counselor collaboratively agree upon will lead to resolution of the problem. For example, if the client and counselor decide together that the career problem is one of inadequate information about self and work, then the desired outcome of career counseling is the client's becoming more knowledgeable in these areas. Whatever the client's problem, all of the major approaches to career counseling are oriented to its solution. More succinctly, the outcomes of career counseling are the solutions which are most appropriate to the client's problems. Too often, however, the outcomes are conceptualized as epiphenomena which have no antecedents. They are frequently seen as appearing only after the career counseling has been completed. Actually, as Grummon (1972) observes, outcomes are part of, and emerge from, process: they can be traced, and assessed, across the course of career counseling (c.f., Kiesler, 1973). In other words, successive cross-sectional assessments of process collectively define a trend line for the outcomes of career counseling. At any one point in time, in comparison with other preceding ones, movement toward the goals which client and counselor established for the career counseling can be determined.

The most generally recognized of these goals—and one which cuts across all of the major approaches to career counseling—is to assist the client in making a career choice. The long-standing societal expectation that everyone is "occupied," preferably in some economically gainful pursuit (particularly males), is an unquestioned assumption of career counseling. Seldom if ever is the avowed outcome of career counseling to help a client decide *not* to work, as legitimate as this outcome may be personally. Sometimes career counselors allow for clients to postpone their decisions, but usually they feel a sense of lack of closure if a decision may be developmentally premature. Super and Overstreet (1960) point out that the exploratory stage of career development should be "open-ended" until the individual has had the opportunity to clarify the self-concept and to learn about the occupational roles which are available and suitable. Similarly, Ginzberg et al. (1951) note the pitfalls in career decision making of pseudocrystallization in choice, stemming from (1) the persistence of childhood interests, (2) powerful fantasies about being admired and successful, and (3) responsiveness to parental pressures (Crites; 1969, p. 171). And Strong's (1955) research on the development of vocational interests indicates that certain interests patterns, specifically Social Service, do not emerge until relatively late in adolescence, whereas others (e.g., Physical Sciences) crystallize earlier on (c.f., Sinnett, 1956). Thus, for the principal outcome of career counseling to be the making of a career decision is theoretically and empirically contraindicated. The *not* making of a career decision may be equally desirable for the client's degree or rate of career development (Crites, 1961).

A second outcome of career counseling, which only recently has been articulated by the developmental and behavioral approaches, is the acquisition of decisional skills. In contrast to trait-and-factor and, to a lesser extent, client-centered and psychodynamic career counseling, the developmental and behavioral orientations have emphasized choice process, not choice content. Both have addressed the question: How can the client best make a realistic career choice? And, in answering this question, they have gone beyond choice content, although this too is seen as an outcome (Thompson, 1954), and have focused upon choice process. Super has enumerated the career developmental tasks with which the client must contend in making a choice (Super, Starishevsky, Matlin, & Jordaan, 1963), and Krumboltz and Baker (1973) have outlined the necessary steps in arriving at a decision. Drawing upon these schemata, as well as general decision theory (Edwards, 1954, 1961), Crites (1973) has constructed the CMI-Competence Test as a measure of the stages in optimal career decision making—information gathering (self and work), goal selection, planning, and problem solving. Presumably a client not only passes through these stages, as needed, in career counseling but also explicitly learns them as a *modus operandi* for decision making in the future. Thus, the client acquires a way of coping with career problems which is not time- or content-bound. S/he has an approach to the decision-making situations of life, whether career or otherwise, which transcends career counseling and changes in the world of work. The problem-specific constraints imposed by career counseling oriented only to choice content are obviated by career counseling which provides a client with a process paradigm for decision making which is "contentless."

Still another outcome of career counseling, and one which has been obscured by its nonvocational nature, is the enhanced general adjustment status of the client. Accruing evidence (Williams, 1962; Williams & Hills, 1962) indicates that career counseling results in the client being better adjusted in areas of life functioning other than just the vocational. There are probably several reasons why this is true. The psychodynamic point of view drawing upon Freud's (1962) conclusion that the hallmarks of maturity are *arbeiten und lieben* (c.f., Shoben, 1956) would contend that the person who can work effectively as well as love fully is better adjusted. Moreover, most of our working hours are spent in either preparing for or engaging in work; it is not surprising, therefore, that the better adjusted worker is also the better adjusted individual generally. A corollary is that, if a client learns to cope with her/his career problem, it is likely that s/he will be better able to cope with other problems. Furthermore, learning to cope with one's career problems generates an overall feeling of greater self-esteem which is reflected in a heightened adjustment level. Unfortunately, this intimate relationship between career and general adjustment is not widely recognized by either career counselors or personal counselors. Rarely do the former explore with a client the implications and applications of what was learned in career counseling to other areas of adjustment, and equally infrequently do the latter discuss with a client what import personality changes have for career development.

Synthesis. In comprehensive career counseling, a basic premise is that all aspects of life functioning and development are interrelated (Super, 1955). If a specific decision concerning career is made, or if career decisional attitudes and competencies are learned, then the impact of these outcomes of career counseling upon philosophy of life, interpersonal relationships, self concept, etc., should be examined. All of the major approaches to career counseling would concur in the humanistic value that their common goal (outcome) is to further the development or growth of clients toward being more fully functioning individuals, whether intellectually, personally, socially, or vocationally. In comprehensive career counseling, the focus is upon the vocational but embraces the others. Super (1957) summarizes it this way:

> By relieving tensions, clarifying feelings, giving insight, helping attain success, and developing a feeling of competence in one important area of adjustment, the vocational, it is possible to release the individual's ability to cope more adequately with other aspects of living, thus bringing about improvement in [his/her] general adjustment (p. 300).

METHODS OF COMPREHENSIVE CAREER COUNSELING

For many years, dating back to Parsons and the early work of the Minnesota vocational psychologists, the methods of career counseling— interview techniques, test interpretation, and occupational information— could be characterized as largely didactic and directive. They came out of an educational tradition which highlighted the expertise of the counselor as the transmitter of information to the client. The Rogerian revolution in the early 1940's, however, wrought a dramatic change in the techniques used by career counselors, who either adopted a nondirective style (Bixler & Bixler, 1946; Seeman, 1948) or alternated between it and a directive one (Kilby, 1949; Super, 1957). In recent years, both have been modified and combined with behavioral methods to the extent that a synthesis can now be extrapolated which reflects the best of the several approaches to career counseling.

Interview Techniques

The techniques available to the career counselor encompass all of those reviewed previously which have been proposed by the major approaches to career counseling (Chapter 2 of this text) as well as others which have been developed in personal counseling and psychotherapy (Kiesler, 1973). The problem in formulating a system of comprehensive career counseling is not one of the availability of interview techniques but rather of how and when to best use them. The developmental and behavioral approaches have been most explicit in addressing this problem, but several issues remain unresolved. One of these is: which interview techniques are most appropriate for *different* client career problems? Neither conceptually nor empirically has the linkage been made between these variables, despite Bordin's observation that "the most vital characteristic of a set of diagnostic classifications is that they form the basis for the choice of treatment. This means that there should be some understandable and predictable relationship between the characteristics which define the construct and the effects of treatment processes" (1946, p. 170). A second issue is: how do differential interview techniques relate to the identifiable stages in the process of career counseling? Presumably, the career counselor would make different responses early in the process, during problem exploration, rather than later on when engaged with the client in problem solution, but this phasing of interview techniques in career counseling has not been articulated. And a third issue is: what relationship exists between interview techniques and the expected outcomes of career counseling? More specifically, are there classes of counselor responses which are more conducive to a particular outcome, e.g., making a specific career decision, than to others (c.f., Robinson, 1950)?

To illustrate how diagnosis and interview techniques can be related, consider the client whose differential diagnosis is "undecided" (no career choice), whose dynamic diagnosis is "indecisive," and whose decisional diagnosis is immature "goal selection," as measured by the CMI. Clinical experience with this type of client indicates that they almost invariably place the responsibility for their career choice upon the counselor. If the counselor responds by saying something such as "I can't make your decision for you; you have to do that for yourself"—a response which is not atypical of most of us— then we have communicated what amounts to a "paradoxical injunction" (Watzlawick, Beavin, & Jackson, 1967). We have said on an "object language" level that we are absolving ourselves of any responsibility for the client's problem, *but* on a metacommunication level we have given the client the injunction that s/he *has* to make the career choice. And this is much the same response that the passive, dependent career client elicits from most people in the extra-clinical situation. Consequently, they react to the counselor as they do to others—they become even more indecisive! If the career counselor "prescribes the symptom," however, by saying to the client "Don't make any decision," the effect is usually for the client to react to this extreme injunction by making a commitment to the career choice process and gradually assuming personal responsibility for it. In other words, the client is faced with the choice of whether to make a choice: If s/he chooses not to make a choice, then career counseling can be terminated with this goal accomplished; if s/he chooses to make a choice, then career counseling can proceed but with the client now actively involved in the decision making.

The interview techniques which are most appropriate to the several stages of the career counseling process range along a continuum from more to less general in form and content. And they correspond to the foci of the stages. In the *first* stage, the career counselor's responses are more general, in order to facilitate exploration of the background of the problem as presented by the client during the early interviews. Of the response repertoire which is available to the counselor, the most frequently used responses are those of (1) restatement and (2) reflection of both content and feeling (Dipboye, 1954;

Robinson, 1950). These kinds of responses serve to "open up" discussion of the etiology and nature of the client's problem. In the *second* stage, the counselor narrows the scope of the problem and moves toward an explicit statement of it through what Colby (1951) calls "interpositions" and "juxtapositions." The former are open-ended questions, such as "How do you mean you never made a *right* decision?" and the latter are comparisons or contrasts, for example: "On the one hand, you have difficulty making decisions, and, on the other, you tell me that your father always told you what to do. Do you see any relationship between these two?" Problem clarification progresses through the counselor's posing of questions like these and the client's responding to them. In the *third*, and last, stage of career counseling, problem resolution is furthered by the counselor's becoming more active and directive. Client responses are openly shaped and reinforced, and the counselor interacts in a way which models a mature relationship between two adults who are collaborating in solving a common problem.

As was mentioned previously, the outcomes of career counseling are intimately related to the process, and both are a function of the interview techniques which the counselor uses. How often do career counselors initiate interviews with a client with no more explicit *rationale* for the responses they are going to make than the "good intention" of helping the client solve a choice problem? Each counselor response should ideally be fashioned to achieve an explicitly agreed upon goal (as part of the collaborative relationship between client and counselor), rather than a random responding to whatever the current content of the interview happens to be. The dictum for the counselor is: "Know why you said what you said." Equally important is the *timing* of counselor responses. If s/he allows the first stage of the career counseling process (problem exploration) to last too long, then the most likely outcome is increased dependence of the client upon the counselor, as manifested in redundant and circuitous recounting of the problem. If s/he moves too quickly to the second or third stages of career counseling, then the client may feel threatened or rejected and "break contact." Pacing responses to coincide with the stages in the career counseling process achieves not only immediate goals but also longer-range outcomes. Still another interview technique, which facilitates personal as well as career development, is *yoking*. The counselor draws implications for life in general from the client's talk about career. Thus, the counselor might point out how dependent the client is upon her/him to make a career choice and then comment: "I wonder whether you rely upon others in the same way to make other decisions in life." Here the focus is upon dependence in career decision making but the extrapolation is to decision making in general—particularly in terms of interpersonal relationships.

Synthesis. The principal *modi operandi* of career counseling are the interview techniques by which diagnosis, process, and outcomes are realized. Each of these facets of the model of comprehensive career counseling is implemented by how the counselor responds to the client. During the beginning of the process, the most relevant interview techniques are those advocated by the client-centered and developmental approaches. Problem exploration appears to be best facilitated by "nondirective" counselor responses. The middle stage of career counseling is characterized by a predominance of "interpretive" counselor responses designed to clarify the predisposing and precipitating factors in the client's problem. These interview techniques come largely from psychodynamic career counseling. And during the terminal stage of career counseling the methods of review and reinforcement from the trait-and-factor and behavioral approaches seem to be most apropos. They are peculiarly suited to problem resolution, which involves instrumental learning and goal-directed behavior. Comprehensive career counseling, therefore, incorporates and applies interview techniques from the other major approaches which implement the diagnostic, process, and outcome model along the communication and relationship dimensions of the client/counselor interaction.

Test Interpretation

From its inception, the heart of trait-and-factor career counseling was test interpretation. The *raison d'être* of this approach was that tests can predict future career adjustment (success and satisfaction) and these predictions provide the client with a rational basis for career choice. When client-centered career counseling emerged, however, the pendulum swung away from test interpretation to a focus upon the emotional side of decision making, and it has not appreciably swung back. Both psychodynamic and behavioral career counseling largely eschew tests, or they use them in unique ways (Chapter 2 of this text), and developmental career counseling has been hung on the dilemma that measures of its central concept—namely, career maturity—have been generally unavailable. Moreover, increasing evidence has accumulated that the initial promise of tests has not been realized; their predictive validity has left much to be desired (Bloom, 1964; Ghiselli, 1966; Holland & Lutz, 1967). The upshot of this disenchantment with tests has been for career counselors to overreact by not using them even when appropriate. That a role for tests in comprehensive career counseling exists, however, can be contended not only conceptually but also experientially (Chapter 2 of this text). Experimentation and experience with tests in career counseling suggest new modes and methods for their integration with diagnosis, process, and outcomes which revitalize their potential for assisting clients with problems in career decision making.

For differential diagnosis, both general aptitude tests and vocational-interests inventory scores, as well as nontest data on career choice, are needed to identify a client's problem within the system described previously (Crites, 1969). These data also provide the basis for dynamic diagnosis but must be supplemented with interview interactions. Process notes on the latter from one contact to another are synthesized with the psychometric data to formulate and test the counselor's understanding of the "hypothetical client." Obviously, the client is intimately involved in this process and collaborates with the counselor in accumulating greater self-knowledge. It should be emphasized that testing is in and through and part of the ongoing career counseling; it is not a separate activity which takes place disjunctively from the client/counselor interaction. Particularly is this true in decisional diagnosis wherein the client and counselor systematically analyze whatever problems may be identified in how choices are made. To illustrate, suppose the differential diagnosis for a client, arrived at mutually with the counselor, is unrealism in decision making due to choice at a level higher than measured aptitude, and the dynamic diagnosis is that of an individual who has been impulsive in decision making. The decisional diagnosis may center, then, upon which phase of the choice process the client is circumventing or subverting. For example, the CMI-Competence Test may reveal low scores on Self-Appraisal and Occupational Information, thus indicating that the client may be impulsively bypassing the information-gathering stage of decision making and prematurely engaging in goal selection (Crites, 1973). Test interpretation in relation to all aspects of diagnosis becomes an integral part of career counseling, not an adjunctive disparate activity.

The relationship of test interpretation to the process of career counseling is that of microcosm to macrocosm. There are not only the beginning, middle, and terminal stages of test interpretation but also, woven through them, the interplay between communication and relationship. From these universal dimensions of client/counselor interactions, in conjunction with the diagnosis, derive the most appropriate techniques for interpreting tests. For example, if a client has "no choice" (either indecision or indecisiveness), tests are probably best interpreted by *not* directly presenting the results to the client. Rather, as questions arise during the career counseling process, which the client and counselor collaboratively agree might be answered with tests, the tests are taken with the understanding that the counselor will "feed back" the information from them to the client as the two of them talk about the choice problem. Thus, in response to a client's expressed indecision about whether s/he might be satisfied with a career in engineering, the counselor might say, depending upon what the test results were, "The interest inventory you took indicates that your interests are very much like those of engineers. The chances are pretty good—about 3½ to 1—that if you went into that occupation you would stay in it and feel relatively satisfied." By interpreting tests in this way, communication is maximized, because the test interpretation is stated within the client's conceptual and linguistic frame-of-reference, *not* psychometric jargon, and the relationship is furthered, because responsibility for interpreting the tests is shared by the client and counselor, *not* assumed almost wholly by the latter as expert. In contrast to the traditional approach to test interpretation, in which profiles are presented and scores are explained didactically, this new technique has become known as "interpreting the tests without the tests."

Its value lies not only in the immediate outcome of facilitating the ongoing process of career counseling but also in the longer term goals of retention and understanding. There is reliable research evidence that test results interpreted in the traditional way are either distorted or forgotten by clients (e.g., Froehlich & Moser, 1954). Counseling experience and preliminary experimental findings suggest that "interpreting the tests without the tests" increases both accuracy and duration of test information and enhances self-understanding. What apparently happens in this approach, although all the dynamics are far from being explicated, is that the test results are translated by the counselor into the vernacular of the client, who, in turn, thinks and talks about them in terms of the decision-making process. The test scores thus become imbedded in the contextual meaning of such considerations as "What kind of person am I?" "What career roles are most compatible with the person I am?" and "What are the problems I have in becoming that person in a career?" Both person and problem appraisal (Super & Crites, 1962) are furthered and, as a consequence, general self-knowledge is furthered. Hence, test interpretation assumes a critical valence in achieving the desired outcome of career counseling: it provides the client with relevant information for making a specific career choice; it models decisional skills and how they can be used in problem solving; and it contributes to better adjustment through greater self-understanding and resultant self-confidence in coping effectively.

Synthesis. Although the procedure of "interpreting the tests without the tests" contrasts dramatically with the trait-and-factor approach, it is nevertheless built upon a common premise—that test information has empirically established usefulness for person and problem appraisal, if not also prognostic appraisal, in comprehensive career counseling. Even contemporary client-centered precepts allow for the value of information about self and reality other than solely from within the phenomenal field (Grummon, 1972; Hart & Tomlinson, 1970). And consistent with this point of view is the technique of "interpreting the tests without the tests," which deliberately casts objective test information into the client's perception of the world. Presumably this new method of test interpretation would also be compatible with behavioral career counseling, in which there is a central focus upon the decision-making process. More specifically, introducing and discussing test results as part of the client and counselor's "examining the consequences of alternatives" (Krumboltz & Baker, 1973) appears to fit the behavioral model of how career choices are made, although this approach is not test oriented (Chapter 2 of this text). Communicating test scores in client/counselor interchanges on the content and process of career choice comes closest to the techniques which are advocated in developmental and psychodynamic career counseling. Both of these orientations emphasize the dynamics of decision making, which are clarified and learned by the client when test results are imparted interactively.

Occupational Information

Of the methods of career counseling, the use of occupational information has been the most inarticulate. Voluminous amounts of occupational information have been published over the years with dubious impact. Some critics (e.g., Barry & Wolf, 1962) have questioned whether it has *any* salience for career decision making, whereas others (e.g., Hoppock, 1963) have highlighted its centrality in both career choice and counseling. Most counselors seem to pay lip service to it, regarding the presentation of occupational information to the client as necessary but uninspiring. As a result, they either do a poor job of it or neglect it altogether. In one unpublished study (Crites, Note 1), for example, it was found that most counselors of a university counseling service engaged in career counseling simply referred their clients to the "occupational file" in the center for information about the world of work. A tally by the receptionist, whose desk was next to the file, of those clients who actually used it indicated that only about 5% availed themselves of it! More novel approaches to the dissemination of occupational information (e.g., Magoon, 1964) may be more effective, but the problem remains that this aspect of decision making does not appear to be integrated with career counseling. There are some new methods, however, which have promise for meaningfully relating occupational information to diagnosis, process, and outcomes in comprehensive career counseling.

If the combined differential, dynamic, and decisional diagnosis suggests that a client's problem is simple indecision, then the use of occupational information by the counselor to increase knowledge of the world of work is appropriate. Clients with this problem typically have had inadequate or insufficient opportunities to learn about occupations, either directly or indirectly, and can benefit from information about job duties and tasks, employment opportunities, lines of advancement, and future trends. In contrast, the client diagnosed as indecisive usually has acquired the necessary occupational information for career choice but is unable to use it in decision making due to antecedent anxiety (Crites, 1969, Chapter 2 of this text). Occupational information only exacerbates the anxiety by emphasizing the presenting problem: the client's decisional processes are paralyzed by anxiety, not lack of information. Once the anxiety has been reduced, then the indecisive client can utilize the previously obtained occupational information and engage in career choice. If the diagnosis is unrealism, then direct presentation of occupational information is indicated. The unrealistic client characteristically "colors" the world of work to look as *if* it is consistent with his/her career choice when it is not. To establish such distortions, and to rectify them, confrontive reality testing against objective occupational information is often the best counseling method.

Three principal processes are available for imparting occupational information to the client: First, the counselor can directly present it to the client in the interview. This procedure has the advantage of integrating the use of occupational information with the overall context of career counseling, but it has the two-fold disadvantage of casting the counselor into the role of "expert," rather than "collaborator," who must then keep abreast of the voluminous information about occupations, which is constantly changing in today's rapidly developing economy. Second, the client can be shaped and reinforced by the counselor to gather information on her/his own outside the interview situation. This approach has merit in fostering client independence in making a career choice, as well as acquiring a relevant competency, but it needs to be incorporated into the ongoing course of the career counseling. Otherwise the information may not be meaningfully used by the client in decision making. And, third, a computerized occupational-information system (Super, 1970) may be utilized as an adjunct to career counseling, in which the client becomes familiar with the world of work by asking the computer questions about possible careers. Again, the potential drawback is that this experience becomes an end in itself, without relation to client/counselor interactions on career choice. The obvious synthesis of these methods, of course, is to use them concomitantly, with the counselor orienting the client to information, including computerized systems, and reinforcing the client in the exploration of this information. The client then discusses the import of the occupational information for career-goal selection with the counselor as part of the career-counseling process.

The immediate outcome of this general method of using occupational information in career counseling is increased knowledge of the world of work, particularly that segment which most closely corresponds to the career choices the client is considering. Until fairly recently there has been no standardized measure of occupational information to assess the extent to which this outcome has been achieved; now, the Occupational Information subtest of the Career Maturity Inventory has been published for this purpose (Crites, 1973). Preliminary findings from research in progress indicate that scores on this subtest increase significantly after exposure to an occupational-information intervention (the Job Experience Kits). The remote outcomes of acquiring occupational information include realistic career choice and greater career maturity. The former can be appraised by the agreement of choice with aptitudes and interests and the latter with the CMI or comparable instruments (Super, 1974). Increased incidence of information—seeking behavior, for example—might be reflected on both the CMI Occupational Information subtest and the Attitude Scale, which can be scored for involvement as well as independence in career choice. Together, the immediate and remote outcomes of occupational information in career counseling should also contribute, through generalization, to the client's effectiveness in functioning in other areas of life adjustment. Thus, having learned how to collect and use information about occupations in making career decisions, s/he might follow the same process in gathering information for a consumer or business decision.

Synthesis. It is difficult to synthesize the positions of the major approaches to career counseling on occupational information, not only because of divergencies among them but also because of the discrepancy between precept and practice. Occupational information is the most neglected aspect of career counseling, yet it is as important as self-knowledge in career decision making, according to the trait-and-factor approach. Similarly, behavioral and psychodynamic career counseling accord a role to occupational information in deciding about a career, although their emphases differ (Chapter 2 of this text). In the developmental orientation, one of the major dimensions of career maturity is occupational information (Super & Overstreet, 1960). Only in the client-centered approach has objective information been eschewed, but even Patterson (1964) allows for it and Grummon (1972) states that it is necessary. Thus, it can be concluded that a comprehensive approach to career counseling would encompass the use of occupational information in assisting a client to make a career choice. The problem is how to integrate this activity, which is largely one of accumulating facts and figures, with the career-counseling process. One solution is to reinforce the client for gathering occupational information outside the contact hour and to use the hour for counseling rather than dissemination. Both the counselor and the client can fulfill the collaborative roles they have assumed for themselves in their relationship, and career counseling can proceed as an interactive process.

MATERIALS OF COMPREHENSIVE CAREER COUNSELING

By the term *materials* of comprehensive career counseling is meant the subject matter of client/counselor interactions, including talk and tests, from the initial interview to the last. Sometimes called case materials or case studies they constitute the warp and woof of career counseling: they give it operational definition. Thus, to provide experiential meaning for the comprehensive approach to career counseling which has been outlined here, the materials of the process must be presented. Ideally, cases which exemplify all of the parameters of comprehensive career counseling would be described, but space obviously does not permit such a survey. A case has been selected, however, which illustrates many of these facets. This was a seven-interview sequence with Karen, a 17-year-old high school senior, who was self-referred for career counseling during the 1974-1975 academic year. She was seen by the author on a weekly basis, with one break over the Christmas vacation period. The materials from the case—interview excerpts, test results, biographical and demographic data, etc.—have been organized according to the model for comprehensive career counseling: diagnosis, process, and outcomes. The method of interviewing, interpreting tests, and using occupational information are discussed in relation to the model, the former being the means for implementing the latter.

Diagnosis

I saw Karen for a relatively short (less than the standard 50-minute hour) screening interview to make arrangements for her career counseling and to gain some initial impression of why she wanted to see me. Her presenting problem was one of uncertainty about her career choice. She said that she had been considering teaching and social work and possibly music but had been having difficulty deciding among them. I responded with largely open-ended questions, such as "How do you mean you are uncertain?" and "Why has it been difficult for you to decide what you want to do?" in order to further problem exploration. Her answers to these and similar questions suggested that her problem might be less one of uncertainty than indecision. For example, she said: "I keep going back and forth between teaching and social work. My mother is a third-grade teacher, and I like what she does, but if I were a social worker I could help people." The reaction she elicited in me was like ones I had had when I could not decide between what appeared to be equally desirable alternatives. I shared this by saying: "I have had much the same feeling of uncertainty you are expressing, or what I call indecision, when I have been trying to make a choice about something. Perhaps it is indecision rather than uncertainty that is troubling you." And, I explained what I considered to be the difference between the two states or conditions, uncertainty being defined as the dissonance which follows a choice, rather than the anxiety which precedes a decision (Crites, 1969; Hilton, 1962; James, 1963). She agreed that she was experiencing indecision, and we settled upon this as her "differential" diagnosis.

Whether the indecision was simple or not, however, had to be determined by making a "dynamic" diagnosis, which continued through approximately three interviews. I had to identify the antecedent conditions in which she had decisional experiences, starting with the family and school. Since she was a high school senior, I asked her what she planned to do after she graduated, and she said she was going to college. Which college or university had she decided upon? Her preference had been a small Southern college, where she felt she could develop closer personal relationships with other students than she had had in high school. But her father questioned her choice, not only because the tuition would be higher, she would be farther from home, and other "objective" reasons, but also because he implied that she really did not know what she wanted for herself. He devalued her need for "closer personal relationships" and encouraged (coerced?) her to attend the state university where she could continue the "reputation of achievement" she had established in high school. She acquiesced and followed her father's wishes. I asked her: "Has this happened with other decisions you have made?" and she answered affirmatively. I continued with questions about how she felt when she was faced with a decision, and she reported what amounted to an accentuated state of anxiety. She observed: "I really feel 'up tight'." "I'm afraid of what he will say." and "I want to do what will please him." From her description of past experiences with decision making, particulary *vis-à-vis* her father, I developed the "dynamic" diagnosis of indecisiveness. Subsequent interviewing and testing tended to confirm that she had considerable difficulty in making not only career decisions but also others.

The pervasiveness of Karen's indecisiveness extended to her self-concept and self-esteem. In one of the early interviews in the overall sequence, I asked her to describe herself, and she said that she couldn't. She added: "I don't know who I am." Since knowing oneself is a central part of mature career decision making I suggested that it might be useful to assess objectively her self-knowledge, as well as some of the other career-choice competencies and attitudes which are related to the decisional process. I described the Career Maturity Inventory, which was designed to measure these variables, and Karen thought that taking it would be worthwhile. She was above average on her scores for all of the parts of the Competence Test except Self-Appraisal. On this subtest she had a raw score of 10 out of a possible total score of 20 and a percentile rank of 15, which placed her considerably below average. In other words, both her degree and rate of maturity (raw score and percentile rank, respectively) (Crites, 1961) revealed that she was career immature in making self-appraisals. Also, although her Attitude Scale score was high, the items which she endorsed in the career-immature direction corroborated both her doubts and uncertainties about herself and her indecisiveness concerning career choice. The "decisional" diagnosis, therefore, was career immaturity in self-appraisal.

Process

The first stage in the process of career counseling with Karen, which included the screening and initial interviews, was primarily oriented to problem exploration. It focused upon diagnosis of her problem. It also opened the complex process of establishing effective communication with Karen and of developing a "working" relationship with her. I found that she interacted readily but rather glibly. The client/counselor "talk ratio," which is a good index of the extent to which each is assuming responsibility for the interaction, was about 50/50. What bothered me was not the quantity of Karen's communication but its quality. Her analysis of her career decisional problem was, at least initially, rather glossy and superficial. To break through this facade I asked open-ended questions designed to expose aspects of her problem which I felt she had not previously considered or been aware of. When she commented that she "didn't know" what kind of person she was, I asked "Why not?" and added "Who is going to know who you are if not you?"

She responded that she usually looked to her parents, particularly her father, for an answer to this question. To clarify the nature of our relationship I came back with: "Do you expect me to tell you what kind of person you are?" Karen: "I guess I did before, but I don't think you're going to." Me: "That's right, but I'll try to help you find out." Her: "O.K. I'd like to do that." Problem explored and explicated, communication opened up, relationship begun, initial contract entered: these goals of the first stage of the career counseling process were achieved.

The second stage in my career counseling with Karen became more *intensive*. We tried to clarify her problem further and identify the factors which had contributed to it. Most of these involved her family. Her father is a hard-driving, achievement-oriented man who expected the same of Karen. In contrast, her mother is a family-centered, elementary-school teacher who encouraged Karen to consider social-service careers. Her indecisiveness thus mirrored the divergent values of her parents and her mixed allegiances to them. I came to see much of her conflict concerning career choice as emanating from anxiety associated with these divided loyalties: If she made a decision, then she was rejecting one or the other parent. Compounded with this dilemma was what emerged as an unwillingness to compromise, since—as was brought out later—to do so would have meant making a career choice and hence running the risk of alienating one of her parents. When I pointed this out to Karen, using the declarative responses more typical of the second stage of career counseling, she cried and said: "But how can I free myself from them? What can I do to be my own person?" At this point in the career-counseling process, I renegotiated our "contract" to include a consideration of Karen's relationships with her parents, in general, and how they impinged upon her career decision making, in particular. We agreed (collaborative relationship) that we would look at how she might resolve her problems with her parents and hence resolve her career-choice problem.

In the third stage of Karen's career counseling, which consisted of the fifth, sixth, and seventh interviews, we talked about various options she had available to her to do what she wanted to do rather than what her parents wanted her to do. She balked at times in considering some of these alternatives, tearing at the prospect of behaving counter to her parents' expectations, but she gradually came to the understanding that her life was her own, if she would assume responsibility for it—which she did. The issue of which college she would attend had been settled, primarily because of financial considerations, but we discussed at some length how she might extricate herself from what appeared to be an *impossible* family situation. The mother tried to have a family reunion at dinner time, but the father subverted this, either by "having" to work late or by playing the stereo at maximum volume when he was at home for dinner, so that dinner-table interaction was impossible. Moreover, her time at home never seemed to be her own; someone was always intruding upon her privacy. The resolution which we arrived at was for her to have time for herself. She felt it was impossible for her to shed any of her home responsibilities, but she was receptive to my suggestion that she go to bed earlier in order to have some "quiet time" to herself in the morning hours before others were up. She did this, as well as exploring possible careers for herself. In discussing these careers, I introduced the results from the tests she had taken—Differential Aptitude Tests, Holland Vocational Preference Inventory, and Career Maturity Inventory—and tried to draw implications from them for her career choice. The third stage of Karen's career counseling ended with a review of the career options which were possibly open to her, in light of current occupational information, and a resolution of her career-choice problem to the extent that she was no longer indecisive, for reasons which had previously been inexplicable to her. She planned to use the summer not only for further career exploration but also to live away from home. Thus, she arrived at a resolution of her choice problem which alleviated the conditions of conflict and posed opportunities for their effective elimination.

Outcomes

Implicit in the process of my career counseling with Karen are the outcomes. First, although she did not arrive at a specific career choice, she learned why she was having difficulty in making a decision. She realized that she was usually unwilling to compromise her lofty ambitions and standards and consequently was frequently indecisive in all areas of her life functioning, not only the vocational. By the end of her career counseling, she was able to compromise more appropriately and to make such decisions as to live away from home during the summer. Second, she started to know herself better and to be able to communicate her self-concept to me. She clarified many of her feelings about her parents, and she moved toward a greater understanding of how she related to peers. She became aware that she often "put them off" by acting toward them much as her father acted toward her—directive and demanding and critical. As a result, she felt "used" by others who sought her advice and help but who kept her on the fringe of their social groups. Karen resolved to "tone down" her active/directive characteristics and to moderate her expectations of others. All these changes contributed to an increased facility for self-appraisal and thus enhanced this aspect of her career maturity. Finally, Karen seemed to be better adjusted upon the completion of her career counseling. Not only did she feel more competent to cope with her career decisions, but she expressed greater confidence in "running her own life." Both her career and her personal adjustment appeared improved from her experience in comprehensive career counseling.

CONCLUSION

The comprehensive approach to career counseling described in this paper and extrapolated from the previous review of major approaches to career counseling is necessarily incomplete. It is a first approximation to a system of career counseling which ideally would be applicable and useful with all possible combinations of clients and counselors, in both individual and group interactions. To test and extend its applicability is the next task. Laboratory studies on what are called career-counseling *modules*, such as "interpreting the tests without the tests," are currently being conducted to determine whether several of these units might be identified which could be used in optimal combinations for different client/counselor parameters. If they can, then research to replicate the laboratory findings in the field will be undertaken, the goal being to make career counseling as comprehensive as possible. In the meantime, clinical work continues as the comprehensive approach is "tried out" with more and different client/counselor diads (and groups).

REFERENCE NOTE

Crites, J. O. *Use of an occupational file by career counseling clients.* Unpublished manuscript, University of Iowa, 1965.

REFERENCES

Barry, R., & Wolf, B. *Epitaph for vocational guidance.* New York: Bureau of Publications, Teachers College, Columbia University, 1962.

Bixler, R. H., & Bixler, V. H. Test interpretation in vocational counseling. *Educational and Psychological Measurement*, 1946, *6*, 145-156.

Bloom, B. S. *Stability and change in human characteristics.* New York: Wiley, 1964.

Bordin, E. S. Diagnosis in counseling and psychotherapy. *Educational and Psychological Measurement*, 1946, *6*, 169-184.

Bordin, E. S. *Psychological counseling* (2nd ed.). New York: Appleton-Century-Crofts, 1968.

Bordin, E. S., & Kopplin, D. A. Motivational conflict and vocational development. *Journal of Counseling Psychology*, 1973, *20*, 154-161.

Colby, K. M. *A primer for psychotherapists.* New York: Ronald, 1951.

Corsini, R. *Current psychotherapies.* Itasca, Ill.: Peacock, 1973.

Crites, J. O. A model for the measurement of vocational maturity. *Journal of Counseling Psychology*, 1961, *8*, 255-259.

Crites, J. O. *Vocational psychology.* New York: McGraw-Hill, 1969.

Crites, J. O. *Theory and research handbook for the Career Maturity Inventory.* Monterey, Calif.: CTB/McGraw-Hill, 1973.

Crites, J. O. Career counseling: A review of major approaches. *The Counseling Psychologist*, 1974, *4*(3), 3-23. (a) (Chapter 2 of this text)

Crites, J. O. A reappraisal of vocational appraisal. *Vocational Guidance Quarterly*, 1974, *23*, 272-279. (b)

Crites, J. O. Career development processes: A model of vocational maturity. In E. L. Herr (Ed.), *Vocational guidance and human development.* Boston: Houghton Mifflin, 1974. Pp. 296-320. (c)

Dipboye, W. J. Analysis of counselor style by discussion units. *Journal of Counseling Psychology*, 1954, *1*, 21-26.

Edwards, W. The theory of decision making. *Psychological Bulletin*, 1954, *51*, 380-417.

Edwards, W. Behavioral decision theory. *Annual Review of Psychology*, 1961, *12*, 473-499.

Ford, D. H., & Urban, H. B. *Systems of psychotherapy*. New York: Wiley, 1963.

Freud, S. *Civilization and its discontents*. New York: Norton, 1962.

Froehlich, C. P., & Moser, W. E. Do counselees remember test scores? *Journal of Counseling Psychology*, 1954, *1*, 149-152.

Gelatt, A. B. Decision-making: A conceptual frame of reference for counseling. *Journal of Counseling Psychology*, 1962, *9*, 240-245.

Gelatt, H. B., Varenhorst, B., & Carey, R. *Deciding*. New York: College Entrance Examination Board, 1972.

Ghiselli, E. E. *The validity of occupational aptitude tests*. New York: Wiley, 1966.

Ginzberg, E., Ginsburg, S. W., Axelrad, S., & Herma, J. L. *Occupational choice*. New York: Columbia University Press, 1951.

Goldman, L. The process of vocational assessment. In H. Borow (Ed.), *Man in a world at work*. Boston: Houghton Mifflin, 1964. Pp. 389-410.

Grummon, D. L. Client-centered theory. In B. Stefflre & W. H. Grant (Eds.), *Theories of counseling* (2nd ed.). New York: McGraw-Hill, 1972. Pp. 73-135.

Hart, J. T., & Tomlinson, T. M. (Eds.). *New directions in client-centered therapy*. Boston: Houghton Mifflin, 1970.

Hilton, T. L. Career decision-making. *Journal of Counseling Psychology*, 1962, *9*, 291-298.

Holland, J. L., & Lutz, S. W. Predicting a student's vocational choice. *ACT Research Reports*, 1967, No. 18.

Hoppock, R. *Occupational information* (2nd ed.). New York: McGraw-Hill, 1963.

James, F., III. Comment on Hilton's model of career decision-making. *Journal of Counseling Psychology*, 1963, *10*, 303-304.

Kiesler, D. J. *The process of psychotherapy*. Chicago: Aldine, 1973.

Kilby, R. W. Some vocational counseling methods. *Educational and Psychological Measurement*, 1949, *9*, 173-192.

Kirtner, W. L., & Cartwright, D. S. Success and failure in client-centered therapy as a function of initial in-therapy behavior. *Journal of Consulting Psychology*, 1958, *22*, 329-333.

Krumboltz, J. D., & Baker, R. D. Behavioral counseling for vocational decisions. In H. Borow (Ed.), *Career guidance for a new age*. Boston: Houghton Mifflin, 1973. Pp. 235-283.

Magoon, T. Innovations in counseling. *Journal of Counseling Psychology*, 1964, *11*, 342-347.

McArthur, C. Analyzing the clinical process. *Journal of Counseling Psychology*, 1954, *1*, 203-208.

Patterson, C. H. Counseling: Self-clarification and the helping relationship. In H. Borow (Ed.), *Man in a world at work*. Boston: Houghton Mifflin, 1964. Pp. 434-459.

Patterson, C. H. *Theories of counseling and psychotherapy* (2nd ed.). New York: Harper & Row, 1973.

Robinson, F. P. *Principles and procedures in student counseling*. New York: Harper, 1950.

Rogers, C. R. *On becoming a person*. Boston: Houghton Mifflin, 1951.

Rogers, C. R. Gendlin, E. T., Kiesler, D. J., & Traux, C. G. *The therapeutic relationship and its impact.* Madison: University of Wisconsin Press, 1967.

Schrader, C. H. *Vocational choice problems: Indecision vs. indecisiveness.* Unpublished doctoral dissertation, University of Iowa, 1970.

Seeman, J. A. A study of client self-selection of tests in vocational counseling. *Educational and Psychological Measurement,* 1948, *8,* 327-346.

Shoben, E. J., Jr. Work, love, and maturity. *Personnel and Guidance Journal,* 1956, *34,* 326-332.

Sinnett, E. R. Some determinants of agreement between measured and expressed interests. *Educational and Psychological Measurement,* 1956, *16,* 110-118.

Strong, E. K., Jr. *Vocational interests 18 years after college.* Minneapolis: University of Minnesota Press, 1955.

Super, D. E. The dimensions and measurement of vocational maturity. *Teachers College Record,* 1955, *57,* 151-163.

Super, D. E. *The psychology of careers.* New York: Harper, 1957.

Super, D. E. (Ed.). *Computer-assisted counseling.* New York: Teachers College Press, 1970.

Super, D. E. (Ed.). *Measuring vocational maturity for counseling and evaluation.* Washington, D. C.: National Vocational Guidance Association, 1974.

Super, D. E., & Crites, J. O. *Appraising vocational fitness* (Rev. ed.). New York: Harper & Row, 1962.

Super, D. E., & Overstreet, P. L. *The vocational maturity of ninth grade boys.* New York: Teachers College Bureau of Publications, 1960.

Super, D. E., Starishevsky, R., Matlin, N., & Jordaan, J. P. *Career development: Self-concept theory.* Princeton, N. J.: College Entrance Examination Board, 1963.

Thompson, A. S. A rationale for vocational guidance. *Personnel and Guidance Journal,* 1954, *32,* 533-535.

Watzlawick, P., Beavin, J. H., & Jackson, D. D. *Pragmatics of human communication.* New York: Norton, 1967.

Williams, J. E. Changes in self and other perception following brief educational-vocational counseling. *Journal of Counseling Psychology,* 1962, *9,* 18-30.

Williams, J. E., & Hills, D. A. More on brief educational-vocational counseling. *Journal of Counseling Psychology,* 1962, *9,* 366-368.

Williamson, E. G. *How to counsel students.* New York: McGraw-Hill, 1939.

A SOCIAL LEARNING THEORY OF CAREER SELECTION

5

JOHN D. KRUMBOLTZ
Stanford University

with ANITA M. MITCHELL
G. BRIAN JONES
American Institutes for Research

A. PROBLEM

Why do people happen to enter the particular educational programs or occupations they do? How or why is it that they change from one educational program or occupation to another at various points throughout their lives? How can it be explained that they express different preferences for various programs or occupations at different times in their lives?

A number of attempts have been made to understand these phenomena. What follows is a social-learning-theory analysis of career decision making. This analysis provides a basis for a series of propositions that lead to some testable hypotheses and provide a framework for a synthesis of existing empirical evidence.[1]

The theory presented here attempts to explain how educational and occupational preferences and skills are acquired and how selections of courses, occupations, and fields of work are made. It identifies the interactions of genetic factors, environmental conditions, learning experiences, cognitive and

Portions of this paper were presented by John D. Krumboltz as his Presidential Address to the Division of Counseling Psychology at the APA Convention in Chicago, August 30, 1975. Work leading to the development of this paper was performed at the American Institutes for Research in Palo Alto, California, with support from the National Institute of Education. Especially appreciated were the efforts of Ivan Charner (Project Monitor), H. B. Gelatt, Waldemar R. Unruh, Barbara A. Sanderson, David "Randy" Black, and Craig Ewart.

[1]A description of the empirical evidence relevant to this theory has been prepared by Anita M. Mitchell and appears as Chapter 3 in Mitchell, Jones and Krumboltz (1975). In Chapter 5 G. Brian Jones has suggested relevant research and development priorities.

emotional responses, and performance skills that produce movement along one career path or another. Combinations of these factors interact in different ways to produce different decisions.[2]

At each decision point the decider has one or more response or decision options. Internal (personal) and external (environmental) influencers (constraints or facilitators) shape the nature and number of those options and the way in which individuals respond to them. Sometimes so many options are available that the individual feels incapable of deciding. At other times options may be so limited or so disproportionate in value that the individual feels only one option is available. In fact, this person might feel s/he has no choice. But always there are options, even if one of them is not to make a decision. A decision—the selection of an option from among two or more alternatives—may increase or decrease options available for future decisions. Some consequences are irreversible. The decision made within an environment becomes part of the new environment and may itself become one of the constraints or facilitators in a new setting. This is another example of the interdependence of any series of learning experiences and decisions.

The theory allows for modifications by future events. In no sense is it intended as a final statement. It should be congruent with presently known facts but it should also suggest further research that may lead to modifying part or all of the theory itself.

B. FACTORS THAT INFLUENCE THE NATURE OF CAREER DECISION MAKING (CDM)

Four categories of influencers are posited.

1. Genetic Endowment and Special Abilities

A person is born with certain inherited qualities that may set limits on that individual's educational and occupational preferences, skills, and selections. Following are some illustrative, although not exhaustive, factors that may well make a difference.

—Race
—Sex
—Physical appearance and characteristics, including physical defects or handicaps that cannot be changed

The evidence is not clear as to the genetic and environmental components of various special abilities. It is not essential for purposes of this theory to know at this point exactly what portion of the variance is due to

[2]Possible practical applications and a summary of the theory are discussed in Krumboltz, Mitchell and Gelatt (1975).

genetic or environmental influencers, but it should be recognized that the possibility exists that certain individuals are born with greater or lesser predispositions to profit from certain types of learning experiences. Aspects of the following abilities might be attributed to such predispositions, while other parts obviously result from interactions with environmental influencers.

—Intelligence
—Musical ability
—Artistic ability
—Muscular coordination

2. Environmental Conditions and Events

Educational and occupational decision making is influenced to a large extent by factors usually outside the control of any one individual. Some events may be planned; many others are unplanned. These environmental conditions and events may be due to human action (social, cultural, political, or economic) or to natural forces (location of natural resources or natural disasters). As a result of these factors, certain events or conditions occur which influence the career preferences, skills, plans, and activities of the individual.

Number and nature of job opportunities. As a result of historical forces and governmental policies, certain occupational opportunities are available in one setting that are not available in another. Opportunities to be an abalone fisherman exist in California but not in Arizona. Opportunities to be a department store Santa Claus are available in certain Western countries but not in Pakistan.

Number and nature of training opportunities. Educational opportunities are available in different cultures through different social institutions. In the United States training is available through public schools, proprietary schools, the armed forces, apprenticeship programs in unions and industry, and through correspondence courses. Accessibility of these training alternatives varies considerably from one location to another.

Social policies and procedures for selecting trainees and workers. Policies and procedures can change as a result of new laws or judicial decisions. For example, the use of certain aptitude tests has been restricted as a result of recent court decisions. Requirements for entering certain jobs may be modified. The requirements may be functional or nonfunctional but still have an influence on the career-selection process. For example, the requirement of a high school diploma may influence certain people to finish their high school education even though a high school education is not necessary for successful performance on the job.

Rate of return for various occupations. The ratio of potential pecuniary and non-pecuniary rewards to the costs of preparing for an occupation varies dramatically from one occupation to another. The rewards, the risks, and the costs of preparing for any given occupation can be different in different cultures and in different groups within the same culture, and can be changed within any given culture as a result of institutional or governmental action. Trends in the rate of return for different occupations may be identified and may affect future planning.

Labor laws and union rules. Rules for joining labor unions can affect the number of new members, the number of job opportunities, and the benefits.

Physical events such as earthquakes, droughts, floods, and hurricanes. Disasters such as these can destroy the economy of a certain location such that individuals employed there can no longer continue the same type of·work.

Availability of and demand for natural resources. The owner of land on which oil was discovered under circumstances where there was a large demand for oil might understandably change his occupational activities.

Technological developments. The invention of new techniques and products produces job opportunities that might have been unavailable a few years previously. Industrialized societies therefore produce different patterns of job opportunities than less developed societies.

Changes in social organization. Setting up the Social Security system in the United States not only provided a large number of jobs for employees in the Federal civil-service system but also affected the career plans of many individuals.

Family training experiences and resources. An individual is born or adopted into a family which has learned a certain religion and adopted certain values and which communicates certain expectations to the new child. Families differ in what they teach their youngsters and in the resources they have available to provide for them. Such differences produce conditions for the individual that may make a difference in that individual's educational and occupational preferences, skills, and selections.

Educational system. The school organization, the administrative policies, and the type and personality of teachers available to the individual can have a big influence on the skills learned and the degree to which the individual strives to achieve success in various endeavors.

Neighborhood and community influences. Communities differ in the extent to which models of people working in different occupations are available, the extent to which peers have learned differential values, and the extent to which various cultural events are available and valued.

3. Learning Experiences

Educational and occupational decision making is also influenced by the individual's past learning experiences. The patterns of stimuli and reinforcement, their nature, and their scheduling are so exceedingly complex that no theory can adequately account for the infinite variations that influence the development of career preferences and skills and the making of career selections. Two categories of learning are used here in an overly simplified form to point out the types of experiences that have an impact on CDM.

Instrumental Learning Experiences (ILEs). In these, the individual acts on the environment in such a way as to produce certain consequences. An H-shaped figure will be used to represent an instrumental learning experience. Figure 1 presents a diagram to show the components in the ILE. Three general components are identified: antecedents, covert and overt behavioral responses, and consequences (including responses to these consequences which in turn become a part of subsequent learning experiences). The antecedents in the general model consist of factors such as those identified in the above three sections (e.g., the cultural setting, the social history of the particular group) and the stimulus characteristics of a particular task or problem that is presented to the individual. Behavioral responses consist of cognitive and emotional responses as well as overt actions. Consequences include both the direct effects produced by the action (self-feedback, verbal feedback from other individuals, observable results of the action itself, immediate or delayed impact on other people) and the cognitive and feeling responses the individual makes when s/he experiences these consequences. Figure 1 also presents a specific example of antecedents, the overt component of behavior, and feedback component of the consequences in the fictitious case of "Roger." Other examples of instrumental learning experiences would include knitting a sweater, reading a book, hitting a baseball, saying hello to a stranger, cutting down a tree, making an angelfood cake, or kissing someone of the opposite sex. The skills necessary for successful career planning, development, and occupational or educational performance are learned through successive instrumental learning experiences.

Associative Learning Experiences (ALEs). Learning experiences also occur when the individual's prevailing response pattern is a reaction to external stimuli. Observational learning in which the individual learns by observing real or fictitious models is included in this category of experiences.

Also incorporated here are experiences in which two events are paired in time or location such that the learner associates a previously neutral situation with some emotionally positive or negative reaction. Thus, for example,

Antecedents	Behaviors	Consequences
Genetic Endowment Special Abilities and Skills		Verbal Feedback from Self and/or Others Direct Observable Results of Action
Task or Problem	Covert and Overt Actions	Covert Reactions to Consequences (Cognitive and Emotional Responses)
Planned and Unplanned Environmental (e.g., Social, cultural, or Economic) Conditions or Events		Impact on Significant Others

GENERAL MODEL

Antecedents	Behaviors	Consequences
Roger, age 17, white, male, poor muscular coordination, superior writing skills		Teacher gives paper an "A" grade and writes "Well done." Roger thinks, "I could have done better if I had to."
Class in Government in which Roger has interacted with teacher and 29 others for 7 months. Teacher assigns paper on "A Famous Person in Government" due in 3 weeks	Roger (who happened to have visited Jefferson Memorial in Washington) writes paper on Thomas Jefferson and turns it in on time	Roger has a stimulating conversation with his father on how the U.S. would be different today if Jefferson had not lived
Government class in U.S. high school where athletic success is dominant basis for male students		Roger's classmate, Jock, sees teacher's comment and calls Roger a "teacher's pet"

SPECIFIC EXAMPLE: "ROGER"

Figure 1. Diagrams representing Instrumental Learning Experiences (ILEs).

hearing or reading words that pair two things together can have an impact. For example, statements such as "All lawyers are crooked" or "Plumbers make a lot of money" or "Those who can, do; those who can't do, teach; those who can't teach, teach teachers." Such verbal stereotypes about occupations influence the relative attractiveness or unattractiveness of each occupation. These associations can be learned not only through words but also through images on film, through reading in books, through observation of people employed in various occupations, and through direct experience. Individuals have a tendency to form generalizations about entire occupations from very few examples, and sometimes the first associations that are formed are the lasting ones.

The pairing of stimuli through the classical-conditioning paradigm is also included here. For example, a boy who becomes nauseous at the sight of blood may generalize the association to conclude that becoming a physician is inappropriate for him.

The general model for associative learning experiences is represented in Figure 2 as an O-shaped diagram. For simplicity, the cognitive and emotional

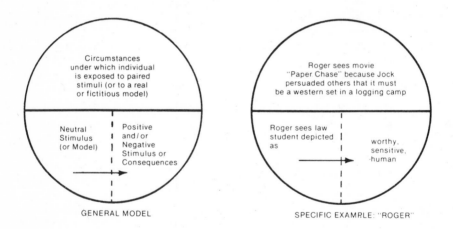

Figure 2. Diagrams representing Associative Learning Experiences (ALEs).

responses the individual makes as a reaction to these associations are omitted from Figure 2. The top of the diagram describes the circumstances under which the individual is exposed to paired stimuli or a model; the neutral stimulus or the model is represented in the lower left quadrant with an arrow pointing to the associated positive or negative stimulus or the consequences received by the model. Figure 2 also presents a concrete example of stimulus pairing. It illustrates how "Roger" might learn that law students could be considered worthy, sensitive human beings.

4. Task Approach Skills

As a result of as yet unexplained interactions between genetic and environmental influences, an individual brings to each new task or problem a set of skills, performance standards and values, work habits, perceptual and cognitive processes (such as attending, selecting, symbolic rehearsing, coding, encoding, reflecting, and evaluating responses), mental sets, and emotional responses. These task approach skills affect the outcomes of each task or problem. As a result of differential outcomes, the task approach skills become modified. For example, in high school Roger may cram for final examinations and get "A" grades, but in college his cramming habit may produce poor grades. The differential feedback may convince him to change his habits. Thus, task approach skills are both factors which influence outcomes and outcomes themselves.

C. OUTCOMES OF INTERACTIONS AMONG INFLUENCERS

Each individual is exposed to innumerable learning experiences throughout the days, months, and years of her/his life. These experiences occur in many sequences. Their combinations and permutations are virtually infinite. Each instrumental learning experience is followed by various rewards and/or punishments at various intervals of time following the behavior, and these varying schedules of reward, in combination with other learning experiences with their varying schedules of reward, produce an array of unique experiences which contributes to the diversity and individuality of the human species. Three kinds of consequences are pertinent to this analysis.

1. Self-Observation Generalizations (SOGs)

As a result of learning experiences, an individual can observe her/his own performance in relation to the performance of others or her/his own past performance and can make generalizations about it. Because the human being is capable of speech, s/he is able to utter statements which report these observations and conclusions. Comparison with others is usually part of the process, but idealized standards can be learned against which one's own behavior is compared. Figure 3 presents a diagram representing such a self-observation generalization. An SOG is defined as an overt or a covert self-statement evaluating one's own actual or vicarious performance in relation to learned standards. Figure 3 also presents a specific example of such an SOG in the case of "Roger." Not all SOGs are necessarily this explicit. A person may have a vague feeling of either confidence or discomfort, for example, when asked to give an impromptu speech. The feeling, as clearly articulated, might be, "I know I can give a succinct summary of my experience which will be well-received by other people because I have done this many times before." Or, if

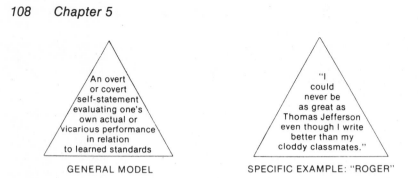

Figure 3. Diagrams representing a Self-Observation Generalization (SOG).

one's past experience had been different, the explicit statement might be, "Everyone will think I'm a fool if I stand up and try to talk in front of them, just like the last time someone made me do this."

Self-observations and conclusions are not necessarily accurate. A child might do an excellent job by objective standards but be told by her/his parents that it was poor. Without any other way to evaluate her/his own performance, s/he will learn to make negative evaluations about that particular behavior. When such negative evaluations are uttered, their expression may be reinforced by well-meaning friends who deny the negative statement and offer a more positive evaluation. Expressing negative self-observations then become a means of eliciting compliments from friends.

Self-observations and conclusions may be a function of the setting or the persons with whom one is associating. A boy may describe his bowling as superior in the presence of his girlfriend but inferior when he is with his buddies at the bowling alley. Such discrepancies can be explained as differential learning, a process involving discriminative stimuli and differential reinforcement. Positive self-observations and conclusions may be reinforced by some and punished by others. An individual accumulates both observations about her/his own performance and the generalizations to various situations but may not necessarily make explicit formulations of these observations or reactions until some suitable occasion for verbalizing them occurs.

Psychologists have devised various procedures for collecting individuals' self-observations and conclusions. Interest inventories are one such procedure. In some approaches to interest assessment, individuals are asked the degree to which they like, are indifferent to, or dislike various activities such as building a birdhouse or writing a letter. An individual may never have formulated an opinion on these questions before but, under the stimulus of the questionnaire, make decisions about her/his degree of liking for each item. These "interests" are merely SOGs generalized from prior learning experiences.

Another such device is an adjective checklist in which the individual circles adjectives which s/he feels are descriptive of herself/himself, e.g., trustworthy, humorous, attractive, shy. These self-descriptive adjectives are the result of the individual's observing herself/himself through one or more learning experiences and arriving at specific self-conclusions.

People tend to remember their reactions to learning experiences but to forget the actual learning experiences themselves, except when such experiences are particularly dramatic or traumatic. So, some individuals can reliably report on whether they enjoy or do not enjoy reading science fiction but cannot give the names of specific science fiction books that they have read. The success of interest inventories in predicting future occupational selection is probably due to the fact that conclusions from various learning experiences are memorable and that people tend to continue doing those activities which produce pleasurable reactions.

Sometimes psychologists speak of interests as if they *cause* occupational selection. However, in the theory presented here, interests are seen as consequences of learning experiences. It is the learning experiences themselves that have an impact on an individual's future development of educational and occupational skills and selection of a course of study, an occupation, or a field of work.

The one most important self-observation generalization for the purposes of this CDM study consists of *preferences*: preferring to work at one task and avoid another; preferring to play one sport but to eschew another. These preferences become an important outcome of learning experiences—the building blocks of career decisions.

2. Task Approach Skills (TASs)

Human beings are capable of relating their observations of themselves and of their environment in such a way as to make possible projections into the future as well as inferences about the past. Task approach skills are defined as cognitive and performance abilities and emotional predispositions for coping with the environment, interpreting it in relation to self-observation generalizations, and making covert or overt predictions about future events. They include work habits, mental sets, perceptual and thought processes, performance standards and values, problem orienting, and emotional responses. Figure 4 presents the general model and a specific example in the case of "Roger."

More specifically related to the purposes of the CDM study documented here, TASs include what may be termed CDM skills. Included are skills in value clarifying, goal setting, predicting future events, alternative generating, information seeking, estimating, re-interpreting past events, eliminating and selecting alternatives, planning, and generalizing (Krumboltz and Baker, 1973). Evidence about the extent to which people can apply these skills can be inferred from their behavior in making decisions and from their self-reports. Here are some self-reports which illustrate TASs: "The last time I faced a problem like this I talked it over with my friends before deciding, and I felt that

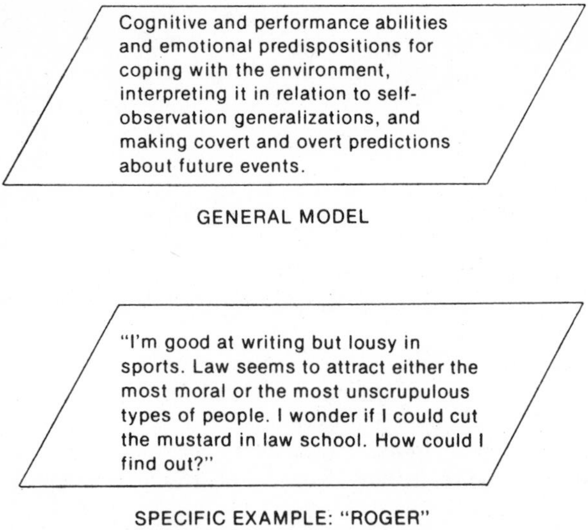

GENERAL MODEL

SPECIFIC EXAMPLE: "ROGER"

Figure 4. Diagrams representing Task Approach Skills (TASs).

it helped me reach a better decision. Maybe I'd better do that now." Or "According to this pamphlet the demand for computer programmers is going to be much less ten years from now than it is now. But I wonder if the person who wrote this pamphlet really knows. I certainly do enjoy working with computers. Maybe by the time I'm old enough to take a full-time job the specific requirements will be quite different than they are now. I wonder if it does any good to plan ahead."

The nature of any TAS for an individual depends upon the sequence of her/his prior learning experiences, including any genetic factors that influenced those experiences. Individuals can acquire and perform sequentially related skills that both build on competencies already in their repertoires and enable them to complete tasks needed for making future career decisions.

3. Actions

Some behavior is the ultimate outcome of the processes described above. Each behavior generates consequences which affect the relative frequency of similar behaviors in the future.

This study of a social learning approach to CDM is specifically concerned here with *entry behaviors*—those actions which represent an overt step in a career progression. Examples include applying for a specific job, applying to a specific school or training program, accepting a job offer or training opportunity, accepting a promotion, and changing a college major.

D. THE PROCESS OF CAREER PLANNING
AND DEVELOPMENT

Consider an individual human being. She is born into the world with certain heredity. Her first view of the world is an antiseptic hospital with trained doctors and nurses in attendance. Immediately, events begin impinging on her. She is slapped on the bottom. She feels cold. She cries. She finds a breast or a bottle. She cannot verbalize it yet but her subsequent behavior reveals that she might have been formulating an SOG which states, "Aha, crying produces warmth and milk for me." From her very first moment on earth, the pattern of learning experiences has begun.

A general model outlining factors affecting educational and occupational decision making is diagrammed in Figure 5. On the left side are the genetic factors represented in the newly-born individual. Time moves from left to right. The underlying environmental, economic, social, and cultural events and conditions impinge upon the individual's learning experiences as the arrows indicate. The individual's learning experiences are represented by the O's and H's defined in Figures 1 and 2, while triangles and parallelograms which have been defined in Figures 3 and 4 represent additional products and thought processes. The triple arrows after certain events represent the fact that the event which subsequently followed did not necessarily have to follow at that point. Each individual can make choices. Other alternatives were equally possible, though not necessarily under the control of the individual involved. The elipses (. . .) indicate that large amounts of time and therefore large numbers of learning experiences as well as environmental events have been omitted in order to save space in this diagram. The general model shows that, as a result of the interaction of genetic factors, environmental factors, and a complex sequence of learning experiences, she arrives at a certain point in time at her current activity. In no sense is that current activity the final career activity. As time continues, further events and learning experiences occur, and educational and occupational activities may change.

As discussed in the preceding sections, learning experiences produce not only preferences (emotional reactions of liking or disliking) for various activities but also cognitive and performance skills. This individual can observe herself engaging in a skilled performance and can obtain reactions from other people about the quality of that performance.

The consequences of each learning experience affect the probability that she will have a similar learning experience in the future. A successful performance or positive feedback from other people increases the probability that certain types of activities will be repeated and therefore that certain types of skills will be developed to a greater extent. If she observes herself writing well and is praised by her teacher and her parents, she probably will continue to write and improve her performance. If she receives more negative feedback, she probably will write as little as possible.

It is the sequential cumulative effects of numerous learning experiences

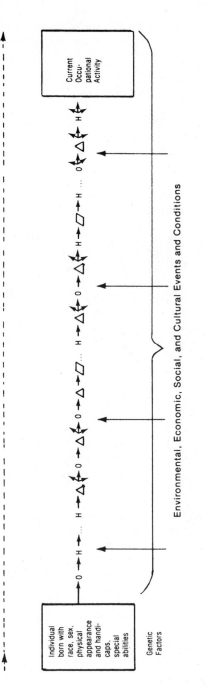

Figure 5. General model of factors affecting occupational selection.

affected by various environmental circumstances and the individual's cognitive and emotional reactions to these learning experiences and circumstances that cause a person to make decisions to enroll in a certain educational program or become employed in a particular occupation. Actual employment or enrollment as a student is not a simple function of preference or choice but is influenced by complex environmental (e.g., economic) factors, many of which are beyond the control of any single individual. A change in learning experiences can produce a change in her stated educational or occupational preferences. Changes in the environment can affect the type of learning experiences she receives. Occupational preferences are highly unstable during adolescence, probably because of the variety of learning experiences to which young people are exposed.

An abbreviated example of the general model applied to the case of "Barbara" is presented in Figure 6. As illustrated there, Barbara was born in the year 1944, influenced by the war, a new public library being built near her home, a charismatic Sunday School teacher, a boyfriend killed in Vietnam, and various social factors affecting women's expectations to have careers. Also diagrammed and illustrated are a very few of the innumerable learning experiences which have some effect on her educational and occupational selections.

Figure 7 presents another example of the general model applied to the case of "Barbara." This one depicts the development of an alternate occupational selection. Genetic factors, early environmental factors, the early learning experiences, and an SOG are left intact from the first example. Then the diagram shows by three arrows that alternate instrumental learning experiences may affect ultimate choice: Figure 7 departs from Figure 6 and shows how different environmental factors and different learning experiences and SOGs may affect the course of Barbara's career development. This diagram also shows that environmental conditions which impinge on Barbara's learning experiences may sometimes be changed by action of the individual, whereas others are so pervasive as to be impervious to an individual's efforts. In the latter case the individual can regress to an early stage or can choose a constructive compromise, as is illustrated in this example.

Figure 8 presents another alternative to Barbara's environmental conditions, learning experiences, and SOGs. In this example, Barbara's early experiences are once again left intact, for purposes of illustrating that the event that followed the triple arrows in the diagram did not necessarily have to follow at that point. These three figures present only three of many alternatives possible. Once again, the environmental conditions impinging on Barbara's options are illustrated. In the first instance she succumbs to the constraints imposed on her occupational selection by rising costs of tuition for graduate school and the high cost of loans. She perceives the constraint as beyond the control of an individual and changes her occupational selection from teacher to secretary. In the second instance she decides to influence the environmental constraints and forms an agency to help remove those constraints.

It should be noted that occupational selections presented in these examples constitute a lifelong process, not one-time choices. Although Barbara is employed as a waitress in 1974 in Figure 6, as a general practitioner in a rural area in Figure 7, and as vice president of an employment agency in Figure 8, it should be recognized that further environmental events and additional learning experiences will occur which will undoubtedly alter Barbara's future educational and occupational activities.

E. THEORETICAL PROPOSITIONS AND ILLUSTRATIVE HYPOTHESES

The preceding analysis suggests a number of testable propositions, several of which follow, and a large number of possible testable hypotheses, only a few of which can be mentioned for illustrative purposes here.

1. Factors Influencing Preferences

As used here, an educational or occupational preference is an evaluative self-observation generalization based on those learning experiences pertinent to any career task. The propositions that follow attempt to explain how these particular self-observation generalizations are acquired.

a. Positive Influences.

Proposition IA1. An individual is more likely to express a preference for a course of study, an occupation, or the tasks and consequences of a field of work if that individual has been positively reinforced for engaging in activities s/he has learned are associated with the successful performance of that course, occupation, or field of work.

> *Illustrative Hypothesis:* Boys who are reinforced for their basketball performance are more likely to indicate an interest in a basketball career than are those who are not so reinforced.

> Why are some boys reinforced for basketball playing and others not? A boy whose heredity and nutritional environment enable him to grow six feet ten inches tall is more likely to be reinforced by his basketball coach than a boy who grows to be only five feet two inches tall. Genetic and environmental factors play a major role in which learning experiences get reinforced.

Proposition IA2. An individual is more likely to express a preference for a course of study, an occupation, or the tasks and consequences of a field of work if that individual has observed a valued model being reinforced for engaging in activities s/he has learned are associated with the successful performance of that course, occupation, or field of work.

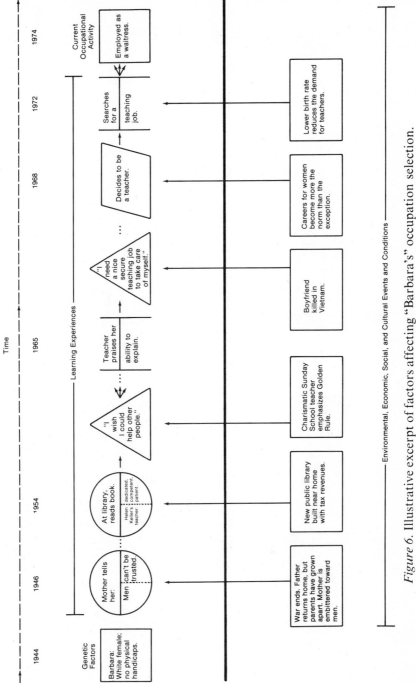

Time

| 1944 | 1946 | 1954 | 1965 | 1968 | 1972 | 1974 |

Genetic Factors

Barbara: White female; no physical handicaps.

Mother tells her: Men "can't be trusted."

At library, reads book. Helen dedicated. Keller's competent teacher: patient.

"I wish I could help other people."

Teacher praises her ability to explain.

"I need a nice secure teaching job to take care of myself."

Decides to be a teacher.

Searches for a teaching job.

Current Occupational Activity

Employed as a waitress.

Learning Experiences

War ends. Father returns home, but parents have grown apart. Mother is embittered toward men.

New public library built near home with tax revenues.

Charismatic Sunday School teacher emphasizes Golden Rule.

Boyfriend killed in Vietnam.

Careers for women become more the norm than the exception.

Lower birth rate reduces the demand for teachers.

Environmental, Economic, Social, and Cultural Events and Conditions

Figure 6. Illustrative excerpt of factors affecting "Barbara's" occupation selection.

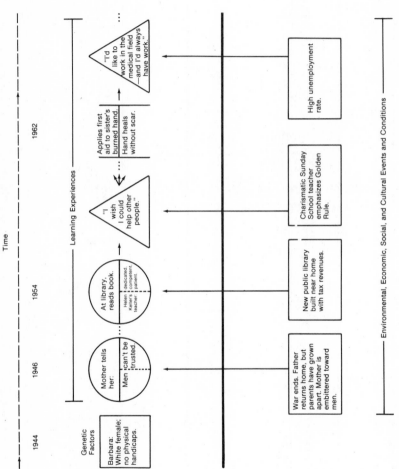

Figure 7. Illustrative excerpt of alternative factors affecting "Barbara's" occupation selection.

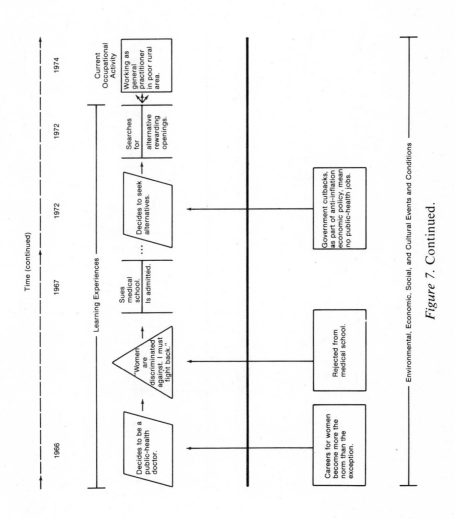

Figure 7. Continued.

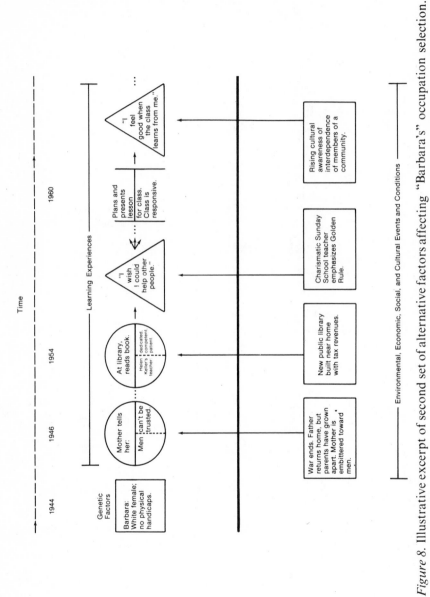

Figure 8. Illustrative excerpt of second set of alternative factors affecting "Barbara's" occupation selection.

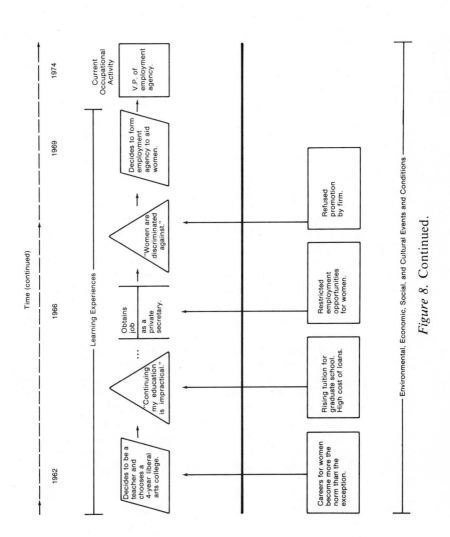

Figure 8. Continued.

Illustrative Hypothesis: Tenth-grade girls assigned to read the *Biography of Florence Nightingale* in English class will subsequently express greater interest in nursing than will those assigned to read *Moby Dick*.

Valued models can be vicarious as well as real. Models presented through literature, television, and motion pictures may well have as much influence as parents, relatives, and friends for at least some youngsters. The books that young people happen to read are a function of a number of environmental and cultural influences, many of which cannot be predicted. The models that young people identify with are those with which they happen to come in contact. Different cultural environments make available quite varied types of models.

Proposition IA3. An individual is more likely to express a preference for a course of study, an occupation, or the tasks and consequences of a field of work if that individual has been consistently positively reinforced by a valued person who models and / or advocates engaging in that course, occupation, or field of work.

Illustrative Hypothesis: Young people whose older friends and / or relatives report satisfaction with the benefits of a military career are more likely to express interest in joining one of the military services than are those whose relatives have not expressed such satisfaction.

Genetic and environmental influences are critical in influencing which people may qualify for and benefit from any given career. Certain physical standards are used by the military services in selecting members. People who are too short or too tall or who were born with certain physical handicaps would not be eligible. Family influences play a big part in whether a given youngster comes in contact with people who model and / or advocate engaging in a particular occupation. Some people simply never come in contact with a person who, for instance, has chosen a military career and has been satisfied with it. Others have had such contact. The accident of birth therefore determines to a large extent the nature and type of models with whom an individual comes in contact.

Proposition IA4. An individual is more likely to express a preference for a course of study, an occupation, or the tasks and consequences in a field of work if that individual has been exposed to positive words and images associated with that course, occupation, field of work, or the activities related to it.

Illustrative Hypothesis: Students presented with a booklet describing and illustrating in glamorous terms a relatively unknown occupation will express more preference for that occupation than will students presented with objective facts about it.

The culture in which a young person grows up influences the type of words and images associated with various occupations. Some cultures will glamorize one occupation; others, another. Furthermore, what constitutes "glamor" depends upon the values that a particular culture manifests.

b. Negative Influences.

Proposition IB1. An individual is less likely to express a preference for and more likely to express a rejection of a given course of study, an occupation, or the tasks and consequences of a field of work if that individual has been punished and/or has not been reinforced for engaging in activities s/he has learned are associated with successful performance of that course, occupation, or field of work.

Illustrative Hypothesis: Children who have received low grades in mathematics are more likely than are those who received high grades to express rejection of any career in which mathematics is said to be an important skill.

Some students happen to be exposed to skillful mathematics teachers; others are less fortunate. Those who are well taught learn mathematics step by step, master it well, and learn to enjoy it. Others find the tasks coming to them in such a sequence or at such a rate that they cannot succeed. The differential reinforcement and punishment provided by the schools undoubtedly leads many people to reject occupations which entail tasks they have come to hate.

Proposition IB2. An individual is less likely to express a preference for and more likely to express a rejection of a given course of study, an occupation, or the tasks and consequences of a field of work if that individual has observed a model receive punishment and/or little or no reinforcement for engaging in activities s/he has learned are associated with the successful performance of that course, occupation, or field of work.

Illustrative Hypothesis: College students whose closest friends were trained to be teachers but could not find jobs upon graduation will be more likely to reject teaching as a career than will those whose closest friends were trained as teachers and did find teaching jobs.

Economic factors play a major role in influencing the number of models which can be reinforced for particular kinds of training activities. The change from a teacher shortage to a teacher surplus has certainly influenced the number of people expressing a preference for teaching as a career. Observing what happens to influential models who fail to be reinforced for their choices can probably lead to lowered preference for those same choices.

Proposition IB3. An individual is less likely to express a preference for and more likely to express a rejection of a given course of study, occupation, or the tasks and consequences of a field of work if that individual has been consistently positively reinforced by a valued person who expresses negative opinions about the activities or persons who engage in that course, occupation, or field of work.

Illustrative Hypothesis: Children of parents who ridicule or degrade occupations requiring manual skill will express more rejection of those occupations than will children whose parents make no value judgments about those occupations.

Comments directed to or even accidentally overheard by children may influence their expressed preferences for certain jobs. People will tend to adopt the opinions of those who positively reinforce them. It is also possible that people will tend to reject the opinions of those who punish them. A number of other hypotheses could be generated on the interactions of reinforcement and/or punishment, the opinions of the reinforcing agent or the punishing agent, and the resulting opinions of the recipient. The persons with whom one happens to come in contact can therefore have a great influence upon the expressed preferences for various occupations.

Proposition 1B4. An individual is less likely to express a preference for and more likely to express a rejection of a given course of study, an occupation, or the tasks and consequences of a field of work if that individual has been exposed to negative words and images associated with that course, occupation, field of work, or activities related to it.

Illustrative Hypothesis: Children seeing a motion picture depicting police officers as corrupt will be more likely to reject law enforcement as a career than will those seeing a factual documentary on law enforcement.

The motion picture and television media probably play an influential role in generating preferences for or against various occupations. It could be speculated that the current popularity of medical and legal training owes a good deal to the influence of Marcus Welby and Perry Mason.

2. Factors Influencing CDM Skills

CDM skills are a subset of task approach skills pertinent to occupational and educational decision making. Propositions in this section attempt to explain how these particular skills are acquired.

a. Positive Influences.

Proposition IIA1. An individual is more likely to learn the cognitive and performance skills and emotional responses necessary for career planning, self-observing, goal setting, and information seeking if that individual has been positively reinforced for those responses.

Illustrative Hypothesis: High school students who are given a structured course in decision-making skills and whose efforts in that course are consistently rewarded and never punished will be more likely to apply those decision-making skills in future decision problems than will those high school students not receiving such a course.

Educational institutions may well be able to influence the degree to which people learn how to take control of their own career decisions. CDM is not exclusively the result of events happening to an individual but can also be shaped by an individual's own actions. But people need to know what kind of actions are likely to have some positive results for them. Systematic instruction can be designed to increase the probability that people can formulate and select intelligently from options that are presented to them or that they may have designed for themselves.

Proposition IIA2. An individual is more likely to learn the cognitive and performance skills and emotional responses necessary for career planning, self-observing, goal setting, and information seeking if that individual has observed real or vicarious models engaged in effective career-decision-making strategies.

Illustrative Hypothesis: Students who observe a CDM film in which the models are depicted as being positively reinforced for engaging in the process of decision making will be more likely to engage in a similar process than will students not exposed to the same film.

Films, books, television programs, as well as the opportunity to observe real people wisely engaging in decision-making activities can probably have a great deal of influence on the extent to which young people will learn decision-making skills themselves. Experiments can be designed to determine the exact nature of such experiences that will make them most effective for youngsters of various backgrounds contemplating decisions of various types.

Proposition IIA3. An individual is more likely to learn the cognitive and performance skills and emotional responses necessary for career planning, self-observing, goal setting, and information seeking if that individual has access to people and other resources with the necessary information.

Illustrative Hypothesis: Students in schools that set up procedures for making career information easily accessible in meaningful ways will develop CDM skills to a greater extent than will students in schools not providing such opportunities.

Educational environments which provide needed CDM resources will probably produce superior decision-making skills. However, the resources need to be tailored to the entering skill level of the students and need to be made interesting and pertinent to the target population. Resources include not merely descriptive materials about occupations, but simulated job experiences, opportunities to talk with people engaged in various occupations, and even opportunities to work for short periods of time in close association with people in various occupations.

b. Negative Influences.

Proposition IIB1. An individual is less likely to learn the cognitive and performance skills and emotional responses necessary for career planning, self-observing, goal setting, and information seeking if that individual has been punished or not reinforced for such behaviors.

Illustrative Hypothesis: Children whose attempts to make their own plans and decisions are consistently punished or overruled will develop less effective decision-making skills than will children whose planning efforts are reinforced or merely ignored.

Planning can be made an aversive activity. When plans are constantly upset by unforeseen factors, a youngster may develop the view that such planning is useless since events are out of her/his control.

Proposition IIB2. An individual is less likely to learn the cognitive and performance skills and emotional responses necessary for career planning, self-observing, goal setting, and information seeking if that individual has observed real or vicarious models receive punishment and/or little or no reinforcement for attempting to engage in CDM activities.

Illustrative Hypothesis: Young people who associate with peers who reject the usefulness of career planning and believe that fate will make their plans are less likely to develop decision-making skills than are those students who associate with peers who are committed to the notion of career planning and the possibility of self-control.

Peer influences play a big part in young people's lives, but peers are only one of the sets of models. Parents whose own careers have been frustrated may explicitly or implicitly model the view that fate controls one's life and that therefore the best course of action is to take the most expedient step at the moment rather than plan for the future.

Proposition IIB3. An individual is less likely to learn the cognitive and performance skills and emotional responses necessary for career planning, self-observing, goal setting, and information seeking if that individual has little or no access to people and other resources with the necessary information.

Illustrative Hypothesis: Persons denied access to simulated vocational problem-solving materials will engage in less career exploration than will individuals who are given successively greater exposure to such simulated vocational problem-solving materials.

Critical experiences may be designed to encourage active career exploration. The fact that many young people have no idea what it is they want to do is probably due to the fact that they have had such limited experience with actual occupational activities. The more activities that can be provided for them related to occupations, the more they can learn what it is they like and dislike, what they can and cannot do, what they want to learn and do not want to learn, and what they want to find out about next.

3. Factors Influencing Entry Behaviors into Educational or Occupational Alternatives

Given the acquisition of preferences, emotional responses, and cognitive and performance skills through various learning experiences, the propositions in this section attempt to explain some factors that account for the actual entry behaviors into occupations, training programs, or educational courses of study.

a. Positive Influences.

Proposition IIIA1. An individual is more likely to take actions leading to enrollment in a given course or employment in a given occupation or field of work if that individual has recently expressed a preference for that course, occupation, or field of work.

   Illustrative Hypothesis: People entering plumbing apprenticeships will express a higher degree of interest in plumbing than will people of the same age and sex who are not entering plumbing apprenticeships.

   Perhaps it seems obvious that expressed preference and actual choice will correspond. However, it is necessary to make explicit that the preferences generated through the procedures described under the first set of propositions above will be reflected in the actual actions taken by those individuals. However, preferences change over time. It is only the most recently expressed preference that is of concern at the time action is taken. This means that recent events can have an influence upon both preferences and actions. Educational and occupational preferences are not established at an early age to remain stable ever after. The process is in a constant state of flux as a result of constantly changing circumstances.

Proposition IIIA2. An individual is more likely to take actions leading to enrollment in a given course or employment in a given occupation or field of work if that individual has been exposed to learning and employment opportunities in that course, occupation, or field of work.

   Illustrative Hypothesis: Communities that make available training opportunities as dental hygienists will find more people in that community seeking to become dental hygienists than will occur in equivalent communities where such training is not made available.

   Again it may seem obvious that the number of trainees will vary as a function of the number of training opportunities. But it is important to note that the economic environment plays a big role in what occupations people actually enter. Individuals make choices among concrete alternatives. Actual entry into occupations or training is a function of available opportunities and the chance to find out about those opportunities.

Proposition IIIA3. An individual is more likely to take actions leading to enrollment in a given course or employment in a given occupation or field of work if that individual's learned skills match the educational and/or occupational requirements.

   Illustrative Hypothesis: Individuals who become professional football players will have superior muscular coordination compared to that of individuals who become accountants.

Traditional aptitude tests have not provided clear distinctions between people entering various occupations. However, for certain occupations there are learned skills (cognitive and performance) which are necessary—skills which are not measured by traditional aptitude tests. Individuals who have learned to pound a nail without bending it are more likely to become carpenters than are individuals who constantly bend the nail after it is halfway into the wood. Opportunities vary for people to learn these skills depending upon the training opportunities they have had, the models they have been exposed to, the cultures that they have grown up in, and the genetic factors that enable them to learn the skills.

b. Negative Influences.

Proposition IIIB1. An individual is less likely to take actions leading to enrollment in a given course or employment in a given occupation or field of work if that individual finds that the cost of preparation for that occupation is excessive in relation to future economic, social, and personal rewards.

Illustrative Hypothesis: Providing scholarship money for medical-school training will increase the probability that poverty-level students who are otherwise qualified will enter medical training.

The cost-benefit ratio of preparation to reward in occupations plays an important part in determining which individuals aspire to which occupations. By reducing the cost of preparation or by increasing the rewards associated with successful performance, a society can alter the nature and number of individuals entering each occupation.

Proposition IIIB2. An individual is less likely to take actions leading to enrollment in a given course or employment in a given occupation or field of work if that individual is denied access to the minimum resources necessary for entering that occupation or field of work.

Illustrative Hypothesis: Among students aspiring to become airline pilots, those who are admitted to Air Force or Navy pilot-training programs will be more likely to enter the occupation of airline pilot than will those who are denied access to such training.

A society can make training for certain occupations so expensive that relatively few people can afford it unless they somehow are given special access that is paid for by the society at large. Pilot training is just one example.

F. IMPLICATIONS FOR COUNSELORS AND CLIENTS

To the extent that this social learning view of career selection bears some resemblance to reality (and the degree to which that resemblance can be checked through empirical research), some important views and implications emerge for counselors and clients:

1. Occupational placement is the result of a complex interaction of genetic components, environmental events and conditions, and learning experiences which result in the development of various task approach skills.

2. Career selection is a mutual process influenced not only by decisions made by each individual involved but also by social forces which affect occupational availability and requirements. People select, and are selected by, occupations.

3. Career selection is a lifelong process. It does not take place at one point in time, but is shaped by events and decisions that occur from infancy through the retirement years.

4. Career selection is caused—not accidental—but the interaction of causal events is so complex that the prediction of occupational selection for any one individual is virtually impossible with any degree of certainty.

5. Career indecision is due to the unsatisfactory nature of an insufficient number of career-relevant learning experiences or to the fact that the person has not yet learned and applied a systematic way of making career decisions. Indecision is a natural result of not yet having had certain learning experiences. An undecided person has no reason to feel guilty or inadequate.

6. Career counseling is not merely a process of matching existing personal characteristics with existing job characteristics, but instead is a process of opening up new learning experiences and motivating a client to initiate career-relevant exploratory activities.

7. The responsibilities of a career counselor, then, are as follows:

(a) to help the client learn a rational sequence of career decision-making skills,
(b) to help the client arrange an appropriate sequence of career-relevant exploratory-learning experiences, and
(c) to teach the client how to evaluate the personal consequences of those learning experiences.

REFERENCES

Krumboltz, J. D., and Baker, R. D. Behavioral counseling for vocational decisions. In H. Borow (Ed.), *Career guidance for a new age*. Boston: Houghton Mifflin, 1973. Pp. 235-284.

Krumboltz, J. D., Mitchell, A. M., and Gelatt, H. B. Applications of a social learning theory of career selection. *Focus on Guidance*, 1975, *8*(3), 1-16.

Mitchell, A. M., Jones, G. B., and Krumboltz, J. D. (Eds.). *A social learning theory of career decision making*. Final Report, Contract No. NIE-C-74-0134. Palo Alto, Calif.: American Institutes for Research, 1975.

RESPONSES TO CRITES AND KRUMBOLTZ 6

A New Synthesis for an Old Method and a New Analysis of Some Old Phenomena

JOHN L. HOLLAND
Johns Hopkins University

The reading of the Krumboltz article in Chapter 5 of this text and the Crites article in Chapter 4 of this text left me feeling like a hungry ant who had discovered the remains of a picnic created by a group of gourmets—I didn't know where to begin (indecision, indecisiveness, ALEs, SOGs, lack of career-development training in high school, or conflicting ideas about fairness, friendship, social obligation, and opportunity for self-expression). Unlike the ant, I am not completely stimulus bound so I have tried to digest these papers in several sittings.

What follows does not exhaust my thoughts, for every time I reviewed these papers I discovered more ideas I wanted to write about. This experience suggests that these papers may be most useful as heuristic devices. Although most people will find something to quarrel about, the papers should lead to some clearer understandings, better research, and more effective practical applications. Unfortunately, there may be very few cogent or prolonged discussions, because the counseling profession is now dominated by big S's who find relating to others more fun than thinking or evaluation. (As a man grows older, he mellows, engages in maintenance activities, reduces emotional involvements, and changes for the better. True or False?)

I have chosen to deal with Krumboltz's speculations (Chapter 4 of this text) first because "K" comes after "C". Although this is only a small step, the systematic discrimination against people in the middle of the alphabet must stop (Title X, 1976.)

SOCIAL LEARNING THEORY AND CAREER DECISION MAKING

I found Krumboltz's application of social learning principles to vocational questions helpful, stimulating, and always clear—probably too clear to be called a theory. His vivid illustrations suggest that social learning theory has many virtues for explaining a wide range of vocational questions and interventions throughout the life span. Equally important, social learning principles appear congenial with most of our speculations about vocational life.

For example, Roe's (1956) hypotheses about parental attitudes and occupational orientation could be reexamined by first translating her hypotheses into characteristic social learning experiences and typical vocational outcomes, and then surveying adolescents or adults for the probable signs of such learning. A learning orientation should structure new kinds of parent/child assessments and suggest new and more explicit hypotheses. Similarly, Krumboltz provides analytical ideas for specifying how the vocational attitudes and competencies embedded in Crites' (1974a) and Super's (1974) models are created as a person interacts with others and with the physical world. In short, whenever someone writes "learn," "develop," or "change." Krumboltz's suggestions can be applied like a microscope to show a more complete and detailed account of the person/environment interaction. Because of its potential supportive and exploratory value for any other vocational speculation, the Krumboltz report is a rare contribution.

Along with its virtues, the social learning (SL) model has a substantial deficiency. Like most process and developmentally oriented theories of career development (CD), it has only weak organizational value. Its greatest strength—explaining variations in CD—is also the source of its greatest weakness. We do not yet have an occupational library organized according to characteristic SOGs, ILEs, ALEs, and TASs, nor do we have a classification for organizing the almost infinite number of learning experiences that people have. In addition the SL model will be exceedingly difficult to apply in daily practice without *parallel* typologies of persons and work environments. In short, the SL model lacks both the organizational property and vocational content necessary for most practical applications. For example, try to describe a client in learning theory terms, try to predict some suitable alternatives in learning theory terms, try to locate occupations that should be compatible, somewhat compatible, or incompatible using only learning theory terms. On the other hand, note that, if a detailed personal history is available, you can visualize how this person learned, changed, and acquired his/her current sense of identity and vocational preferences. The figures in Krumboltz's proposal provide a variety of vivid illustrations, but also note that much of the required information is not readily accessible.

In formal terms, theories of personality, interests, or vocational decision making require both a classification to describe and organize what we know about both people and jobs and some speculations to explain change and personal development. (I am indebted to Adam Lackey for this insight.) Theories and speculations about vocational choice, careers, and vocational adjustment are always much more useful for one of these purposes rather than both. For example, the vocational-development people need to create or acquire a compatible classification scheme to use with their developmental speculations; vocational speculations with strong classificatory virtues need to acquire, revise, or strengthen their developmental speculations. The classification scheme recently proposed by Dawis, Lofquist, and Weiss (1974) illustrates an attempt to strengthen a theory of vocational adjustment that has had strong empirical support but lacked a comprehensive classification scheme. Both Maddi (1968) and Levy (1970) provide extensive discussions of the relative virtues of learning and organizational approaches to personality and, by implication, to the present formulations.

At present, I would estimate that social learning ideas will be most helpful for filling in the blank spaces in all other speculations about vocational life. Next, social learning will be especially helpful in the design of comprehensive programs of vocational assistance in which large environments are assessed for their impact on children, adolescents, or adults. Some social learning formulations force you to look at events and environmental characteristics that we often overlook. Finally, I assume that social learning principles will have little to add to the current practice of one-to-one vocational counseling over and beyond the current applications of general learning principles.

A NEW SYNTHESIS FOR VOCATIONAL COUNSELING

The "comprehensive approach" to career counseling is especially difficult to evaluate. Crites (1976) provides his subjective integration of five major approaches to vocational counseling. He presents no persuasive evidence that his particular synthesis is unique, valid, or effective, but it would be premature and unfair to expect him to demonstrate immediately that his approach is worthy of special attention. On the other hand, my earlier failure to cope more directly with his historical summary (Chapter 2 of this text) has been construed by some as an attempt to avoid the issues. This time I will comment more directly. However, as I wrote earlier (Holland, 1974a, 1974b), I believe vocational counseling should be the treatment of last resort. Its only other valuable use would be as a special experience for sensitizing counselors and researchers about interpersonal relations and vocational problems.

A Comprehensive Model

When you look closely at the proposed model, it has a marked resemblance to the old trait-and-factor model. The counselor works hard to establish a diagnosis ("nosological classification" of a client's problem and a "dynamic diagnosis"). These are followed by "decisional diagnosis of disjunctions" using the Career Maturity Inventory (CMI). That is a lot of diagnostic activity, and only an exceptional counselor could avoid the client dependency generated by such extensive, strenuous diagnostic work. In addition, the evidence does not appear to support Crites' conclusion that these diagnostic activities will "allow the counselor to draw better than chance conclusions about what the problem is . . . ." If it does, better-than-chance is still a very low standard. Bordin and Kopplin's (1973) recent proposal for a diagnostic scheme is only a first sketch with an N of only 82; Bordin's (1946) earlier scheme—insightful as it still seems—goes largely unused; and Crites' (1969) scheme has received only weak support (Goen, 1965). Even my proposal (Holland, Gottfredson & Nafziger, 1975), which I love, is inefficient. In short, we don't have the tools to implement an approach with a heavy reliance on a diagnostic base.

Crites' brief description of the "process" of vocational counseling appears like a reasonable integration of what most counselors understand. In his use of the CMI, Crites appears to have substituted the CMI structure for the old crossroads-of-life model. "The counselor can locate the place the client has reached on the continuum of career development." His discussion and synthesis of counseling outcomes (like his diagnostic ideas) are controversial. Although he enumerates the making of vocational choices, the acquisition of decisional skills, and the enhancement of general adjustment as major goals, his discussion indicates that he depreciates the making of vocational choices.

The neglect of finding satisfying alternatives is reminiscent of those piano teachers who show mothers how well their children have learned to play difficult, sometimes dazzling technical exercises, but the same children cannot play a simple piece of music in an attractive manner. In short, methods should never obscure our goals.

My impression is that consumers of vocational counseling want most of all to arrive at or confirm one or more vocational alternatives they can feel good about. Other outcomes—decision-making skills and enhanced general adjustment—are desired more by professionals than consumers. It is possible that a few highly skilled people can foster all three goals simultaneously, but the inherent conflict involved in pressing for all three goals should prevent their attainment by most counselors. I do not believe that you can integrate the client's definition of the problem with vigorous attempts to redefine the problem by the counselor—giving decisional training and fostering general adjustment.

I have reluctantly resolved this dilemma for myself in the following way. Until our diagnostic techniques are much more efficient, we should rely on the consumer for the direction of treatment. At this point, the long-range value of decision-making training remains untested. Likewise, the CMI—perhaps the best engineered assessment for decisional training in a developmental context—may have only a limited validity (Holland, Gottfredson, and Nafziger, 1975). Finally, acknowledging the consumer's right to define his/her goals is consistent with our increased awareness of human rights—it is the consumer who must live with counseling outcomes, not the counselor. At the same time, diagnostic hypotheses can be shared with the consumer in the course of simple, routine vocational assistance. If various vocational-assistance attempts fail to bring desired results, diagnostic discussions can come as ordinary conversations as the person ends one form of vocational activity and prepares to try another. In this context, diagnostic activity becomes problem-solving, planning, and educative activity rather than probing interviews. Perhaps this is what Crites also means.

Methods

The synthesis of interviewing methods is a smorgasbord of all points of view. It is hard to believe that it would not confuse and block many users as they proceed from a client-centered, developmental orientation to the trait-and-factor and behavioral approaches as their clients approach termination. Likewise, the introduction of test results in such a deliberate way must convey to a person his/her inadequacy. "Interpreting the tests without the tests" seems like an exaggeration of the old trait/factor, directive orientation.

Having counselors transmit occupational information epitomizes one aspect of the expensive waste in much vocational counseling. I like Crites' solution—reinforcing the gathering of information outside the contact hour—but such activity is not only the accumulation of "facts and figures" but also the tryouts of roles and life styles.

The Case of Karen

As a taxpayer in Maryland, I was appalled that a person of John Crites' talents and potential would use my income-tax money to instruct a young woman about the difference between indecision and indecisiveness in the course of seven interviews—especially when I know there are more than 35,000 students in his university.

John Crites' seven-interview case report of a high school student is especially valuable because it provides a concrete illustration of what Crites has in mind for his synthesis. His report is also a new projective device. I found it helpful to speculate how I would have acted if this student had appeared at my door. I think other readers would profit from a similar comparison of orientations to counseling. The following paragraphs summarize the differences I see between the Comprehensive Synthesis and the Exploratory Approach (Holland & Gottfredson, 1976).

Crites begins with a brief screening interview, explores Karen's "presenting problem," discovers that she vacillates between "teaching and social work," explains the difference between indecision and indecisiveness and settles on indecision as her "differential diagnosis." I might have seen Karen for about 5 to 15 minutes. I would have started with "What do you have in mind?" When she talked about whether it should be social work or teaching, I would have mumbled to myself: "There is not much difference between an SIA or SAE, and music (ASI) is a related alternative; looks like a girl with consistent alternatives; should have little difficulty in making a decision." I then would have asked, or she might have asked to take the Self-Directed Search (SDS). (My reputation is "the professor who has a thing you can take and score yourself, who gives you books to read or fill out, and who doesn't listen long.") I would have loaned her a copy of the Occupational Outlook Handbook and told her to come back when she was ready.

Like Crites, I agree that there is a need for some diagnostic activity, but the comprehensive approach seems much too intrusive to promote exploration, growth, and independence. Although I engage in diagnostic thinking, it consists initially only of some gross observations such as "Is this person very upset?" If so, my initial interview would be longer, more supportive, and perhaps I would decide that our psychological clinic would provide more useful help and make a referral. Finally, I expect the treatment experiences—taking the SDS, using the Occupational Outlook Handbook or other workbook materials, and subsequent reports about these experiences— to provide unobtrusive information about decision-making skills, origins of current difficulties, and some progress toward goals.

Crites next devotes three interviews to making "a dynamic diagnosis." If Karen came back to see me for a second interview (I lose some), I would have asked "How did the SDS go?" "What did you get out of the Occupational Outlook Handbook?" Or, she might have taken the initiative because the SDS supported social work more than teacher, or because she now saw more alternatives. Our discussion would have focused on the alternatives— questions she might have, where to get more information about training, what it is like to be a social worker, what led to the current alternatives, how she justified each alternative, and so on.

In the second interview, I would have relied on the SDS to learn whether or not she was a well-differentiated person and therefore a good decision maker. If her SDS profile were well-defined and if her vocational daydreams appeared to cohere (her initial preferences did), I would conclude that she probably needed only informational assistance. I would not have attempted to help her work through her conflict with her family. Instead, I would have reinforced the need to continue exploring those vocational alternatives that were appealing via reading and work experiences, and I would have told her that it is not necessary for people to always know what they are going to do. If you are going to college, you usually have about a two-year period to explore yourself and your future.

Crites reports three process interviews and indicates some outcomes of his work with Karen. She didn't make a choice but understood why; she knew herself better; and she appeared better adjusted. My fictitious work with Karen might have increased the options she considered, clarified why some made more sense than others, given her more understanding of herself in vocational terms, and given her a structure she might use to relate to the vocational world. Her family relationships would have gone largely unexamined (I would have listened to her account of family conflicts, but I would not have interfered unless they appeared severe), but she might feel more confident about her tentative choices (and thus able to resist family pressures) and have some ideas for coping with the next steps in her life. She would be no poorer (I don't charge) and possibly more independent (my consumers do nearly all the work).

In general, the exploratory view consists in focusing on the exploration of vocational alternatives with the subordination of the concerns of diagnosis, personal adjustment, examining one's values, and similar counseling concerns.

SOME AFTERTHOUGHTS

Even my incomplete attempt at reviewing the case of Karen demonstrates the innumerable variations that must be evaluated empirically if we are to make vocational counseling a more effective experience. The complexities of Crites' eclectic view also suggest why more easily defined views of counseling may have come about; they are not only easier to define but also easier to use and test. I cannot imagine how we could evaluate the comprehensive plan in an empirical manner.

At this point, I still see little value in the strategy of trying to renovate traditional vocational counseling: (1) The evidence for its effectiveness so far is no better than that for simpler, less expensive methods (Holland & Gottfredson, 1976). (2) The possibility of developing a clear knowledge of vocational-counseling effects appears remote despite more than 25 years of handwringing and some research. Bordin's (1974) *Research Strategies in Psychotherapy* is an eloquent account of the complexities involved. Although he concludes that "we are entering a period with potential for great success," we have already demonstrated in only five or six years that paper materials and computer-assisted forms of vocational assistance, for many purposes, usually do as well as counselors. These are results, not promises. This evidence suggests that it is time for a full exploration of a new strategy—namely, the exploration of standard treatment modules.

I confess that I titled an old APGA talk in 1970 "The Self-Directed Search—A Device to Replace Counselors" more to attract attention than to represent my beliefs. Now five years later, we have better evidence for the actual effects of these paper booklets than we have for the virtues of counselors.

Paper materials and computer programs have great potential for explicating the vocational treatment process. Unlike counselors, they come in standard models which do not vary from day to day or give off individualistic cues. The long list of troubles usually involved in the experimental study of vocational counseling is greatly reduced—cost, time, attempts to standardize counselors, ambiguities about counselor behavior, maintaining morale, and administration support. The danger of "over-simplification" (Bordin, 1974) of the treatment process now seems minimal because these standard treatments already compare favorably with counselors. The next step should be to dissect what special aspects of these impersonal modules are most responsible for their effects. Perhaps we also might profit from more attempts to study the effects of other impersonal but standard forms of assistance such as films, books, and vocational exercises.

REFERENCES

Bordin, E. S. Diagnosis in counseling and psychotherapy. *Educational and Psychological Measurement*, 1946, *6*, 169-184.

Bordin, E. S. *Research strategies in psychotherapy.* New York: Wiley, 1974.

Bordin, E. S., & Kopplin, D. A. Motivational conflict and vocational development. *Journal of Counseling Psychology*, 1973, *20*, 154-161.

Crites, J. O. *Vocational psychology.* New York: McGraw-Hill, 1969.

Crites, J. O. Career development process: A model of vocational maturity. In E. L. Herr (Ed.), *Vocational guidance and human development.* Boston: Houghton Mifflin, 1974. (a)

Crites, J. O. Career counseling: A review of major approaches. *The Counseling Psychologist*, 1974, *4*(3), 3-23. (b)

Crites, J. O. Career counseling: A comprehensive approach. *The Counseling Psychologist*, 1976, *6*(3), 2-12.

Dawis, R. V., Lofquist, L. H., and Weiss, D. J. *Minnesota occupational classification system.* Department of Psychology, University of Minnesota, 1974.

Goen, J. N. Explorations of Crites' vocational diagnostic system (Doctoral dissertation, University of Iowa, 1964). *Dissertation Abstracts International*, 1965, *25*, 5111-5112. (University Microfilms No. 65-460)

Holland, J. L. Some practical remedies for providing vocational guidance for everyone. *Educational Researcher*, 1974, *3*, 9-15. (a)

Holland, J. L. Career counseling: Then, now, and what's next? *The Counseling Psychologist*, 1974, *4*, 24-26. (b)

Holland, J. L, & Gottfredson, G. D. Using a typology of persons and environments to explain careers: Some extensions and clarifications. *The Counseling Psychologist*, 1976, *6*(3), 20-29.

Holland, J. L., Gottfredson, G. D., & Nafziger, D. H. Testing the validity of some theoretical signs of vocational decision-making ability. *Journal of Counseling Psychology*, 1975, *22*, 411-422.

Krumboltz, J. D. A social learning theory of career selection. *The Counseling Psychologist*, 1976, *6*(1), 71-81.

Levy, L. H. *Conceptions of personality.* New York: Random House, 1970.

Maddi, S. R. *Personality theories.* Homewood, Ill.: Dorsey Press, 1968.

Roe, A. *The psychology of occupations.* New York: Wiley, 1956.

Super, D. E. Vocational maturity theory. In D. E. Super (Ed.), *Measuring vocational maturity for counseling.* Washington, D. C.: American Personnel and Guidance Association, 1974.

Reactions to
Krumboltz and Crites

ANNE ROE

COMMENTS ON "A SOCIAL LEARNING THEORY OF CAREER SELECTION"

Krumboltz (Chapter 5 of this text) presents a very thorough analysis of all of the possible factors which he sees as influencing the nature of career decision making (CDM). I find it very comprehensive and persuasive in its thoroughness and effectively organized. There is little I would add, and nothing of great moment.

To his statement that technological developments have produced job opportunities that might have been unavailable a few years previously, I think it should be pointed out that they have also made a considerable number of jobs obsolete and will probably continue to affect more and more of those in the semi-skilled as well as unskilled categories.

He points out the importance of family training and background, referring to the family of origin without mentioning one of the most important indicators of the general status—father's occupation.

He includes the influence of peers in learning differential values. But to his list of environmental conditions affecting career development I would add the marital family. This may of course not be very relevant, but it may have a strong influence. Among the younger persons, marriage may well force choices that would otherwise not have been made, but this is also true for older persons, in whose case the wishes or needs of spouse or children may have a potent influence in decisions, particularly with regard to job changes.

I find Figure 1 in Krumboltz's article somewhat confusing, since the antecedents and consequences do not appear necessarily directly related, except in the middle section. In Figure 5, although it is clear that O and H refer to environmental factors, I can find no explanation of how they differ, either by reference to earlier figures or to the text. Figures 6 and 7 seem to me to be quite helpful presentations of the developmental process as it may occur.

I don't think contrasting reading a book on the life of Florence Nightingale with reading *Moby Dick* brings out very clearly what he means to say about the influence of such models. I would guess that as many girls, after reading *Moby Dick*, would choose nursing as would choose it before. A better contrast would involve the life of another woman which has been very different from Nightingale's.

Although he nowhere mentions chance as a separate category of influential factors, he does indeed note it indirectly in several places. I would like to see somewhat more attention paid to this, if only because in our studies of career changes in later ages Baruch and I found so many persons ascribing so much to chance, even though to us it often seemed as though it was of much less importance. There seemed to be a surprising lack of conscious decision making, as though the subjects were not convinced of their own ability to make appropriate decisions or perhaps did not wish to accept that responsibility.

I am particularly pleased with Krumboltz's underlining of the importance of the general and specific economic environmental influences throughout.

COMMENTS ON "CAREER COUNSELING: A COMPREHENSIVE APPROACH"

Crites' article (Chapter 4 of this text) is a thoughtful analysis of the models and methods of career-counseling approaches, and a synthesis of these for each of the phases he uses. The model does indeed include a comprehensive analysis of the current schools of counseling in terms of the models each exemplifies (diagnosis, process, and outcomes) and the methods they use (interview techniques, test interpretation, and use of occupational information).

Some form of diagnosis is common to all the systems (even the client centered), and Crites distinguishes between differential, dynamic and decisional diagnoses. He mentions most standard tests only in passing, except the Career Maturity Inventory (CMI) on which he places great reliance. The distinction between indecision and indecisiveness is a crucial one, and it may be that this cannot be made by any test or combination of them, although I am not sure of this. However, I find it very curious that there is no mention of making use of the client's previous academic, or even work, history. Yet it is well established that past performance is a very good predictor of future performance. He does, however, recognize this in his discussion of whether or not indecisiveness has been characteristic generally or only in specific situations in the client's past.

His whole discussion relates to career counseling which has been sought by a client and concerns the interaction between client and counselor. This is certainly a legitimate limitation for the discussion. But it gives no suggestion of any mechanism by which persons in need of some assistance in career decisions can be helped in any other way or indeed can be found other than by referral by self or others. He makes only the briefest reference to any occupational-information system which can be used by anyone without personal counseling, although there are a number of these presently available, besides the one he mentions (Super, 1970). Tiedeman's information system for vocational decisions is ignored. There is also the computerized system developed by Harris and one presently in development by Miller-Tiedeman. There is the Washington Pre-college Career Planner, an extremely comprehensive survey which can be self-administered and which includes biographic information, school achievement, educational goals, planned major, and so on, as well as a vocational-interest inventory and extensive information about the training necessary for different careers. Such procedures, comprehensive as they are, may not be in themselves sufficient for many students, but they would readily pick out those who need personal counseling and relieve the counselor of much of the time required for the more usual systems, thus making him/her available for more clients in serious need. They have also the great advantage of tending to encourage personal responsibility for decisions—a problem often faced by counselors, as Crites notes.

REFERENCES

Crites, J. O. Career counseling: A comprehensive approach. *The Counseling Psychologist,* 1976, *6*(3), 2-12.

Krumboltz, J. D. A social learning theory of career selection. *The Counseling Psychologist,* 1976, *6*(1), 71-81.

Super, D. E. (Ed.). *Computer-assisted counseling.* New York: Teachers College Press, 1970.

This Chevrolet Can't Float or Fly: A Rejoinder

JOHN D. KRUMBOLTZ
Stanford University

I probably would not have bothered to write this rejoinder to Holland's and Roe's critiques (pp. 128 and 136) if I had not received an inciting letter from our esteemed editor, John Whiteley, who reported, "Holland said that your theory lacks both the organizational property and vocational content necessary for most practical applications." To be an effective editor one must be like my 8th-grade acquaintance, Jasper I. Middlebroker, who would tell George "Sam says you're a jerk" and would tell Sam "George says your mother eats nails" and then would step back to watch the fight.

I had read Holland's comments earlier and somehow had overlooked this undigestible statement hidden as it was among the more palatable pellets of praise. So, aroused beyond my action threshold, I will deal with Holland's comments before Roe's because of the penalties associated with failure to follow the affirmative-action program for middle-of-the-alphabet people (Title X, 1976).

PRACTICAL FOR WHICH PURPOSES?

Let's start with Holland's challenging assertion that the social learning theory of career selection (Krumboltz, 1975; Krumboltz, Mitchell, & Jones, 1976) lacks both the organizational property and vocational content necessary for most practical applications. If Holland were writing for *Motor Trend Magazine*, he would probably state: "This Chevrolet lacks practical value because it can neither fly nor float on water."

One must first ask: What was the product designed to accomplish? Then: How well does it perform its purpose? Of course, Holland is right. (The last time he made a mistake was in 1933.) We do not yet have a table of organization for self-observation generalizations, for instrumental or associative learning experiences, or for task approach skills related to each possible occupation. Nor do we know how to organize the infinite sequence of learning activities so as to produce a coherent account of precisely what occupational preferences will result. The social learning theory was not intended to supply such an organizational property nor the vocational content.

The social learning theory of career selection was designed as a first step toward understanding more precisely what specific kinds of learning experiences contribute to the development of occupational preferences. It posits certain environmental and cultural events that facilitate or inhibit the reinforcing and punishing consequences which contribute to various occupational preferences. It was designed to make more explicit how certain skills in decision making and other task approach skills are developed as a result of the interaction of genetic endowment and learning experiences in a cultural context. It was designed to show how specific occupational entry behaviors result from the interaction of skills and preferences generated in the past with current cultural, social, and economic forces.

The nineteen propositions in the theory are not the only possible propositions but are merely a starting point. Associated with each proposition is at least one testable hypothesis (not necessarily the best one) to illustrate that the proposition is subject to empirical test.

One purpose of the theory is to explain the cause of occupational preferences and behaviors. If I were to be critical of Holland's theory (the kettle talking to the pot), I could point out that it lacks explanatory value since it does not attempt to explain how the expressed interests in various occupations originated. Holland could then reply that it was not his intention to explain how interests originated, merely to organize and categorize the interests that do eventually emerge. I see no conflict with Holland's theory. The two views simply address different problems. Mastery of the social learning theory of career selection would not constitute a sufficient tool for counselor practice. After all, the theory may not even by true. It is set forth as a series of propositions whose veracity can be ascertained. Some preliminary evidence tends to support certain of the propositions (Mitchell, 1975), but many of them are simply in dire need of empirical evidence.

However, if the theoretical propositions do tend to be supported as evidence accumulates, I believe there will be a number of practical implications that will make a big difference in the way in which vocational counselors operate.

1. Decision making will be taught as a skill. A traditional vocational counselor works with people who report being undecided about their choice of an occupation. To help them move from the undecided to the decided category, the counselor must somehow enable them to accept the name of some occupational category as their career goal. In a social learning model, however, the goal of counseling is not seen as that of merely identifying an occupational label as a goal, but as that of helping clients to realize that this particular career decision is merely one of hundreds of decisions that will be required in the future and that there are some logical steps that one can take in order to improve the likelihood that the resulting decisions will be more satisfactory. Therefore, the process of counseling is to help the person learn a wise decision-making strategy by giving that person some practice in using this strategy for the first time, perhaps even by enabling the client to name a tentative occupational goal. Since circumstances and preferences change as a result of the continuous stream of new experiences, it must be recognized that all such choices are tentative. But with the career decision-making skill mastered, the client will be able to cope with the inevitable future decision problems in a coherent and rational manner.

Holland doubts that counselors can teach decision-making skills to clients who simply want to arrive at or confirm a vocational alternative. Some algebra students want their teacher to tell them the answers instead of teaching them how to solve problems independently, but a good teacher uses the students' current problem as a specific instance for teaching a more generalizable skill. Similarly, counselors can benefit their clients more by using the current decision problem as a way to develop decision-making competency instead of taking the easier path of providing answers. The client still gets "an answer" but discovers a method for solving future career problems too.

2. Criteria of vocational counseling success will be different. How can we tell that vocational counseling has been successful? If the goal is to have people convinced that they know what their life goal is, then we can simply count the number of people in the graduating high school class who report being certain of their occupational goal. But might not that very certainty be a disadvantage? What happens to the student, certain that he wants to be a medical doctor, when he discovers that he is not admitted to medical school? What happens to the potential plumber who is not accepted as an apprentice? What happens to the engineering graduate after he finds that he really dislikes designing machines and prefers more human interaction? In other words, helping people become more certain of their life goal may be an outcome that later has severe disadvantages.

If the social learning view of career development is upheld, we might expect the criteria of successful vocational counseling to be evidence that certain decision-making processes were being used in a variety of decision-making settings. We might expect to hear more students making statements such as "Let's not decide until next week and spend some time investigating the alternatives in the meantime" instead of "I already know what I want to do, so don't confuse me with any more facts." We would look for evidence that students could cope successfully with new decision problems, not that they were certain of their past decisions.

3. Development of occupational preferences and skills will be more systematic. The recognition that occupational preferences are learned, not preexisting, might well change the whole orientation of career education and vocational education. If in fact occupational interests are learned from a sequence of associative and instrumental learning experiences, as the theory specifies, then school systems will have a big role to play in providing a large variety of educational experiences that might lead students to clarify their occupational preferences. A greater emphasis would be placed on career-relevant activities. Feedback from these activities could be articulated with various occupations. Both the joys and frustrations of various occupational activities would be consequences experienced by students in advance of a more permanent career choice. Ways of making career exploration more enjoyable would be sought. Students might be encouraged to form teams to explore occupational possibilities. Simulation activities could be provided for occupations that could not be experienced more directly. The reason that so many young people are undecided about their occupational choices is simply due to the fact that they have not had a sufficient number or the sufficient kinds of learning experiences that would enable them to discover which occupational activities they enjoy and which ones are distasteful. Being undecided is no reason to feel guilty, it is only a sign that more needs to be learned.

Students can respond to occupational titles with a high degree of reliability, but are their impressions about those occupations based on accurate facts? I doubt it. A practical value of the social learning approach would be to encourage a large number of learning activities that will enable students to respond with increased accuracy to items such as are found on the *Self-Directed Search* (SDS). Other practical applications are described in Krumboltz, Mitchell, and Gelatt (1975).

Having now convinced you that the social learning view of career selection will neither fly nor float, but will get 20 miles per gallon on dry land, let us turn to Roe's comments (delayed justice for end-of-the-alphabet persons).

CHANCE, "NO"; UNPREDICTABLE EVENTS, "YES"

"Chance" was deliberately omitted as a separate category of influential factors. Certainly each of us could testify about the unpredicted events, indeed unpredictable events, that influenced the course of our own career development. Perhaps we signed up for a course with a particularly charismatic teacher who just happened to be visiting our school that one semester. If we had taken the same course from any other teacher we would have hated it, not majored in it, and have been in a completely different career as a result. Are we then to attribute our choice of major and subsequent career to chance? Or to the influence of a particular model and sequence of learning experiences? While no one could have predicted that a particular student and teacher would have interacted at one particular moment of history, we would be making a big mistake to attribute the influence of that significant interaction to "chance." If we know that the interaction of particular kinds of teachers and students at crucial moments in their respective developments has indeed an influence on occupational preferences and subsequent actions, then some practical implications follow in terms of discovering exactly what the nature of those interactions is, identifying the kinds of teachers that have significant impact and discovering how to produce more inspirational moments for more students and teachers.

"Chance" almost never influences career development, but unpredicted and unpredictable events have a massive effect. To think of them as "chance" would absolve us of any responsibility for doing something about them. To think of them as unexpected learning opportunities enables us to take best advantage of whatever happens. A tennis player never knows exactly where her opponent's serve will land, but she prepares herself to respond in a timely manner to many eventualities. Thinking of unpredictable events as "chance" discourages the active preparation which makes constructive responses possible.

WHO'S IN CHARGE HERE?

Roe mentions some environmental factors that may influence career decision making, such as the fact that technological developments may make certain jobs obsolete and that father's occupation and one's marital family are also influences on career choice. I subsume these variables under other categories listed under environmental influences, but it is, nevertheless, helpful to have them pointed out specifically. Undoubtedly there are many other specific factors that could be identified. The crucial point is that the environment (social customs, national policies, availability of resources, and so on) exerts a potent effect upon the types of alternatives from which one may be able to choose.

Roe reports some confusion about Figure 1, noting that the antecedents and consequences do not appear necessarily directly related. They are not. In a specific example in Figure 1, Roger was reported as having a stimulating conversation with his father about how the United States would be different today if Jefferson had not lived. If Roger's father had been too tired to talk that evening, Roger might not have had that conversation and its associated positive reinforcement. Another student in similar antecedent circumstances might well have received quite different consequences. The H-shaped figure in Figure 1 represents an instrumental learning experience, which consists of antecedents, behaviors, and consequences. The particular antecedents, behaviors, and consequences will be quite different for every person, but it is important to realize that every person is going through a continuous sequence of instrumental learning experiences that is shaping occupational preferences.

I apologize to Anne Roe and to other readers who may be confused by the absence of self-contained explanatory notes in Figure 5 (though the symbols are explained in the text). The H's in Figure 5 refer to instrumental learning experiences which were represented in Figure 1 as an H-shaped figure. The O's represent associative learning experiences which in Figure 2 were represented as circles. The triangles represent self-observation generalizations, as diagrammed in Figure 3; and parallelograms represent task approach skills, as defined in Figure 4.

Roe expresses concern that there appeared to be a surprising lack of conscious decision making, but the triple arrows in Figure 5 are designed to represent choice points where conscious decision making does occur. The intent of the diagram is to show that conscious decision making takes place in a context of complex cultural, social, environmental and economic events, conditioned by a long history of instrumental and associative learning experiences. An individual has the power to exercise choice over the direction of his or her own life, but decisions and their outcomes are inevitably influenced by the environmental setting and prior learning experiences.

I am pleased that both Holland and Roe saw fit to make many favorable comments about the possible contributions of this social learning theory and hasten to add that I thoroughly agree with every nice thing they said. They were too kind to point out other defects in the theory, so I would like to state some of them now.

WANTED: NEW FACTS AND PROPOSITIONS

The social learning theory of career selection is far from complete. Although it specifies some types of learning experiences that may facilitate or inhibit the development of specific career preferences, it does not explain how those various learning experiences are combined to yield a certain preference. We do not know, for example, how many positive reinforcement experiences would be cancelled out by one negative modeling experience. We do not know whether 33 positive associations of words and images with a particular occupation supplemented by 12 positive reinforcements by three valued persons who advocate engaging in that occupation would be negated by one observation of a model being punished for engaging in that same field of work. The theory does not specify any algorithm for combining the number and intensity of experiences, simply because our knowledge of the way in which these experiences are combined is so totally inadequate. Perhaps some day we will learn enough to be able to specify how people cognitively process combinations of experiences to generate preferences, at which time an additional proposition can be added to the theory.

The theory is also inadequate in that it does not specify exactly what cognitive or behavioral processes represent effective decision-making skills. It is assumed that there are some steps or processes that can be learned. To date the theory remains silent on exactly what they are until further research defines them.

The theory does not make explicit how people learn which activities are associated with which occupations. Many of the associations that are learned (through observing TV programs, observing models, reading books, and so on) may be inaccurate. People may consequently reject a potential occupation, or set of occupations, needlessly on the grounds that they believe they could not master the necessary skills when in fact those skills are not even needed. However, people will act upon the associations they have learned whether accurate or not. Part of the responsibility of counselors may be to make sure that the career-exploratory experiences bring clients into contact with accurate representations of reality.

While much more needs to be learned to verify or disconfirm already stated propositions, to add organizational and vocational content, to devise new propositions on the basis of accumulating evidence, the social learning theory of career selection offers this tentative picture to clients and potential clients: Although you are born with certain characteristics into a time and place where certain unpredictable events will be occurring, you have some power to shape your own destiny by devising learning experiences of your own choosing, by exploring creative alternatives, and by learning a logical process of weighing the potential consequences of your various alternatives to pick those that most nearly fit your own values.

REFERENCES

Holland, J. L. A new synthesis for an old method and a new analysis of some old phenomena. *The Counseling Psychologist*, 1976, *6*(3), 12-15.

Krumboltz, J. D. A social learning theory of career decision making. In Mitchell, A. M., Jones, G. B., and Krumboltz, J. D. (Eds.), *A social learning theory of career decision making*. Final Report, Contract No. NIE-C-74-0134. Palo Alto, Calif.: American Institutes for Research, 1975. Pp. 13-39.

Krumboltz, J. D., Mitchell, A. M., and Gelatt, H. B. Applications of a social learning theory of career selection. *Focus on Guidance*, 1975, *8*(3), 1-16.

Krumboltz, J. D., Mitchell, A. M., and Jones, G. B. A social learning theory of career selection. *The Counseling Psychologist*, 1976, *6*(1), 71-81.

Mitchell, A. M. Analysis and synthesis of CDM literature as related to this theory. In Mitchell, A. M., Jones, G. B., and Krumboltz, J. D. (Eds.), *A social learning theory of career decision making*. Final Report, Contract No. NIE-C-74-0134. Palo Alto, Calif.: American Institutes for Research, 1975. Pp. 40-53.

Roe, A. Reactions to Krumboltz and Crites. *The Counseling Psychologist*, 1976, *6*(3), 16-17.

USING A TYPOLOGY OF PERSONS AND ENVIRONMENTS TO EXPLAIN CAREERS: SOME EXTENSIONS AND CLARIFICATIONS

7

JOHN L. HOLLAND
GARY D. GOTTFREDSON
The Johns Hopkins University

Any large-scale, long-term investment—writing a textbook, teaching a course, or developing a theory—requires occasional reexamination of its value, scope, and potential use. The purposes of this paper are: (a) to show more completely than before how a theory of careers (Holland, 1973) can be used to explain common career phenomena and concepts, (b) to report some new insights and supportive data, (c) to rectify some theoretical misunder-standings, and (d) to spell out the implications of these ideas for counseling practice and vocational interventions. These goals are incorporated in the following sections: What Vocational Questions Require Explanation? How the Theory Explains. Typological Interpretations of Developmental Concepts. Extending the Typology to the Life Span. Practical Implications for Vocational Assistance.

This article will be of most benefit to readers who have an understanding of the theory and its associated classification (Holland, 1973). Some knowledge of recent research is also helpful but not essential. Interested readers should see Lackey's (1975) annotated bibliography concerned with the theory, the Vocational Preference Inventory (VPI), and the Self-Directed Search (SDS) for the period 1972-1975. Likewise, Campbell (1974), Harmon (1974), Osipow (1973), Walsh (1973), and Warnath (1974) provide independent views of the theory's strengths and weaknesses.

In this article, "career" is defined as a person's work history and his/her

We are indebted to the following persons for their helpful reviews of earlier drafts of this article. Because we did not always follow their advice, they do not necessarily endorse the ideas expressed here. They include: Linda S. Gottfredson, Geoffrey Kelso, Charles F. Elton, Nancy K. Schlossberg, Laurel Oliver, Thomas M. Magoon, Samuel H. Osipow, Joseph P. Schnitzen, Richard W. Bolles, John H. Hollifield, Adam Lackey, Douglas T. Hall, Douglas R. Whitney, and Ellen Greenberger.

history of vocational aspirations (both kind and level) from birth to death.

WHAT VOCATIONAL QUESTIONS REQUIRE EXPLANATION?

The theory attempts to provide explanations for some important vocational questions. We have assumed that an understanding of careers requires useful answers to four fundamental questions.

1. What personal and environmental characteristics lead to vocational choice, involvement, satisfaction, and career achievement? Or, what personal and environmental characteristics lead to alienation, dissatisfaction, failure, and dropping out of the work force?

2. What personal and environmental characteristics lead to stability of the kind and level of work a person performs? Why do most people have orderly or stable careers when their individual jobs are categorized in any one of several classification schemes?

3. What personal and environmental characteristics lead to change or instability of the kind or level of work a person performs? Or, why do people change jobs? And, what influences the search for new jobs?

4. Why do some people make choices that are congruent with their vocational assessments, others do not, and still others are undecided?

Most of the problems and questions about careers can be restated in terms of these more fundamental questions. Subsequent sections use these questions to illustrate the use of the theory, to explain common career behaviors, and to reinterpret developmental concepts.

HOW THE THEORY EXPLAINS

The theory attempts to answer the four fundamental questions by using a few carefully defined ideas to explain vocational behavior.

A person's resemblance to each of six theoretical personality types is assessed by the use of several special techniques (SDS, VPI, Strong-Campbell Interest Inventory, major field, or vocational preference). These techniques also provide an assessment of the supplementary concepts of consistency (the degree of compatibility of primary dispositions) and differentiation (clarity) of a person's personality pattern. Likewise, environments are assessed for their resemblance to each of six environmental models by use of several special techniques (the Environmental Assessment Technique, code of current job). These techniques also enable an assessment of the supplementary concepts of consistency and differentiation. The classification of both persons and environments provides a plan for summarizing, organizing, and understanding the voluminous information about people's psychological characteristics as well as the voluminous data about jobs.

The relations among types, among jobs, and between types and jobs are estimated according to a hexagonal arrangement or model. The hexagonal model arranges both types and jobs according to their psychological similarities and differences. According to the hexagonal model, the similarity of the types is inversely related to the distance between them. The hexagonal model is also used to estimate degrees of person/job congruency. For example, a Realistic person in a Realistic job is in a more congruent situation than a Realistic person in an Investigative job; a Realistic person in a Social job is in the most incongruent situation possible; and so on.

The last step consists of applying the formal account of the theory (typological and environmental formulations and the hypotheses about their interaction) and the personal and environmental constructs (including differentiation and consistency) to explain and predict the most probable personal characteristics and performance. In short, the typology can be applied using a small number of constructs and explicit definitions.

In general, career phenomena are explained by following the theoretical formulations as explicitly as possible. The most recent statement of the theory (Holland, 1973) summarizes how careers are explained or understood, but some additional clarification is needed.

1. *How do personal development, initial vocational choice, work involvement, and satisfaction come about?*

People grow up to resemble one type or another because parents, schools, and neighborhoods serve as environments which reinforce some behaviors more than others and provide different models of suitable behavior. The reinforcement consists of the encouragement of selected activities, interests, self-estimates, and competencies. The modeling occurs because parents, peers, and friends engage in (model) some behaviors more than others. This experience contributes to the development of a characteristic, typological disposition, which, in turn, leads to a characteristic cluster of personal traits. Consequently, when the need for choice or employment occurs, a person is predisposed toward some groups of occupations more than others (see Grandy & Stahmann, 1974). Different cultural influences, as well as other aspects of the interpersonal milieu, such as sex-role socialization, race, religion, and social class, promote the development of some types more than others by differential encouragement of the experiences (activities, interests, competencies, and so on) that lead to different types.

Satisfaction and success result from a congruency of person and environment. People who possess the competencies required by their environment and who desire the rewards the environment yields are expected to be more satisfied and involved. In contrast, people who are not in an environment congruent with their personal characteristics are expected to be uninvolved, dissatisfied, and unsuccessful. Lack of involvement may result from a failure to find a congruent environment or from a lack of a clearly defined and consistent personality pattern so that no environment is clearly congruent with the individual's personality type. Caplan (1973, pp. 18-34) illustrates how a lack of match between a person's competencies and a job can result in a decision not to work when non-work provides more rewards than the incongruent work.

The secondary concepts of consistency and differentiation indicate the degree of precision that is expected for the explanation; that is, consistent and well-defined types are more predictable (their expected behavior is more likely to occur) than are inconsistent and poorly defined types.

2. *Why do most people have orderly careers when the individual jobs in their work histories are categorized using an occupational classification scheme?*

The majority of people manage to find work that is congruent with their type. More explicitly, the average person searches for or gravitates toward work environments in which his/her typological predilections and talents (activities, competencies, perceptions of self and world, values, traits) are allowed expression and rewarded. The person/job congruence of the majority of people (Nafziger, Holland, Helms, & McPartland, 1974) occurs because we assume that most adults are differentiated, and by definition well-defined types know what activities and competencies bring them satisfaction and achievement. They act on this knowledge to achieve congruency. In this instance, "know" includes both conscious and unconscious knowledge of self and environment.

Economic standing, race, and sex are important determinants of careers. All of these influence and restrict occupational choice—vocational self-concepts and skills are not developed in a social vacuum. Everyone's personality is the result of a developmental process influenced by economic standing, race, sex, and myriad other influences. To the extent that any of these influences are actually incorporated in an individual's self-theory, they are within the scope of the present theory and are expected to promote orderly careers. Gottfredson, Gottfredson, and Holland (Note 1) have recently argued that the occupational structure in our society does not currently allow everyone to be employed in congruent jobs.

Orderly careers are also encouraged by the stereotyped ways in which employers perceive a person's credentials. In addition to the influences of education, race, and sex, employers seek people with "the right kind of experience." Consequently, it is easier to remain a plumber, an administrator, a secretary, or a teacher than it is to change occupations or roles within an occupation. To change usually requires energy, initiative, money, persistence, and the ability to persuade a potential employer that the desired change is rational and in the employer's interest.

3. *Why do people change jobs? What influences their search for new jobs?*

People change jobs because they are dissatisfied, because they are incompetent, because other workers wish them to leave, and for other personal and environmental reasons: better climate, physical disability, dissatisfied relatives, more money, and other influences. In theoretical terms, people leave because of excessive person/environment incongruency or because of an opportunity to increase their congruency. Other things being equal, a particular person's departure should be explainable by a careful assessment of the structure and formulations specified earlier (Holland, 1973, pp. 40-43). What is the person's type, degree of differentiation and consistency? What was the degree of person/job congruency? Using these concepts to review the interaction for the reinforcement or match between preferred and rewarded activities, competencies, self and world views, values and traits should indicate the character of the incongruency that led to a job change. If no incongruency is evident, then the job change is likely to be based on an opportunity for increased congruency—a similar job at better pay, a higher-ranking position in the same field, and so on. Some other reasons for job change—such as a physical disability or closing of a company—cannot be interpreted in theoretical terms, but the job search that follows can be.

The search for the next job should follow the same principles. The person should search for jobs that are congruent with his/her type. If a consistent and well-defined type moves, he or she is expected to move between similar jobs because he/she has integrated consistent personal characteristics, and because he/she has a clear sense of vocational identity. Consequently, this person readily recognizes potentially congruent jobs when they become visible. In contrast, an inconsistent and poorly-defined type is expected to move between dissimilar jobs because he/she has incorporated diffuse and divergent personal characteristics, or because no clear patterning of characteristics has developed. Because of an ambiguous vocational identity, the potential congruency of a particular job often appears ambiguous—a perception which frequently leads to an inappropriate job. A further hypothesis, not yet studied, is that poorly-defined people may appear confused or ambiguous to potential employers so that the search for congruency is complicated by the potential employer's inability to clearly determine what the applicant's desires and competencies are.

At the same time, people with substantial and varied personal resources, such as money, good looks, and health will have greater job-searching ability and may have more subsequent vocational success. A variety of liabilities such as ethnic origin, sex, poverty, prison records, or infirmities frequently interfere with job seeking. Similarly, some people leave congruent jobs and take incongruent jobs to get more money. Researchers and practitioners must control for these assets and liabilities in order to test and use the typology. Like all psychological theories, the present one must be supplemented by a host of personal and environmental contingencies.

4. *Why do some people make vocational choices that are congruent with assessment data, others do not, and still others are "undecided"?*
People with consistent and well-defined personality patterns are expected to be "good" decision makers because of the implications of

differentiation and consistency: integration of preferred activities, competencies, occupational preferences and self-estimates, and compatibility of primary dispositions.

Research supports this explanation. A recent large-scale study by Holland, Gottfredson, and Nafziger (1975) found that differentiation and consistency predicted decision-making ability more efficiently than a group of rival predictors (age, social class, personality variables, CMI variables). Other findings (Holland, Gottfredson, & Nafziger, 1975) reveal that some types may be better decision makers than others. The investigative type appears to be the best and the conventional type the worst. The formulations for these types appear to be consistent with these findings.

The making of decisions at appropriate times (end of high school, end of sophomore year; when to change jobs, when to marry, and so on) may reflect only different rates of personal development and different environmental contingencies. A large-scale study by Baird (1969) found no important and substantial differences between "decided" and "undecided" students. Similarly, a study by Kelso (1975) found that choice "realism" is highest for young people when they are about to enter the job market. Some findings do suggest that "decided" students score slightly higher on a measure of interpersonal competency (Holland, Gottfredson, & Nafziger, 1975; Baird, 1969) and slightly lower on measures of anxiety (Kimes & Troth, 1974) and dependency (Ashby, Wall, & Osipow, 1966). Taken together, these data suggest that not having made a choice may appropriately cause some uneasiness for college students, but that this "indecision" does not necessarily have important adverse consequences. Needless to say, severe cases of indecision such as "cannot decide which shoes to wear" and extreme cases of parental dependency or family conflict lie outside the scope of the theory.

TYPOLOGICAL INTERPRETATIONS OF DEVELOPMENTAL CONCEPTS

There are two main traditions for understanding careers: the developmental view (Super, 1974; Crites, 1974a; Levinson, Darrow, Klein, Levinson, & McKee, 1974) and the differentialist view (Williamson, 1972; Lofquist & Dawis, 1969; Holland, 1973). Both perspectives are useful for interpreting career data, but the purpose of this section is to illustrate how a typology—more properly a modern differentialist view—can be used to reinterpret some common vocational developmental concepts. These interpretations are intended to demonstrate the versatility of the typology and its usefulness for understanding and clarifying vocational developmental concepts.

This task is desirable because this application of the typology is not always understood and because it is desirable to rectify some misinterpretations of the modern differentialist point-of-view. Some authors (Osipow, 1973; Crites, 1972-73; Super, 1969; Borow, 1973; Gysbers & Moore, 1975) have suggested that a matching or typological model cannot or does not cope with the role of development in career decisions and problems. They often bolster their case by criticizing Parsons' (1909) model rather than a contemporary version. (What did the developmental model look like in 1909?) Equally important, developmentalists frequently ignore the main strengths of person/environment typologies: useful forecasts of achievement and satisfaction, practical structures for understanding person/environment interaction, and practical structures for organizing occupational and personal data, including work histories. The following paragraphs show how the present typology can be used to interpret developmental processes and concepts. Some of these interpretations are clearly speculative; others are supported by data.

The career development (CD) perspective has multiple origins in life-stage theory and developmental psychology. Likewise, the CD perspective has multiple definitions and techniques for assessing vocational-development concepts. To simplify discussion, Crites' (1974b) summary of the assessment of career development (Figure 1) is used to exemplify the CD view.

In Figure 1, "Degrees of consistency of career choices" is readily translated into typological terms. Consistency of vocational choices or jobs over time can be assessed in degrees by categorizing successive choices using the classification scheme and by using the hexagonal model. (See Holland & Whitney, 1968, for a concrete illustration or Holland, 1973, for the general method.) Agreement between choices according to level can also be obtained by simply noting the GED levels assigned to a person's vocational choices. Equally important, the act of classification automatically ties the data to the theory, including a tested explanation of the meaning of consistency.

The CD construct, "realism or wisdom of career choices," is conceived of as agreement between a person's interests, preferences, abilities, and social class and his/her choices. In the typology, realism of career choices is assessed by the degree of differentiation of a person's SDS profile. A differentiated SDS profile can only be obtained when a person's competencies, interests, and self-estimates are in close agreement with each other. (Here a person's career choice is equivalent to vocational preferences in the SDS.) Social class also influences the profile because different social classes press for different types. Information about a person's economic and family resources, access to training or credentialling agencies, and job availability must be used to supplement information from the SDS profile in assessing realism.

Consistency of a person's SDS profile (i.e., the degree to which the types the person most resembles are compatible versus divergent) appears to be an aspect of personal integration that is not operational in the career-development model, but which nevertheless appears to contribute to the realism or wisdom of career choices. Some evidence indicates that people with more consistent profiles or job codes have more predictable vocational preferences (Holland, 1968) and job changes (Holland, Sorensen, Clark, Nafziger & Blum, 1973) and are "better" decision makers (Holland,

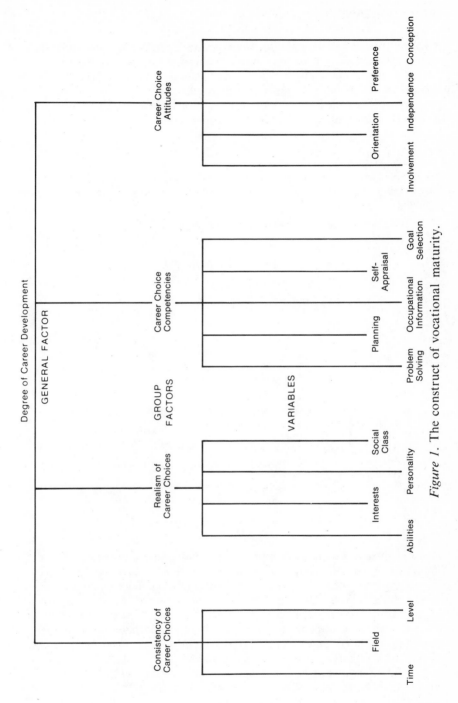

Figure 1. The construct of vocational maturity.

153

Gottfredson, & Nafziger, 1975). Here, "better" pertains to close correspondence between SDS assessment and desired alternatives.

"Career choice competencies" are measured by Crites' CMI competency scales. In the typology, choice competencies are indirectly assessed by a person's score on the Future Possibilities item, a decision-making task. Table 1 shows the task and how it is scored and interpreted in typological terms.

Table 1. Future possibilities

List all the jobs or occupations you could do and would like, if you had enough money to get the necessary training and if you could get that job when you finished your training or education.

I could do and would like the following kinds of jobs:
 1.
 2.
 3.
 4.
 5.
 6.
 7.
 8.
 9.
10.

Scoring Procedure

1. Get first-letter code from the SDS.
2. Get first-letter code for each response to the future possibilities.
3. Using the hexagon, assign scores as follows for *each* future possibility listed.
   If the letters are the same, give a score of 4.
   If the letters are adjacent, give a score of 3.
   If the letters are not adjacent and not opposite, give a score of 2.
   If the letters are opposite on the hexagon, give a score of 1.
4. Add up the scores and divide by the number of future possibilities listed.

Note: See Holland, Gottfredson, and Nafziger (1975) for more information.

High scores on this quasi-performance measure of decision making are obtained by having current vocational aspirations that are supported by a comprehensive vocational assessment (the SDS) of interests, competencies, and self-estimates. This test (Future Possibilities) asks a person to demonstrate his/her decision-making ability rather than querying him/her about knowledge of problem solving, planning, occupational information, self-appraisal, and goal selection. The assumption is that getting high scores on the task requires "career choice competencies."

"Career choice attitudes," as conceived of by Crites (1974b), are related to the consistency and differentiation of a person's SDS profile, as well as intelligence and social class. The translation of this developmental concept is admittedly ambiguous and speculative in contrast to the other concepts.

Finally, a person's "degree of career development" as a general construct incorporates a person's score on the Future Possibilities task, constancy of aspiration type and level over time, and the degree of differentiation and consistency of the SDS, VPI, or SCII profiles. Other operational definitions may have potential value for defining "degree of career development": for example, the summary code for a person's entire work history, or the summary code for the last three jobs, or variations on these ideas. Summary codes can be obtained by assigning 1, 2, or 3 letter codes to aspirations or jobs and by following the SDS scoring procedure (see Holland & Gottfredson, 1975, for an example).

In addition to the concepts associated with the vocational-maturity work, some other development concepts from diverse sources can be reinterpreted in typological terms. For example, "personal integration" becomes the possession of a consistent and well-defined SDS, VPI, or SCII profile. "Identity" appears related to differentiation. After all, "identity" means knowing who you are and what you are not, what you want and what you don't want. Holland, Gottfredson, & Nafziger (1975) have observed that a scale devised to assess vocational identity had low but significant correlations with differentiation scores. "Crystallization of interests" is likewise related to differentiation of the SDS, VPI, or SCII, or a series of similar aspirations or jobs. Perhaps degree of differentiation in typological terms also equals differentiation of personality or level of personal development (Edwards, Nafziger, & Holland, 1974). And "vocational adjustment" (i.e., satisfaction and success) is assumed to be the outcome of a congruent person/job interaction. The reinterpretation of mid-career crises and life-stage problems is taken up in the next section.

EXTENDING THE TYPOLOGY TO THE LIFE SPAN

The purpose of this section is to spell out more completely how the typology can be used to cope with career problems throughout the life span— adolescence through retirement. The earlier speculations (Holland, 1973, pp. 40-44) about how a person lives through successive environments (parents, neighborhoods, schools, social institutions, and jobs) will be elaborated.

The main assumption in this elaboration is that the typology of persons and environments is more useful than any of the life-stage strategies for coping with career problems. Life-stage speculations suffer from myriad scientific and practical difficulties: (a) they usually treat people as a single type, differing only in stage of development, so they fail to deal adequately with the diversity of human personalities; (b) they have weak research and theoretical foundations (small N's have been used to generate a life-time plan); and (c) they provide ambiguous guidance for practical interventions ("her children have left the home, she must be. . ."). In addition, the boundaries assigned to life stages may vary from type to type and may be functions of the stability of a person's home and work environments. For these reasons, the prospect of ever getting life-stage speculations in workable order now appears remote. In contrast, typologies of persons and environments do not make any assumptions about characteristic vocational crises or problems at different stages of life. Instead, they provide an explicit structure for assessing a person and his/her current situation at any age. This structure (What type of person is involved? What environment is he/she coping with? What environments are possible?) can be applied from adolescence to retirement, can be readily understood by the person, incorporates the differential tradition, incorporates many developmental speculations, and has a comprehensive and strong research and theoretical base. It has the added virtue of avoiding "ageist" stereotypes. These ideas are amplified in what follows.

Coping Styles

At any age, the level and quality of a person's vocational coping is a function of the interaction of personality type and type of environment plus the consistency and differentiation of each. Among these, type and personality pattern appear especially important. The formulations for the types clearly imply that some types have higher aspirations than others, that some types are more likely to plan than others, that some types are more apt to remain lifelong learners than others, and that some types are better decision makers than others. Consequently, different types will manage their careers and life problems in different ways and with different degrees of success. (See Holland, 1973, pp. 24-26, for other more explicit hypotheses about the expected life styles of the types.)

For example, a woman with a well-defined Investigative-Artistic personality pattern would be expected to have high educational and vocational aspirations, to have good decision-making ability, to have a strong and lifelong interest in learning, to have moderate personal competency, and to have a marked interest in creative and high-level performance rather than in leadership. In addition, such a person would be prone either to remold her environment or leave it in the face of adversity (Holland, 1973, p. 42).

In contrast, a man with a poorly defined Social-Artistic pattern would be expected to have low educational and vocational aspirations, to have poor decision-making skills, to have a weak interest in lifelong learning, to have a modest degree of interpersonal competency, to lack interest in high-level performance (vocational or educational), to readily accede to environmental adversity rather than struggling to revise his environment or moving to a new environment. In short, a review of the typological formulations implies a comprehensive set of expectations for characterizing how we might expect a particular person to cope with common vocational problems. Such hypotheses should, however, be modified by environmental assessments and any contingencies beyond the scope of the theory.

Ages and Stages

The person/environment model is applicable to any age—adolescence through retirement. At any age, the counselor and the person can use the typology to review the congruency of the current job (environment) for its implications for staying, going, revising a current job, or changing one's self. The person's personality, as expressed in an interest profile and in the scoring of his/her aspirations and work history, should imply some useful diagnostic and treatment ideas. The principal value of life-stage speculations is that they provide additional hypotheses about the nature of the person's current difficulties, which can be reviewed if the typological hypotheses are found wanting. Because maturity is a complex construct composed of skills and dispositions presumed to lead to adjustment, CD measures may provide clues about the origins of problems. At the same time, they will seldom suggest explicit remedial actions a person can take or reassure a person about a tentative choice or goal. In addition, diagnoses resulting from the CD perspective usually specify "inadequate self-knowledge" or other intrapsychic problems to the exclusion of problems of person/environment interaction. Many vocational problems result from lack of opportunity, undesirable environments, or unsatisfactory person/environment interactions.

Age is primarily important for two reasons: (a) it moderates the clarity of predictions based on interest and ability assessments because people change or become clearer about themselves over time; and (b) important events in people's lives differ systematically with age. Nevertheless, the similarities of vocational problems at different ages appear to outweigh the differences. For example, selecting and worrying about work in high school, deciding on or being forced into a first job, being fired from a job, being promoted, getting fed up with a job, worrying about failing or imagined incompetency—all can culminate in a crisis, or can produce a high degree of tension, and all can be structured and explained as person/environment interactions and their consequence. Likewise, questions of identity, self-confidence, sexuality, work involvement, personal expression, interpersonal competence, satisfaction, achievement, and family relations are intertwined with most vocational decisions at any age and can also be examined as person/environment interaction.

Because some tasks are characteristically encountered at specific times, groups of people sometimes show patterns of similar responses. The "dissertation anxiety" that sometimes occurs when students with high aspirations realize that their scientific contribution will be modest, the uneasiness that occurs when some aspiring workers see that they have reached a plateau, and the "culture fatigue" characteristic of Peace Corps Volunteers (Brein & David, 1971) are examples of these patterns. Knowledge of the characteristic "crises" provides some hypotheses about vocational problems, and the normative information may be a source of reassurance to clients. Unfortunately, the incremental value of these speculations over a detailed examination of person/environment interactions is not known. At this time, life-stage hypotheses form a rickety roulette wheel of possibilities which counselors should spin only after the more obvious hypotheses have been explored.

The evidence about adolescents and adults implies that person/job congruence and job satisfaction increase with age and that the majority of the population maintain stable work histories or careers. The evidence for this conclusion now is pervasive and compelling. (See the following studies, many of which are based on national representative samples of adolescents and adults: Holland et al., 1973; McLaughlin & Tiedeman, 1974; Nafziger et al., 1974; Parsons & Wigtil, 1974; Quinn, Staines, & McCullough, 1974; Statistical Policy Division, 1973.) Most recently, Gottfredson, Gottfredson, and Holland (Note 1), using Nafziger et al. (1974) data, have shown that, although areas of divergence exist, most people wish to remain in jobs of the same general category as their present job. Finally, the evidence for the stability of vocational and avocational interests over long timespans is substantial (Strong, 1943; Campbell, 1971). Campbell (1971, p. 82) reports that stability coefficients of interests of men for periods of 20 years range from .64 to .72; and for periods of 11 to 20 years, they range from .64 to .80. These stability coefficients tend to increase with increasing age of initial measurement.

The results of the diagnostic test, Future Possibilities, also suggest that vocational decision-making ability varies only slightly with age from adolescence on; the decision-making score distributions of high school juniors, college juniors, and employed adults are characterized primarily by their marked overlap rather than their differences. This is additional evidence for the similarity of some vocational principles at different ages.

Change and Crisis

As we indicated earlier, change in career direction is amenable to the typology at hand. For example, many (we are inclined to believe most) mid-career shifts are not drastic shifts in direction. Gilbride (1973) found that 80% of his resigned priests (a Social job) entered other Social occupations. Clopton (1972) compared 20 men, characterized as having made radical mid-life changes, with 20 comparable men who had not made changes. A coding of the pre- and post-change jobs again reveals that the majority fall in the same major category—for instance, minister to vocational counselor. The typology also provides a single method for assessing the *degree* of change or shift (Holland & Whitney, 1968; Holland et al., 1973).

At the same time, some people do undergo change or develop somewhat different personalities (become more like another type than an earlier type, become a more differentiated person of the same type, become a more inconsistent person, or undergo some other change). In general, these changes occur in accordance with the same principles outlined for the development of the types. Persons in congruent work situations will change very little, for they are rewarded for the expression of their current interests, self-views, competencies, and personal traits. Because the majority of people have success in finding congruent work, stability of type is the rule rather than the exception. In contrast, persons in incongruent situations will change the most, for they are ignored or punished—their personal dispositions do not fit the reward structure.

It is reasonable to expect that many career shifts attributed to special events or special experiences can be explained as particular person/environment interactions. For example, some major life experiences are enabling or facilitating, because they carry with them the possibility of a type being more able than before to act out his/her central goals, preferred activities, values, and so on—promotion, sudden wealth, special training, or personal development. Some subsequent behavior may then be explained as due to an increased opportunity for an Enterprising type, for instance, to assume the enterprising role more completely, with more power, more resources, and so on. The person has not changed—the environment has.

Other life experiences involve deprivation or thwarting influences: loss of job, poverty, divorce, loss of close relatives, demotion, declining energy, declining competency. Again, how a person copes with these experiences is expected to be, in part, a function of his/her type, differentiation, and so on.

Some real-life examples appear to illustrate these principles. A minister with social and enterprising skills was fired for the first time in his career and became interested in the process of job finding to such an extent that he has now become an expert in the placement process. True to form (we should say, true to well-defined type), he continues to counsel and preach by conducting numerous workshops and by writing self-help books. In short, his job loss resulted in an opportunity to use nearly all of his old skills, to reach a larger audience (ministry), and to attain more personal fulfillment in terms of greater self-expression, fewer employer restrictions, and greater income.

In contrast, other people sometimes deteriorate after a job lay-off by failing to face the situation, remaining inactive, or drinking. Kroll, Dinklage, Lee, Morley, and Wilson (1970) document how workers in a shoe factory (largely Realistic people) coped with a factory closing in divergent ways. Some saw the signs of closing six months in advance; others ignored the signs. Some made a smooth transition by planning and had a new job ready the day the factory closed (higher levels of S and E?); others waited until the actual closing, went home, and watched TV for several weeks (low levels of S and E?).

Finally, some experiences will be thwarting to one type but will be enabling to another. For example, divorce for a Social type married to an unsociable Investigative type may allow a gregarious person the freedom to satisfy social needs that the restrictive marriage did not. Some of the positive outcomes of widowhood discovered by Maas and Kuypers (1974) can be interpreted in this way. The death of a husband may open the door that previously blocked career or personal development.

Special Groups

Suggestions that special theories are needed for women or minority groups are made from time to time (Psathas, 1968; Zytowski, 1969). Three arguments converge in suggesting that the most useful and wisest approach is a single theory for all. First, because all groups are members of the same species, the psychological principles underlying vocational behavior are presumably the same for all groups. Different distributions of types in different groups are some of the phenomena that a theory of vocational behavior must explain; these differences are not grounds for separate theories. In principle, the effects of sex, ethnic identity, or religion contribute to the development of the types just as do any other social, personal, or environmental influences—social class, geography, physical size, physical or social stigmata, and intelligence. Interest or personality inventories and achievement tests are tools for assessing the result of these processes, and group differences are data with which any theory must jibe. The present theory predicts differences in personal development when personal history differs: people given Social opportunities, rewarded for Social behavior, and provided with Social models are expected to develop Social preferences and competencies.

Second, the data do not support the hypothesis that different psychological processes exist for different groups (group-by-type interactions). For example, Rose and Elton (1971) argue for separate theories for men and women with some of the strongest data anyone has presented, but the sex-by-type interactions they found, although statistically significant, are tiny compared to the main effects in their data, making these interactions of little practical value. Vocational assessments for men, women, Blacks, and Whites reveal both similarities and differences among the distributions of types (Gottfredson & Holland, 1975a; Gottfredson, Holland, & Gottfredson, 1975; Nafziger et al., 1974), and there is good evidence that these assessments have useful validity for all groups (Gottfredson & Holland, 1975b; Holland & Lutz, 1968; Kimball, Sedlacek, & Brooks, 1973). In addition, different assessment devices all show common patterns of sex and ethnic-group differences (Allport, Vernon, & Lindsey, 1970; Campbell, 1971; Gordon, 1975; Hanson, 1975; Lamb, 1974).

Third, using the same typology and assessments for all groups to organize vocational information has important practical uses: (a) *to assess people's current status*—the cumulative effects of heredity and socialization (including the effects of racism and sexism); (b) *to plan more advantageous career development* by visualizing areas of desirable vocational development. Instead of ignoring a person's history we can use this classification and others to estimate the psychological distance between current status and one or more vocational alternatives. The width of the chasm to be jumped is important information for anyone wishing to go from here to there. A knowledge of current status and deficiencies allows a person to plan action leading to his or her goals. For example, a young man or woman who desires a career as a mechanic but lacks mechanical skills is best served by learning of this deficiency. Sound decision making requires the acquisition of these skills—or in some cases abandoning the goal, if the skills cannot be acquired or if the activities prove to be distasteful. Likewise, a young man or woman who desires a career as a marriage counselor but who lacks social skills can use this information to try to develop these talents or to revise his or her goals. (c) *To design job-seeking strategies* by specifying the most promising alternatives. A Social type might seek a higher level Social job, a Conventional person, a better Conventional job, or people might explore jobs in related categories of the classification. In general, women and men who capitalize on their greatest strengths are expected to maximize their satisfaction and success. The indiscriminate encouragement of women and men to try any kind of work is not in their best interests, for it will result in some people trying jobs for which they have little interest or competency and ignoring jobs for which they have more. Part of this misleading emphasis may result from a failure to distinguish between type and level of occupations in efforts to improve the standing of minorities or women (Gottfredson, Holland, & Gottfredson, 1975).

PRACTICAL IMPLICATIONS FOR VOCATIONAL ASSISTANCE

The practical implications of the typology for vocational guidance have been summarized earlier (Holland, 1973, pp. 85-93). In short, the typology can be used to organize occupational materials and experiences, to explain and interpret vocational data and behavior, and to plan remedial activities. The purpose of the present discussion is to clarify and extend some of these ideas using more recent experience, data, and thinking.

Personal and Group Counseling

The main functions proposed earlier—organization, explanation, and remediation—now appear to have some unanticipated but desirable side effects. Organizing occupational information according to the typology was intended to make the use of such materials easier and to reduce counselor work. At the same time, the typological organization of materials may have increased people's independence and competency for dealing with their vocational questions and problems. Likewise, the use of the typology to explain vocational problems and to plan developmental or remedial activities appears to generate some of the same effects. Users (students and employed persons) become actively engaged in understanding their current situation because they can understand the assessment (SDS, VPI, SCII, coded work history), comprehend the theory and classification scheme, and see the reasonableness of some next steps (Zener & Schnuelle, 1972). The dependency often observed after vocational assessment appears to occur less frequently (Krivatsy, 1974). In short, the typology and its tools appear to give understanding and power to the user throughout the vocational counseling process.

Earlier, the implications of the typology for counseling theory were unclear and were ignored. Now it may be helpful to outline how the use of the typology in counseling can be related to other points of view.

In many ways, the typology is neutral with respect to theories of counseling and learning, but it also is congenial with many of them. For example, the theory suggests that people *learn* to become types. All major theories of learning seem useful in explaining learning in this context. Cognitive theory can be employed to help explain how people with increasing work experience acquire different views of themselves (self-estimates) that lead to job changes. Or, social learning theory (models, and occasional or vicarious reinforcement) can be applied to explain how people become more like some types than others. Likewise, Cochran, Vinitsky, and Warren (1974) have shown how the typology and the SDS can be used in a developmentally oriented counseling program to facilitate self- and environmental exploration and their integration.

We now see a new vocational-assistance orientation evolving out of the typology, the increased need for service, the hard times, the use of self-administered inventories, and the remnants of other points of view.

It is hard to give this new orientation a name, but the Exploratory View is helpful as a beginning. Using materials that a person can use with little aid (self-administered and self-scored inventories and vocational information), a person defines his/her vocational questions and begins to help him/herself. The counselor acts as a consultant or resource person who encourages (reinforces) exploration of self and potential environmental solutions (jobs, training, and so on), but the counselor assumes that most people (those not seriously disturbed or mentally defective) can resolve vocational questions if they are provided a rich climate of information and exploratory reinforcement. Attempts to clarify self-concepts, to reduce psychological conflicts, or to facilitate development via person-to-person learning are minimized and are engaged in only after self-directed and informational programs have been tried. Counselors emphasize the client's need to explore and to come to his/her own conclusions. Counselors do not intervene with a person who exhibits "premature crystallization." Making choices under any circumstances may be more constructive in the long run than postponement, because choices lead to involvement, learning, and responsibility. In short, this view accepts the person's definition of the problem and helps him/her deal with it by providing resources and information, but, above all, this approach emphasizes exploration of self and the world as the road to vocational decision making, planning, and problem solving. Finally, professional information—what the counselor really thinks, test manuals, texts, and so on — is available, rather than hidden, so that the traditional balance of knowledge and resources is more even. This openness is a built-in safeguard against counselor ineptitude and inadvertent sexist or racist responses.

In this framework, person-to-person counseling then becomes the treatment of last, rather than first, resort. In this way, counselors are more likely to serve people most in need of their skills and to avoid people readily served by simpler and cheaper methods. People who have found the typological materials insufficient will arrive with some preparation for engaging the counselor. Likewise, the counselor will have some "open" diagnostic information immediately at his/her disposal for discussion with the person.

The counselor can continue to work with the person using the typology as a means of communicating and use whatever counseling theory and program appears useable and congenial. Or the counselor can use the typology in a thorough fashion to assess the person's current situation and any proposed alternatives, to understand the person, to propose possible explanations of the difficulties in decision making, to characterize a person's work history and its implications, or to engage in activities designed to promote needed personal growth in order to facilitate a person's vocational decisions.

As it stands, the typology is assumed to be especially useful because it provides a comprehensive set of concepts for organizing and understanding personal and vocational data, assessment techniques using the same constructs (SDS, VPI, SCII, ACT II), a diagnostic scheme, and now an outline of a closely related approach to vocational assistance.

Still unexplored is the possibility of using the typology to assign or suggest treatment according to type. For instance, I's may profit more from reading, S's from group activities, C's from structured workbooks. Some clinical experience suggests that these hypotheses may be too simple. At any rate, it is clear that the typology can be used to orient an entire vocational-assistance program including associated vocational counseling, or the typology can easily be integrated with other orientations to vocational counseling. In that situation, the typological view becomes one more approach in a counselor's repertoire.

The application of the typology to impersonal forms of vocational assistance has recently been outlined (Holland, 1974, outlines how the typology can be applied to the vocational needs of high school and college students as well as employed adults). In contrast to traditional vocational counseling, these plans are concerned with improving the vocational environments in schools and at work to help resolve the majority of vocational questions by the provision of information and self-administered help in more accessible and inexpensive ways.

Effects and Evaluation

In the end, whether or not anyone has benefited from these ideas is the paramount question. Although evaluations of vocational treatments are not a popular enterprise, they form the only avenue for a reliable and consensual understanding of what works and, perhaps more important, of how to design more potent and economical forms of vocational assistance.

Recent research on the effects of computerized counseling and paper guidance systems provides some provocative results. Studies of the effects of computer-assistance systems are usually positive (Harris, 1974). The effects of group vocational guidance using highly structured materials have received very positive evaluations by college students (Magoon, 1965). And the effects of the Self-Directed Search have been positive (Redmond, 1973; Zener & Schnuelle, 1972) and essentially equal to the effects of counselors (Nolan, 1974; Krivatsy, 1974). Even programmed-test interpretations have sometimes received high marks when compared to counselor interpretations (Forster, 1969; Graff, Danish, & Austin, 1972; Tipton, 1969).

These results lead to the next question—why do impersonal forms of assistance work as well as they do? Because impersonal interventions primarily provide information, a likely hypothesis is that many people can readily use well-organized information to resolve vocational questions. The function of the typology in the SDS may be largely to organize personal and vocational information in ways which are easily comprehended. Only a rare counselor can communicate as much personal and occupational information at the same rate and accuracy. It is even conceivable that person-to-person communications (counseling) about many vocational difficulties actually interfere with the transmission of accurate personal/environmental information. Put another way, impersonal vocational-counseling devices may provide a kind of limited empathic experience by giving back to the person some vocational alternatives and understandings that are often congruent with a person's self-perceptions. This experience may then generate feelings of being understood that resemble the feelings generated by empathic therapists (Rogers, 1975), and such positive feelings may, in turn, generate self- and occupational exploration. These speculations are untested but they appear worth further exploration.

If impersonal devices continue to receive positive evaluations, perhaps we should explore other ways of making needed personal and environmental information more accessible and clear. Unsettling as it is to say, we may have over-rated the virtues of vocational counseling and under-rated the potential of simpler methods.

DISCUSSION

This report has been an unabashed attempt to illustrate the virtues of a particular typology. Consequently, it is important to attempt a stocktaking of both its strengths and weaknesses, to delineate some pressing research needs, to cope with some remaining complaints and misunderstandings, and to reiterate some vocational-assistance issues. For balance, the reader should consult the book reviews and texts cited in the introduction.

Strengths and Weaknesses

The virtues of the typology are easily summarized: (a) it is easily grasped; (b) it has many of the virtues of a useful theory—clear definitions, internally consistent structure, broad scope, and formalizations for dealing with both personal development and change; (c) it has a broad base of research support using samples of children, adolescents, college students, and unemployed adults; and (d) it is easily applied to practical problems—the development of vocational-assessment devices, the classification and interpretation of personal and environmental data, and the conduct of vocational counseling.

The weaknesses of the typology appear as follows: (a) the hypotheses about vocational environments are only partially tested and require much more exploration; (b) the hypotheses about the person/environment interactions in the last account of the typology (Holland, 1973) have received recent strong support (Helms & Williams, 1973), but they also require more testing; (c) the formulations about personal development (Holland, 1973, pp. 11-13) and change (pp. 41-44) have received some support (Edwards, Nafziger, & Holland, 1974; Grandy & Stahmann, 1974; Holland, 1973, pp. 53-54), but they need a more comprehensive examination; (d) the classification of occupations may differ slightly for the different devices used to assess the types; and (e) many important personal and environmental contingencies lie outside the scope of the typology. For example, the distribution of power or influence within a person's environment (at home or at work) makes a difference, so researchers must control for power, and practitioners must make some estimate of the role of power in evaluating environments for their clients. The role of social class, intelligence, and special aptitudes is incorporated only indirectly and incompletely in the typology so these personal characteristics must also be allowed for.

Complaints and Misunderstandings

The typology suffers from multiple misunderstandings of its formulations, scope, and empirical support. Some of these are contrary to the facts, some are meaningless complaints, and some represent genuine controversy.

Some misunderstandings arise from reading incomplete, unclear, out-of-date, or inaccurate textbook accounts of the theory instead of reading the 1973 version. Other misunderstandings probably result from the author's penchant for brevity.

Some complaints can be disposed of with facts. Contrary to some reports, National Merit Finalists were used in only five of 250 investigations. Large scale investigations, using nationally representatives samples of high school students and employed adults, document that the typology is not limited to the psychology of college students (Holland et al., 1973; McLaughlin & Tiedeman, 1974; Nafziger et al., 1974; Parsons & Wigtil, 1974). (See Lackey's, 1975, bibliography for other investigations using employed adults.)

Some critics (McConnell, 1968; Yonge, 1965) believe that the assessment of types and environments is flawed by "circularity." They fail to see that the actual assessment of types and their environments is performed by using different populations and methods. In addition, once a code has been established for an occupation or major by conducting a census of types, the use of the environmental code is completely independent of individual assessment in subsequent research or applications. Richards, Bulkeley, & Richards (Note 2) have shown that environmental assessments based on different kinds of information (faculty, curricula, or degrees granted) lead to similar environmental assessments. In short, critics fail to differentiate the rational parallelism of the types and environments from the independent assessment of each.

The belief that the typology does not explain the development or changing of types no longer holds; the belief that the theory is "mostly descriptive" also appears contrary to its formalizations and the illustrative explanations provided earlier. Much of this kind of criticism revolves around an unresolvable issue: some counselors and psychologists still prefer deep-seated, inner forces as explanations. In contrast, the present typology provides more easily tested explanations, using well-defined constructs, although even these have considerable ambiguity or surplus meaning.

The arguments that the typology and associated assessments apply only to the status quo (Cole & Hanson, 1975; Warnath, 1974) form complex questions when they are carefully examined. In one sense, any speculations about the way the world is in any formal theory can only be consistent with the current situation, not the future. So far, the effects of the present typology, as translated into the SDS, are positive and liberating (more alternatives) and equal to the effects of counselors; no negative effects are documented. Finally, typologies that are open to public examination and revision appear to be more socially beneficial and responsible than subjective speculations about their effects in an ambiguous future.

New Research and Practice

Although we have suggested that many of the career problems of adults are amenable to understanding using the typology, the need for large-scale studies of adults and their careers is acute. Articles about mid-career crises are popular but precious little data has been accumulated, and what we have is usually limited to small, unrepresentative samples of middle-class men.

In practice, the typology would benefit from a comprehensive trial in a few settings. Although counseling and career centers often use the assessment devices (SDS and VPI) and the classification scheme to organize materials, none has tried to apply the typology to an entire vocational-assistance program in a thorough-going way. That kind of experience is also needed to evaluate the practical virtues and limitations of the typology.

In research, workers usually make use only of selected constructs (for instance, single types) so that the complete theory goes unused or untested—a practice which leads to an underestimation of the theory's explanatory and predictive power. We need more studies like the recent experiment by Helms and Williams (1973) in which all the personal and environmental constructs and their interactions were tested. Finally, we need studies of the proposed explanations of change (Holland, 1973, pp. 41-44). Although the evidence for the organizational virtues of the typology is abundant, the hypotheses about change are largely untested and form complex and difficult questions in the study of careers and of human behavior generally.

REFERENCE NOTES

1. Gottfredson, L. S., Gottfredson, G. D., & Holland, J. L. *A complementary perspective on occupational structure.* Unpublished manuscript, Johns Hopkins University, Center for Social Organization of Schools, 1975.
2. Richards, J. M., Jr., Bulkeley, E. M., & Richards, B. M. *Faculty and curriculum as measures of two-year college environments.* Paper presented at the American Educational Research Association Convention, New York, 1971.

REFERENCES

Allport, G. W., Vernon, P. E., & Lindsey, G. *Manual: Study of values* (3rd Ed.). New York: Houghton Mifflin, 1970.

Ashby, J. D., Wall, H. W., & Osipow, S. H. Vocational certainty and indecision in college freshmen. *Personnel and Guidance Journal,* 1966, *45,* 1037-1041.

Baird, L. L. The undecided student—How different is he? *Personnel and Guidance Journal,* 1969, *47,* 429-434.

Borow, H. (Ed.) *Career guidance for a new age.* Boston: Houghton Mifflin, 1973.

Brein, M., & David, K. H. Intercultural communication and the adjustment of the sojourner. *Psychological Bulletin,* 1971, *76,* 215-230.

Campbell, D. P. *Handbook for the Strong Vocational Interest blank.* Stanford, California: Stanford University Press, 1971.

Campbell, D. P. Have hexagon, will travel. *Contemporary Psychology,* 1974, *19,* 585-587.

Caplan, N. *Competency among hard-to-employ youths.* Ann Arbor: Center for Research on Utilization of Scientific Knowledge, University of Michigan, 1973.

Clopton, W., Jr. *An exploratory study of career change in middle life.* Unpublished doctoral dissertation, Department of Psychology, University of Cincinnati, 1972.

Cochran, D. J., Vinitsky, M. H., & Warren, P. M. Career counseling: Beyond "test and tell." *Personnel and Guidance Journal,* 1974, *52,* 659-664.

Cole, N. S., & Hanson, G. R. Impact of interest inventories on career choice. In E. Diamond (Ed.), *Issues of sex bias and sex fairness in career interest measurement.* Washington, D.C.: National Institute of Education, 1975.

Crites, J. O. Career maturity. *Measurement in Education,* 1972-73, *4*(Winter), 1-8.

Crites, J. O. Career development process: A model of vocational maturity. In E. L. Herr (Ed.), *Vocational guidance and human development.* Boston: Houghton Mifflin, 1974. (a)

Crites, J. O. Problems in the measurement of vocational maturity. *Journal of Vocational Behavior,* 1974, *4,* 25-31. (b)

Edwards, K. J., Nafziger, D. H., & Holland, J. L. Differentiation of occupational perceptions among different age groups. *Journal of Vocational Behavior,* 1974, *4,* 311-318.

Forster, J. R. Comparing feedback methods after testing. *Journal of Counseling Psychology,* 1969, *16*, 222-226.

Gilbride, T. V. Holland's theory and resignations from the Catholic clergy. *Journal of Counseling Psychology,* 1973, *20*, 190-191.

Gordon, L. V. *The measurement of interpersonal values.* Chicago: Science Research Associates, 1975.

Gottfredson, G. D., & Holland, J. L. Some normative self-report data on activities, competencies, occupational preferences, and ability ratings for high school and college students, and employed men and women. *JSAS Catalog of Selected Documents in Psychology,* 1975, *5*, 192. (Ms. No. 859) (a)

Gottfredson, G. D., & Holland, J. L. Vocational choices of men and women: A comparison of predictors from the Self-Directed Search. *Journal of Counseling Psychology,* 1975, *22*, 28-34. (b)

Gottfredson, G. D., Holland, J. L., & Gottfredson, L. S. The relation of vocational aspirations and assessments to employment reality. *Journal of Vocational Behavior,* 1975, *7*, 135-148.

Graff, R. W., Danish, S., & Austin, B. Student reactions to three kinds of vocational-educational counseling. *Journal of Counseling Psychology,* 1972, *19*, 224-228.

Grandy, T. G., & Stahmann, R. F. Family influence on college students' vocational choice: Predicting from Holland's personality types. *Journal of College Student Personnel,* 1974, *15*, 404-409.

Gysbers, N. C., & Moore, E. J. Beyond career development—life career development. *Personnel and Guidance Journal,* 1975, *53*, 647-652.

Hanson, G. R. *Assessing the career interests of college youth: Summary of research and applications* (Report No. 67). Iowa City: American College Testing Program, 1975.

Harmon, L. W. Review of Making vocational choices: A theory of careers. *Measurement and Evaluation in Guidance,* 1974, *7*, 198-199.

Harris, J. The computer: Guidance tool of the future. *Journal of Counseling Psychology,* 1974, *21*, 331-339.

Helms, S. T., & Williams, G. D. *An experimental study of the reactions of high school students to simulated jobs* (Research Report No. 161). Baltimore: Center for Social Organization of Schools, Johns Hopkins University, 1973. (ERIC Document Reproduction Service No. ED 087 882)

Holland, J. L. Explorations of a theory of vocational choice: VI. A longitudinal study using a sample of typical college students. *Journal of Applied Psychology Monograph,* 1968, *52*(1, pt. 2).

Holland, J. L. *Making vocational choices: A theory of careers.* Englewood Cliffs, New Jersey: Prentice-Hall, 1973.

Holland, J. L. Some practical remedies for providing vocational guidance for everyone. *Educational Researcher,* 1974, *3*, 9-15.

Holland, J. L., & Gottfredson, G. D. Predictive value and psychological meaning of vocational aspirations. *Journal of Vocational Behavior,* 1975, *6*, 349-363.

Holland, J. L., Gottfredson, G. D., & Nafziger, D. H. Testing the validity of some theoretical signs of vocational decision-making ability. *Journal of Counseling Psychology,* 1975, *22*, 411-422.

Holland, J. L., & Lutz, S. W. Predicting a student's vocational choice. *Personnel and Guidance Journal,* 1968, *46*, 428-436.

Holland, J. L., Sorensen, A. B., Clark, J. P., Nafziger, D. H., & Blum, Z. D. Applying an occupational classification to a representative sample of work histories. *Journal of Applied Psychology,* 1973, *58,* 34-41.

Holland, J. L., & Whitney, D. R. *Changes in the vocational plans of college students: Orderly or random?* (Research Report No. 25). Iowa City: American College Testing Program, 1968.

Kelso, G. I. The influences of stage of leaving school on vocational maturity and realism of vocational choice. *Journal of Vocational Behavior,* 1975, *7,* 29-39.

Kimball, R. L., Sedlacek, W. E., & Brooks, G. C., Jr. Black and White vocational interests in Holland's Self-Directed Search (SDS). *Journal of Negro Education,* 1973, *42,* 1-4.

Kimes, H. G., & Troth, W. A. Relationship of trait anxiety to career decisiveness. *Journal of Counseling Psychology,* 1974, *21,* 277-280.

Krivatsy, S. *Differential effects of three vocational counseling treatments.* Unpublished doctoral dissertation, College Park: University of Maryland, 1974.

Kroll, A. M., Dinklage, L. G., Lee, J., Morley, E. D., & Wilson, E. H. *Career development: Growth and crisis.* New York: Wiley, 1970.

Lackey, A. An annotated bibliography for Holland's theory, the Self-Directed Search, and the Vocational Preference Inventory (1972-1975). *JSAS Catalog of Selected Documents in Psychology,* 1975, *5,* 352.

Lamb, R. R. *Concurrent validity of the American College Testing Interest Inventory for minority group members.* Unpublished doctoral dissertation, University of Iowa, 1974.

Levinson, D. J., Darrow, C., Klein, E., Levinson, M., & McKee, B. The psychosocial development of men in early adulthood and the mid-life transition. In D. F. Ricks, A. Thomas, & M. Roff (Eds.), *Life history research in psychopathology* (Vol. 3). Minneapolis: University of Minnesota Press, 1974.

Lofquist, L. H., & Dawis, R. V. *Adjustment to work.* New York: Appleton-Century-Crofts, 1969.

Maas, H. S., & Kuypers, J. A. *From thirty to seventy.* San Francisco: Jossey-Bass, 1974.

Magoon, T. M. *A model of effective problem solving applied to educational and vocational planning with students* (Research Report No. 13-65). College Park: Counseling Center, University of Maryland, 1965.

McConnell, T. R. What college for whom? *Contemporary Psychology,* 1968, *13,* 99-101.

McLaughlin, D. H., & Tiedeman, D. V. Eleven-year stability and change as reflected in project talent data through the Flanagan, Holland, and Roe occupational classification systems. *Journal of Vocational Behavior,* 1974, *5,* 177-196.

Nafziger, D. H., Holland, J. L., Helms, S. T., & McPartland, J. M. Applying an occupational classification to the work histories of young men and women. *Journal of Vocational Behavior,* 1974, *5,* 331-345.

Nolan, J. J. The effectiveness of the Self-Directed Search compared with group counseling in promoting information-seeking behavior and realism of vocational choice (Doctoral dissertation, University of Maryland, College Park, 1974). *Dissertation Abstracts International,* 1974, *35,* 195A. (University Microfilms No. 74-16, 569)

Osipow, S. H. *Theories of career development.* New York: Appleton-Century-Crofts, 1973.

Parsons, F. *Choosing a vocation.* New York: Houghton Mifflin, 1909.

Parsons, G. E., & Wigtil, J. V. Occupational mobility as measured by Holland's theory of career selection. *Journal of Vocational Behavior,* 1974, *5,* 321-330.

Psathas, G. Toward a theory of occupational choice for women. *Sociology and Social Research,* 1968, *52,* 253-268.

Quinn, R. P., Staines, G. L., & McCullough, M. R. *Job satisfaction: Is there a trend?* (Manpower Research Monograph No. 30). Washington, D.C.: U. S. Government Printing Office, 1974.

Redmond, R. E. Increasing vocational information-seeking behaviors of high school students (Doctoral dissertation, University of Maryland, College Park, 1972). *Dissertation Abstracts International,* 1973, *34,* 2311A-2312A. (University Microfilms No. 73-17, 046)

Rogers, C. R. Empathic: An unappreciated way of being. *The Counseling Psychologist,* 1975, *5,* 2-10.

Rose, H. A., & Elton, C. F. Sex and occupational choice. *Journal of Counseling Psychology,* 1971, *18,* 456-461.

Statistical Policy Division of the Office of Management and Budget. *Social indicators.* Washington, D.C.: U. S. Government Printing Office, 1973.

Strong, E. K., Jr. *Vocational interests of men and women.* Stanford, California: Stanford University Press, 1943.

Super, D. E. Vocational development theory. *The Counseling Psychologist,* 1969, *1,* 2-14.

Super, D. E. Vocational maturity theory. In D. E. Super (Ed.), *Measuring vocational maturity for counseling.* Washington, D.C.: American Personnel and Guidance Association, 1974.

Tipton, R. Relative effectiveness of two methods of interpreting ability test scores. *Journal of Counseling Psychology,* 1969, *16,* 75-80.

Walsh, W. B. *Theories of person-environment interaction: Implications for the college student* (Monograph 10). Iowa City: American College Testing Program, 1973.

Warnath, C. F. Review of Making vocational choices: A theory of careers. *Personnel and Guidance Journal,* 1974, *52,* 337-338.

Williamson, E. G. Trait-factor theory and individual differences. In B. Stefflre, W. H. Grant (Eds.), *Theories of counseling* (2nd ed.). New York: McGraw-Hill, 1972.

Yonge, G. D. Students. *Review of Educational Research,* 1965, *35,* 253-263.

Zener, T. B., & Schnuelle, L. *An evaluation of the Self-Directed Search: A guide to educational and vocational planning* (Report No. 124). Johns Hopkins University, Center for Social Organization of Schools, 1972. (ERIC Document Reproduction Service No. ED 061 458)

Zytowski, D. G. Toward a theory of career development for women. *Personnel and Guidance Journal,* 1969, *47,* 660-664.

BEHAVIORAL SELF-CONTROL AND CAREER DEVELOPMENT

8

CARL E. THORESEN
CRAIG K. EWART
Stanford University

CAREER DEVELOPMENT

One of the most important things counselors do is help people find intelligent solutions to life's major questions. Selecting a career is one such question. The seemingly simple steps of career decision making encourage many to see the process of helping others to make vocational decisions as far simpler than helping them to overcome anxiety, depression, or other more ambiguous difficulties. Yet, trying to make career-related decisions in a systematic fashion can involve stressful and personally threatening experiences—ones that we often avoid by letting things "take their natural course." The stress and turmoil experienced in selecting careers and pursuing vocations have been dramatically portrayed by Studs Terkel (1974) in his book *Working*. Many persons interviewed by Terkel presented themselves as adrift in jobs that they somehow got into—jobs that they now find depressing, discouraging, and debilitating. Those not fatalistically resigned to their "career" appear anxious to do something else. But what? And how? What can people do to change their vocations?

Career choice today is rapidly becoming an on-going, life-long process as people demand greater fulfillment from work, as more people change their careers in mid-life, as women re-enter the job market, and as workers discover that there is no longer a need for their skills. Counselors are finding that men

Preparation of this article was supported in part by the Stanford Boys Town Center for Youth Development, a contract (OEC-0-74-1701) between the National Academy of Sciences and the Office of Education (HEW), and the Stanford Research and Development Center for Teaching, School of Education, Stanford University. The assistance of Guy Browning, David Campbell, Thomas J. Coates, John L. Holland, and John D. Krumboltz in critically reviewing earlier versions of this article is gratefully acknowledged.

and women of all ages need help in making changes for which they are unprepared. Many people (perhaps most) rarely make explicit, systematic choices about how to spend their working lives. "Deciding by not deciding" is more norm than exception. Economic factors, family pressures, and other environmental influences ("I just happened to be at the right place at the right time. . .") limit opportunities for systematic decision making. In addition, most people fail to learn the skills they need to make and to implement career-relevant behaviors. The counselor's task in many ways is that of teacher: helping people learn skills and persevere in new ways of thinking, feeling, and acting. Here as elsewhere in counseling and psychotherapy the problem is to help individuals function in new and often more demanding ways—ways which demand conscious attention, sustained effort, and some delay of gratification. Clearly more is required than simply telling people what to do— no matter how sage and emphatic the advice—and providing some bits and pieces of career information (computer assisted or otherwise). As we'll see, people need specific help in learning how to self-manage their actions so that change is made and sustained.

The requirements of decision making are not hard to state: specifying the task, gathering relevant information, identifying alternatives, selecting an alternative, and taking action toward a tentative decision. Indeed, the steps involved are closely akin to the scientific method (Platt, 1964; Thoresen, 1969; Thoresen, in press). The empirically oriented scientist often cycles in dynamic fashion through the same steps, sometimes converting observations into an alternative stated as a testable hypothesis and then conducting a probe or experiment. Although the basic steps of modern science as a framework for inquiry can be described, the actual sequence of behaviors engaged in by a scientist remain obscure (Feibleman, 1972; Mahoney, 1976). There is far more complexity to science as a human endeavor than the several steps (e.g., observing, experimenting, inferring) enumerated in introductory research textbooks. Similarly, there is more to career decision making than memorizing the steps and gathering up some information.

What Options and Which Alternative?

Besides clarifying the problem situation, two important activities are involved in career decision making: *identifying options* and *selecting an alternative* for further action. Granting the diversity of ways that persons process information and develop inferences (cf. Mahoney, 1974) it is still possible to set forth a logical, systematic sequence of operations for generating and selecting alternatives. Clients can learn to apply this sequence in a wide variety of choice situations (Krumboltz & Baker, 1973). How they will later use these activities remains unknown, but these activities can be conceived of as basic skills needed to create a personally meaningful product. All artists and craftsmen learn basic skills that become ingredients of a unique performance. The same holds true of the basic or the applied scientist (Thoresen, in press).

Some basic inquiry skills must be acquired *before* a creative contribution can emerge.

Decision making involves prediction; that is, the person needs to anticipate possible outcomes of his or her actions. In general, two kinds of outcome predictions can be made: *probability* estimates and *utility* estimates (Mischel & Masters, 1966; Thoresen & Mehrens, 1967). Probability estimates are used in establishing the range of alternatives and the likelihood of attaining them. Utility estimates predict which alternatives will prove most useful or satisfying. Thus a decision can be represented as a function of the probability and the utility of any given alternative. Together they determine its value. A career decision involves weighing the probability of entering a given occupation ("Do I have what it takes to get through law school?") against its utility ("How much would I enjoy being a lawyer?").

Although a theoretical decision model can be quite explicit, its actual implementation with clients offers problems. Probability estimates of a client's chances of qualifying for a given occupation are not difficult to develop. Current information on particular career openings, together with the academic or other credentials required can be used. A counselor can develop tailored expectancy tables based on the experiences of others relevant to the client (e.g., students in a particular school or college who have gone to law school). Such tables can provide probability estimates which are helpful in predicting future performances (Goldman, 1961; Yabroff, 1969). Thus a university student with a B average could be shown an "experience table" based on the past performance of students from the same institution. The table would provide estimates of getting admitted to a given graduate school, based on such factors as grade-point average, scholastic aptitude, or other qualifications.

The counselor could function primarily as an occupational-information specialist, searching out, organizing, and transmitting "objective" data relevant to each client's interests. One limitation with this approach, however, is that clients often fail to recognize and use such information. Subjective expectancies of the clients often disagree with the objective information and estimates provided by the counselor (Thoresen & Mehrens, 1967). For example, a premed student with average grades may decide to apply only to prestige medical schools because he or she believes a chance to get in still exists. On the other hand, a more academically successful premed student may greatly underestimate chances of acceptance. Such a student may not believe he or she has much of a chance against the thousands of other applicants. The counselor must know how to clarify and resolve certain contradictions between a client's expectations and other more objective estimates. There is much more to counseling for career selection than "giving them the facts." Facilitating change in a client's way of thinking and acting calls for knowledge and skills not included in the information-giving model.

The desirability or usefulness of alternatives merits attention. The counselor's task is to help the client decide what needs, interests, or values are possibly involved in a particular career option. What rewards, for example, might a certain occupation provide? Apart from providing information, counselors are often expected to facilitate career decisions by helping clients discover what they value. Interest inventories and occupational value scales are numerous; most of these devices help the counselor assign a client to one or several vocational types or categories. These instruments are sometimes viewed by counselors (and almost always by clients) as providing a kind of "x-ray" view of an individual's vocational personality. They are seen as capable of telling us something about our career needs and interests that we do not already know. Thus, if I am trying to choose between careers in social work and sales management, feeling equally attracted to both, I might see the results of an inventory as capable of telling me which career I *really* want to enter, or which occupational type I am. If my type fits the helping professions more than it fits the business-sales occupational type, then I should go into a helping field. I may even assume that this data can be used to predict my future happiness in a given area of work.

Information about my vocational type may be of little use to me if my membership in that type in no way enhances my enjoyment of one occupation over another. Standard interest inventories are generally helpful in counseling only to the extent that they actually tell clients more than they already know about their *ability* to enjoy a given line of work. Results of standard tests and inventories have yet to demonstrate this result. The *capacity to enjoy* an occupation is determined by a host of personally subjective and specific environmental factors that interest inventories do not tap. The assembly-line worker might score low on an inventory measuring managerial interests, but does this mean that he or she lacks the qualities needed to find satisfaction in becoming a manager and performing the job well? Thus it is more difficult to predict potential vocational satisfaction from a few simple indicators (e.g., responses to inventory items) than it is to predict career entry from level of formal education, social-economic status, or equivalent data. The counselor must be able to help the client define conditions of "success," "meaning," and "enjoyment" in his or her own life and to explore the possibilities for fulfilling these conditions in various kinds of work. The counselor must go well beyond the information-and-testing role suggested by the objective requirements of the simple decision model (Thoresen & Mehrens, 1967). Career selection involves self-exploration and change; a counselor should be able to facilitate these activities.

Engineering Decision Behaviors

Roughly stated, the counselor's job is one of helping people "engineer" their own decisions. In effect, the counselor teaches the client to clarify problem situations, make tentative choices, and, most importantly, to act on his or her decision. Counseling involves teaching clients to approach life in a way that is new, demanding, and possibly threatening. Thus counselors find themselves in need of practical knowledge about how to help clients:

1. To clarify the nature and scope of the decision they must make and the goals they seek to achieve.

2. To commit themselves to undertaking and persevering in personal and environmental explorations.

3. To acquire a more accurate understanding of their needs, interests, and abilities.

4. To change self-attributions and beliefs, along with inaccurate stereotypes and misperceptions.

5. To restructure their environment to help them engage in desirable behaviors.

6. To evaluate and maintain progress in the direction of personal goals.

The information needed to help achieve these goals can be provided by well-designed research. It may be helpful at this point to review briefly the kinds of questions and methods currently being pursued in career research with an eye to their limitations and possibilities.

EXISTING VOCATIONAL THEORIES AND RESEARCH: CURRENT AND CHOICE

Career decision making is one of those gardens of human activity in which theories blossom and grow numerous but produce little fruit. Attempts to explain vocational behavior have increased in quantity and sophistication during the last twenty years (Osipow, 1968). Even so, this theoretical diversity is not apparent at the level of empirical investigation; one or two major orientations appear to predominate.

In terms of the sheer number of studies, John Holland's vocational typology currently inspires the most research activity. The Self-Concept theories of Donald Super and others (Super, 1963, 1969) account for much of the remaining effort. A recent review (Mitchell, Jones, & Krumboltz, Note 4) of empirical studies reported in the five-year period from 1969 through 1974 illustrates this fact. A search of approximately 600 books, monographs, dissertations, and other sources identified 45 empirical studies of psychological factors that influence career decisions. Nearly half of these studies (48%) investigated Holland's theory, while a second major orientation (17%) reflected the self-concept approach. The remaining third of the investigative effort represented a variety of theoretical viewpoints. Vocational research continues on lines sketched by Osipow (1968) in his thorough review. This review, together with others (Bailey & Stadt, 1973; Borow, 1973; Crites, 1969), obviates any need to characterize the theoretical literature here. Let's focus for the moment on how much the current research tells us about how to do effective career counseling. In this section we will look at the two theories that are generating the most empirical research activity and will attempt to indicate their practical contributions and limitations.

Holland's Types

John Holland (1973) provides the counselor with a plausible and appealing vocational typology. His system identifies six major "vocational types" or clusterings of vocational preferences: Realistic, Investigative, Artistic, Social, Enterprising, and Conventional. A person's type is indicated by his or her responses to Holland's (1975) system.

The typology is an intuitively sensible and empirically tested scheme for classifying people's interests, job skills, and work environments. It does not, however, constitute an explanation of how such skills or preferences develop and how they change. Although he has proposed a learning or behavioral account of how people come to fit certain types (Holland, 1973, 1975), basic research on learning issues within the Holland framework remains to be done.

As a typology, Holland's system does entail an important theoretical presupposition: it is based on an enduring-trait conception of personality. An individual's responses on the Vocational Preference Inventory (VPI) are treated as direct and additive signs of underlying personal dispositions (traits) which presumably do not vary greatly over time or across situations. For example, the more mechanical interests you endorse on the test, the stronger your Realistic orientation (trait) is thought to be. If you score higher on this category than on any other, then you might be advised to consider jobs that require you to work with things more than with ideas or people. Because you checked more mechanical items (Realistic) than people items (Social), you are thought to have a strong and enduring preference for things over persons.

Holland (1973) makes the interesting suggestion that the six major vocational orientations (VPI types) are not all equally consistent with one another; a given vocational preference can be viewed as closer to some VPI categories than to others. The six types are depicted as forming the corners of a hexagon (Figure 1); moving about the perimeter one passes from Realistic to Investigative, Artistic, Social, Enterprising, and Conventional (which is again adjacent to Realistic). Recent interpretative material presented with scores of the Strong Vocational Interest Blank uses this format (Campbell, 1974). VPI types that are adjacent on the hexagon are thought to be consistent with one another, whereas those hexagonally opposite are deemed mutually inconsistent. In this scheme, a person would find it somewhat easier to reconcile interests in the Investigative career domain (e.g., biological research) with a Realistic career preference (e.g., engineering) than with an interest in work that falls in the Enterprising category (e.g., sales person).

Typical questions and methods. Most of the research on Holland's theory (roughly half of the empirical work reported in the career decision making area) pursues one or more of the following questions and methods:

1. *Question:* Does my VPI type indicate the type of job I am likely to choose after college?

   Method: Test the predictive validity of the typology by measuring the

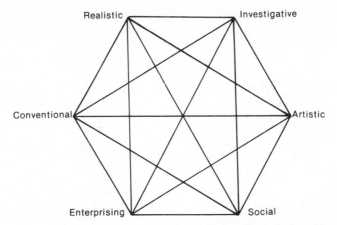

Figure 1. Holland's hexagonal model for defining the relationships among VPI types. The shorter the distance between any two types, the greater their similarity is thought to be. (Adapted from *Making Vocational Choices: A Theory of Careers*, by J. L. Holland. Copyright © 1973 by Prentice-Hall, Inc. Reprinted by permission of Prentice-Hall, Inc., and American College Testing Program.)

correlation between students' VPI types in college and the VPI type of the job they seek after graduation.

Answer: Research on large student samples indicates that student VPI types predict the types of their majors and initial job choices (Holland, 1973). However, it should be noted that some investigators have failed to verify this association (Hauselman, 1971; Hughes, 1972); in these cases, factors such as sample size or differences in aptitude or social-economic status may have been more decisive than one's vocational preferences. While most research results indicate that your future job type can be predicted from your VPI score, this prediction is only *half* as good as the one you could give if someone asked you directly (Holland, 1968).

2. *Question:* What does the VPI tell me about my personality?

Method: Correlate students' responses to the VPI with their responses to a battery of personality tests and rating scales.

Answer: The answer depends in part on your theory of personality. If you define personality as whatever is measured by standard personality tests, the VPI does not tell you very much about personality. Of 856 correlation coefficients estimating the association of VPI scales with 7 personality tests (e.g., CPI, Cattell 16PF) only $3\frac{1}{2}\%$ exceeded a value of .36. VPI types can be said to account for less than 10% of personality test score differences (Folsom, 1971; Holland, 1975). But career-related behaviors are important characteristics of individuals, and the VPI does predict these as we have just noted.

3. *Question:* Does the *consistency* of my current job preferences indicate how happy I will be in my future job?

   Method: a. Correlate students' VPI consistency measures with the frequency with which they change majors or report that they are dissatisfied with their field of study.

   b. Analyze work-history data to see whether people with "inconsistent" codes tend to change jobs more often than people having consistent VPI types.

   Answer: The consistency of a person's dominant vocational interests has been found to be significantly related to measures of stability and satisfaction in academic settings (Holland, 1968). A work-history analysis performed by Holland and his associates (Holland, 1973) on a large national sample of working adult males showed that VPI type predicted job choice, stability, and achievement over 5- to 10-year periods. The analysis indicated that people "tend to keep doing the same things." Further, analysis of preference patterns for men in the Realistic category permitted predictions of job stability and achievement with significant accuracy (also see Parsons & Wigtil, 1974).

   Again, inconsistent or negative findings have been reported by some investigators (e.g., Werner, 1969). VPI consistency failed to predict job satisfaction in a sample of employed males in their twenties and early thirties (Hughes, 1972). In this last group, the consistency between a person's VPI orientation and the VPI type of job actually held was not associated with reported job satisfaction.

   On the whole, it seems that people are happier and accomplish more in environments that encourage them to do what they enjoy most.

   In sum, the evidence on the code consistency/job satisfaction relationship is inconclusive. The work-history analyses, while well designed and extensive, leave important questions unanswered. Frequent job changes can be seen as a function of unhappiness or as an indication that a person has interests and talents in diverse job areas and is successful in expressing them. People frequently "keep doing the same thing" not because they enjoy it, but because they see no other alternative. If your code is inconsistent, i.e., if you enjoy doing very different things, the data indicate you are likely to explore a wider variety of job options than if your interests happen to be more focused. Whether or not you will be happy probably depends more on the satisfactions your work skills can win you than on the "consistency" of your code.

4. *Question:* Will I enjoy my job more if my personal VPI type is consistent with the VPI types of the people I work with?

   Method: Correlate measures of student/environment VPI congruence with tendency to change majors or report dissatisfaction.

   Answer: The degree of congruence between an individual's VPI type and the VPI types of other persons in the work environment has been found to be positively associated with academic achievement and "good conduct" in high school students (Dayton & Uhl, Note 2). Holland reports that students in universities having a wide array of VPI types are more likely to change their majors and to report satisfaction with their choice than are students in schools having a more homogeneous VPI profile (Holland, 1968).

In short, Holland has established a way to *group* career interests, a system which has led to the creation of useful guidance materials (e.g., the SDS) and has stimulated considerable research (Lackey, 1975). Although the typology constitutes an important contribution to career counseling as an intelligible and empirically sound system for organizing vocational information and instruction, the research inspired by it has not been directed at some major needs of the career counselor. By examining some limitations of the theory and of the methods used to test it, we may gain a better idea of needed research to answer some important questions.

Some limitations. In terms of current counseling needs, the Holland typological approach encounters several major difficulties. In the first place, characteristics of the samples and research strategies typically used limit the practical applications of the results. The counselor who is trying to help men or women "engineer" a career change in mid-life will need information that applies to working adults. More than two-thirds of the studies supporting Holland's theory have been done with college or high school students (cf. Lackey, 1975; Mitchell et al., Note 4). While greater attention is now being given to employed adult samples, most of the data cited in support of the typology may reflect the typical structure of American academic institutions more than the world of work. An additional difficulty for practical interpretation arises from the fact that studies of the VPI have used very large samples. The problem of obtaining statistically significant predictions in large samples differs in important ways from the problem of helping an individual decide on a career. The latter case calls for *intensive* as opposed to *extensive* research—one has to discover what works for *this person in particular,* not for college students in general.

To verify a typology, a researcher must sample extensively; the problem is to discover what generalizations seem valid on the average for the largest possible number of cases. Problems of large-scale sampling and category definition are paramount concerns. Whether enduring generalizations are really possible is, of course, debatable since so many variables may interact to obscure findings (cf. Cronbach, 1975). The problem facing the counselor is different: to help a particular person explore career options and tentatively pursue some. To do so one must discover what situational and intrapersonal factors are at work in this particular case. Specific techniques for discovering what these factors might be and how they operate for a given person become the primary focus of the counselor. The counselor's job is to help a client identify and assess factors that might influence his or her choice, as well as create conditions needed to implement a given decision. A vocational-classification scheme with an extensive empirical base can provide valuable information, but it inevitably ignores important situational and intraindividual variables that can affect a person's choice. Average occupational-interest profiles provide useful points of reference; however, in themselves they offer no guide to how one might develop the mastery of self and environment needed to make and implement career-related decisions.

A second major limitation results from an overdependence on correlational techniques. Experimental investigations of possible cause-and-effect relationships in career choice must be undertaken if we are to further our understanding of the processes and conditions of vocational development and change. How do career orientations develop? How difficult are they to alter? What experiences have the greatest impact on our choices and on our ability to enjoy the work we have chosen? Our inability to answer such questions severely limits the effectiveness of counseling. If we knew more about the origins and the antecedents (the "causes") of career interests and the kinds of influences which make them change or stay the same over the years, then we might know more about how to help people select, develop, and maintain satisfying careers. A vocational typology can help us classify vocational leanings, but it does not tell us all we need to know if we are to develop them into a career.

The case of Jessica: An "indecisive type." Consider Jessica, a recent college graduate with a major in economics ("It wasn't all that interesting, but I figured it would get me a job"). Her major and some of her interests type her as Enterprising—she likes to sell people on her ideas and aspires to leadership—but she also speaks of the importance of "being original" and "having a philosophy of life" (Artistic). After considering a number of career alternatives, she finds herself with two major options. One possibility is to get a degree in business administration and pursue a career in management. Another alternative is to study journalism with a view to writing about social and political issues. A business career would be consistent with many of Jessica's past interests and experiences; her background in economics is a sound base for business. But Jessica's experiences as an economics major have made her aware of problems women face in a male-dominated field. She believes that as a writer she might help change people's attitudes toward women in business and industry. An interest in writing belongs more to the Artistic category: it seems inconsistent with an Enterprising orientation.

Should a counselor warn Jessica that she will be unhappy as a writer? Actually, the fact that Jessica enjoys persuading people and has strong verbal skills may predict success in journalism. In actual counseling it is necessary to focus on specific skills and job functions; each VPI category embraces a wide array of job possibilities and must be narrowed considerably before it can be of much use.

For better focus, Holland advocates a 3-point code which assigns a person to half of the six categories in order of preference, as judged from the pattern of responses to the VPI. This makes good sense *if* one is trying to increase the number of accurate predictions in a large sample—the more information you have about someone the better your chances of predicting what they will do. But the usefulness of this practice to the counselor remains in doubt.

Let's look at Jessica. Upon completing the *Self-Directed Search* she is assigned a three-point code ASE (Artistic, Social, Enterprising). She discovers that this code is used to characterize reporters and journalists. Soon after making this discovery, she learns of a job opening in an advertising agency in New York. An old friend of the family is in a position to offer her the job if she wants it. Jessica is thrilled at the thought; the challenge and glamor of Madison Avenue entice her but she discovers that the advertising job code (AES) differs from her own in the second and third points. Should she take the job? Upon further reflection, Jessica notes her increasing concern for women's rights and wonders if perhaps a degree in law might put her in a better position to fight for some of the changes she desires. The code for attorneys is EAS; it includes all of Jessica's interests but in a different order of priority. As the counselor with whom Jessica shares her dilemma, should I advise her that an advertising career in New York is likely to prove more satisfying than a career in law because the former is more congruent with her Artistic high point emphasis than the latter? Should I encourage her to study journalism?

Having read work history and other investigations of code stability, I might conclude that I should advise Jessica to stay within her current ASE job category. This research shows that people tend to stay in the same job categories (e.g., doctors continue to see patients and truck drivers continue to drive trucks). Further, people who remain within the same job category may even tend to achieve somewhat more "prestige" and report more job satisfaction than people who shift back and forth among widely differing job types. On the other hand, I might consider the possibility that work-history data reflect the stability of environmental contingencies in our society over recent years. It is usually easier and more lucrative to keep on doing the same job than to change; further, loyalty is usually rewarded. The data tell me nothing about the *capacity* of individuals to explore new ground. Further, Jessica insists that she wants to create her own kind of career, that none of the established job labels or stereotypes are appropriate for her, and that there are things in her self and in society that she wants to change. To her, job prestige and stability matter less than the opportunity to master a wide variety of skills and express her own personal values. It is clear—as Holland would probably concur—that a simple interpretation of the typology and stability data would be grossly inappropriate. Too many other important factors must be considered. In large part, Jessica's dilemma arises out of questions concerning her own capacity for self-mastery and change—questions the typology cannot answer.

It would be possible to explore issues of change within the Holland framework. Indeed, this is a much-needed endeavor, but the effort requires a shift to an expanded research perspective—one that includes controlled experimental studies as well as large-scale correlational ones. While a promising step in this direction has been made by Helms and Williams (1973), much more remains to be done if the typology is to be helpful to people like Jessica. In addition, it will be necessary to explore the question of how individuals learn skills of self-mastery and change—a question vital to career choice and implementation but thus far barely recognized (Holland, 1975). In summary, the current VPI type codes help draw a client's attention to various personal interests and job possibilities but remain too broad to provide specific answers to many basic questions that clients ask. Once a VPI code has been determined, major problems of interpretation and self-analysis still face the client.

Do types predict choices? In the final analysis, much of the practical usefulness of the typology rests upon its power to predict future choices and satisfactions. Helms and Williams (1973), in an experimental test of Holland's system, found that the degree of congruency students reported between themselves and simulated job kits could be predicted from the VPI codes of the students and the kits. Wiggins (1976) reports that VPI categories predicted job satisfaction in a group of female teachers of retarded children. However, some evidence (Hughes, 1972) suggests that the amount of agreement between the VPI category of the job that a client eventually chooses and the client's own VPI type may bear little relation to the amount of satisfaction he or she experiences in the job. A counselor might want to know whether the VPI or SDS can predict a person's future job choice any more accurately than the person's own directly stated opinion; in other words, does it tell you something more about your future job choice than you could already state if someone asked you directly instead of by means of a questionnaire? Holland's (1968) conclusion is that it does not. As noted earlier, within large samples VPI type predicts students' actual vocational *choice* after graduation at better than chance levels *but is only half as effective as the student's own prediction.* The best single predictor of the career that the student will choose is the student. Even the extensively developed and researched Strong Vocational Interest Blank does not give a more accurate prediction of future jobs a person will hold than does the person's own directly stated opinion (Dolliver, 1969).

But even where the predictive accuracy of the typology is relatively high (e.g., work-history analyses), we should not assume that these measures tell us much about people's capacity for change and satisfaction. In recent years personality research and studies of aptitudes have seen a growing recognition among investigators that assessment techniques must take account of considerable *situational* variability in what people feel, think, or do (cf. Block, 1968; Cronbach, 1975; Mischel, 1968). As mentioned earlier, people translate the same self-descriptive labels into action in radically different ways. Characteristics of persons such as interests are not expressed in identical ways over time and across situations (Insel & Moos, 1974); some trait researchers have tried to account for this fact by hypothesizing various "moderator" variables such as sex or intelligence of subject or characteristics of the setting in which a trait is assessed (Kogan & Wallach, 1964). Unfortunately the yield of moderator-variable research has been very meager; individual variability still persists, causing generalizations to be sharply limited (Thoresen, 1973b). The stability of VPI choices may be more a function of *environmental limits* than of intrapersonal limitations.

Super's Concept

Self-concept theories (Super, 1963) account for a sizeable portion of career-decision research activity. Self-concept theorists assume that people have global conceptions of themselves, their abilities, and interests, which they express or "implement" through their work. Job choice is determined by a person's idea of himself or herself—an idea that is reasonably stable yet subject to change over time. Self-concepts are elicited by means of self-descriptive instruments; Q-Sorts and adjective checklists are commonly used. People are often asked to indicate adjectives that describe themselves as they really are or as they would ideally like to be. These self-descriptions are then correlated with actual job choice, with the person's description of his or her "ideal" job, reported job satisfaction, or level of occupational attainment.

The following are some questions and results of self-concept research:

1. *Question:* Does the need to implement a self-concept cause a person to choose a career that suits his or her *abilities?*

   Method: Correlate people's self-esteem ratings with how they rate their own competence in their chosen vocation.

   Answer: Higher self-esteem is often, but not always, associated with higher levels of self-reported job skills (Greenhaus, 1971; Hughes, 1972; Mansfield, 1973).

2. *Question:* Do people tend to implement their self-concepts by choosing roles that match the way they view themselves?

   Method: Measure the correlation between the descriptions people give of their personalities using an adjective checklist and the descriptions they give of their jobs on the same instrument.

   Answer: People in different occupations differ somewhat in the adjectives they choose to describe themselves. For example, high school science teachers, engineers, ministers, and business managers use slightly different "vocabularies" to describe themselves (Hunt, 1967). Also, college students tend to see themselves as more similar to people in jobs they prefer than to people in jobs they dislike (Ziegler, 1970).

3. *Question:* Are people happier when their self-concept (self-esteem) matches the view they take toward their work role than when evaluations of self and one's work do not agree?

Method: Correlate measured consistency between people's self-descriptions and their descriptions of the jobs they hold with their self-reported levels of job satisfaction.

Answer: People who report higher skill levels tend to be happier in their work than less skilled people, and occupational prestige has been found to be related to job satisfaction for people who are low in self-esteem (Greenhaus, 1971).

Self-concept: Cause or effect? Self-concept researchers have shown that there is often a significant association between the way in which people view themselves and the work they currently are performing. These associations show that there can be an important relationship between the work one does and one's sense of personal identity. A question this research does not resolve, however, is the causal link between self-descriptions and job choices. As one self-concept researcher notes, the simple observation that self- and occupational concepts are significantly related does not demonstrate that self-concepts determine occupational choice (Hunt, 1967). Self-descriptions may be as much the consequence of occupational choices or achievements as their antecedent or cause; what people do in their work may determine how they view themselves. Self-perception research suggests just this kind of consequence: perceptions of myself *follow* from observations of my actions (Bem, 1972). Do people select careers in which they are likely to do well because they hold themselves in high esteem (thus implementing positive self-concepts) or is the high self-esteem measured by the adjective checklist a consequence of the fact that they have chosen jobs in which they perform well?

Assume, for example, that we see medical students and practicing physicians using some of the same words to describe themselves. We note that these words differ from some of the adjectives that business students and corporate executives often use to characterize their own personalities. How do we account for this? Do people who see themselves as "kind," "compassionate," "patient," and "exact" implement these concepts in medical careers while persons viewing themselves as "bold," "persistent," and "innovative" seek to express these self-evaluations in business occupations? Or do medical students tend to see themselves as "compassionate" and "dedicated" because they are trying hard to become good doctors and these are qualities doctors should possess? Do people in business call themselves "innovative" merely because they find they are forced to spend much of their time on the job thinking up new ways to get ahead of the competition?

In vocational counseling it is important to know how self-concepts develop and whether they undergo much change over time. Can inaccurate self-concepts be altered? If so, how? Recall Jessica's situation. Her responses to a self-descriptive adjective checklist are somewhat more similar to those given by business entrepreneurs than one would expect of a professional writer. A counselor tries to help her interpret the practical significance of this information. If self-concepts reflect relatively enduring dispositions to feel and act in certain ways, then perhaps she will be more likely to enjoy a business career. However, if one views self-concepts as more malleable, as consequences of current experiences and influences, then the counselor might place less emphasis on the checklist responses. Instead, the counselor may suggest some specific actions that Jessica might take in order to find out more about her interests or to develop her skills. Jessica's self-view would be expected to change as a function of new work experiences and feedback in whatever career she chooses. If Jessica wants to become a writer, how can a counselor help her develop the self-attitudes and skills she will need to enjoy this work and to do it well? Again, the question is how to engineer a choice. In this case, how can Jessica be helped to change her self-concept in the direction she desires?

Few, if any, researchers in the career-decision field are devoting efforts to solving this problem. Personality and social psychologists, however, have conducted explorations of the relations between performance feedback and a person's attitudes toward himself or herself (e.g., Bem, 1972; Rotter, 1954). Again, an experimental, as opposed to an exclusively correlational, research approach has been necessary. Individuals, for example, may be asked to predict their performance on a series of tasks; changes in expectancies of success on future tasks are related to positive or negative feedback regarding one's performance over the course of successive trials. Results of such studies suggest that self-concepts are changed as a result of feedback, but that this change is mediated by a number of other factors, such as achievement orientation or fear of failure (e.g., Atkinson & Feather, 1966; Heckhausen, 1968). Also, changes on one task sometimes generalize to others, thus suggesting that overall self-concepts may be altered by specific success or failure experiences.

Self-concepts (self-esteem) have been shown to play an important role in human behavior (e.g., Hannum, Thoresen, & Hubbard, 1974). Further, what is termed self-concept can be directly modified by specific training in self-instructions, reattributions, and cognitive restructuring (e.g., Goldfried & Goldfried, 1976; Mahoney, 1974; Meichenbaum, 1974). The responses people give to checklists are not simply and directly related to what they do or feel about career choices. Much self-concept research highlights the fact that people are capable of viewing themselves in many different ways, *depending on the situation* in which they find themselves. The self-concepts that people express to others have been shown to change with the setting in which they are elicited, with the person who requests the self-description, and with the perceived consequences of the self-revelation (e.g., Jones, Gergen, & Davis, 1962). Current self-concept research in career decision making does not take these factors into account. At best, this research does a good job of telling us what we already know—that self-concepts and work roles tend to be related. But it does not help us untangle the complex network of causal interactions between self-estimates and occupational feedback that influences career choice and satisfaction.

SOME LIMITATIONS AND A FEW POSSIBILITIES

Let us try to summarize some major areas needing research. From what has been said thus far, it should be clear that we will not solve the practical problems in career counseling by continuing to ask the same kinds of questions using correlational methods that currently prevail. Instead, several major changes of focus are needed.

1. *Whom are we trying to help?* Most of the career research reviewed above was conducted with student samples. This fact reflects realities of convenience and need for the researcher (Thoresen, 1969); student samples are the easiest to obtain and much counseling is directed at helping students select academic majors and first careers. With changing attitudes toward work, including the concept of continuing career development and mid-career change, and the re-entry of women into the world of work outside the home, there is a growing need to help postcollege-age persons implement good career choices. Thus, future research should take account of a wider range of clients, including women, minorities, and adult career-changers.

2. *Sample size: How large?* In most cases, career-decision researchers employ samples numbering in hundreds or even thousands of subjects. While extensive sampling has the advantage of allowing the investigator to report low-magnitude correlations that would not reach statistical significance with a smaller number of subjects, this technique alone cannot give us the knowledge we need to help people make major self-changes. Further, the exclusive search for statistically significant correlations using large samples often obscures the relationship between theory and research. Improving theory to make it more useful in understanding career-related processes requires a deemphasis on statistical-significance testing and more stress on experimental control (Cronbach, 1975; Meehl, 1967).

In a very large sample, one simply does not have the degree of control or immediacy of observation possible with a smaller number of subjects. Research capable of producing specific information of greater relevance to counseling must make more use of carefully constructed mixed-analysis-of-variance designs along with intensive, single-subject experimental studies (Thoresen, 1969; Thoresen, in press). Especially needed in the earlier stages of the scientific inquiry are well-documented, intensive, single case studies devoted to problems of careful observation and systematic measurement of career-relevant behaviors (cf. Lackenmeyer, 1970). These "short-run empirical studies" (Cronbach, 1975) can reveal a great deal of information about how cognitive and emotional behaviors influence career aspirations, decisions, and satisfactions. Simply put, we should *first* work closely and intensively with relatively few people over time to improve our understanding of what people do. Later comes the need for extensive studies with larger Ns seeking generalizations. (For a brilliant statement of the need for careful, intensive experimental studies, see Claude Bernard's classic on experimental medicine, written in 1865.)

3. *Traits and situations.* As noted above, current research on vocational typologies and self-concepts does not sufficiently account for the complexity of individual behavior. The relationship between self-attitudes and overt behavior is complex; how people feel about themselves and how they behave varies considerably with the situation in which they find themselves. Researchers need to consider the various situations in which individuals live, work, and make choices. Knowledge of ways in which situational factors influence a person's self-attitudes and occupational decisions could enable counselors to help their clients analyze and restructure their environment to help themselves develop and maintain the life style of their choice. Behavioral self-control techniques, to be discussed later, can provide the necessary bases for self-analysis and environmental change.

4. *To categorize or to change?* Most career research tends to show, for large groups, what self-statements are associated with what other self-statements at a better-than-chance level. This kind of information gives us few clues about how to help people make real-life decisions and enact them. What experiences help people discover what they want in life and permit them to commit themselves to moving toward their goals? We need to know what personal and environmental events tend to facilitate the decisions of individual clients. An experimental approach that seeks to find causal factors through systematic control and observation could contribute much to our understanding.

A Social Learning Model of Career Selection

A learning account of career development is needed to explain how vocational types or self-concepts develop and change. Krumboltz (Note 3) has suggested a rationale based on a social-learning-theory model of human behavior. The theory recognizes career preferences, occupational skills, and the individual's selection of courses, occupations, and fields of work as a composite of many past and present experiences, as well as the anticipation of future experiences. These experiences are composed of four general factors, each of which interacts to influence the other factors over time. Just how these variables function is not yet understood.

Four major factors have been identified: (1) genetic endowment and special abilities, (2) environmental conditions and events, (3) specific learning experiences, and (4) a set of "task approach" skills. Table 1 illustrates some of the characteristics of these four factors. The advantages of a social learning rationale are at least two-fold. First, it suggests the means by which client self-

Table 1. Social learning analysis: Factors influencing career decisions

---

A. "Environmental" Factors
(These factors influence the individual but are generally beyond his or her control, at least in any immediate sense. They are not amenable to change through counseling.)

  1. Genetic Endowment and Special Abilities
      Race
      Sex
      Physical characteristics
      Intelligence
      Music and art abilities
      Muscular coordination
  2. Environmental Conditions and Events
      Number and nature of job opportunities
      Number and nature of training opportunities
      Social policies and procedures for selecting trainees and workers
      Rate of return for various occupations
      Labor
      Natural
      Technological
      Social
      Educational
      Family and neighborhood structures

B. "Psychological" Factors
(These processes and skills determine a person's thoughts, feelings, and actions. Counselors try to help clients understand and change these "inner influencers.")

  1. Learning Experiences
      Instrumental learning experiences
      Associative learning experiences
  2. Task Approach Skills
      Problem solving skills
      Performance standards and values
      Work habits
      Perceptual and cognitive processes

Adapted from Krumboltz, 1976.

attitudes and behaviors are acquired, maintained, and changed. Understanding how career attitudes and choices are formed could permit the counselor to help clients take an active role in *changing* the direction of their lives. Second, the theory relates directly to a cognitive-social-learning perspective for self-managed change, which we will present shortly. For now it is important to note that career decision making requires a variety of effective self-control competencies—from controlling the common impulse to "simply avoid doing something about careers" to rearranging one's social environment to encourage behaviors such as preparing for final exams or maintaining one's commitment in a challenging apprenticeship program.

Instrumental learning. Under the Learning Experiences factor, two basic types are noted: instrumental and associative. An instrumental learning experience is one in which a person "acts on the environment in such a way as to produce certain consequences." Self- and career attitudes can be understood as resulting in part from our past actions and their consequences (e.g., comments from people we respect, direct results of the action itself, the impact on others, and so on). The consequences of our acts are also determined by the context or situation in which we act (e.g., where we are, with whom, what prior beliefs or preconceptions we bring to the situation).

Recall Jessica's dilemma about journalism or business. Her growing interest in a writing career, a change that is difficult to explain within the framework of a static vocational typology, is readily understandable. A series of situational or behavioral analyses of Jessica's career-relevant actions and their outcomes in various settings would be enlightening. We would note what things Jessica does that are relevant to her career interest (e.g., writes an economics paper, contributes to class discussions, reads a woman's account of sex biases) and examine the consequences of these actions. We might find that her paper received an A and many enthusiastic comments from the professor, that her male classmates ignored or belittled her remarks in a discussion, and that the woman who wrote the interesting article is well respected by a number of her professors. We might help Jessica estimate her enjoyment and satisfaction of possible future careers by performing additional situational analyses. What specific actions would she perform in the job and what would be their probable outcomes? Counseling would involve *teaching* Jessica to notice and evaluate her reactions and those of others to certain behaviors in past and current situations. She could then use this knowledge to guide her choices.

Associative learning. The second kind of learning experience is associative. In this type, the focus is on the person's reactions to external events or stimuli. ". . . Two events are paired in time or location such that the learner associates a previously neutral situation with some emotionally positive or negative reaction." In this way, we acquire associations such as "Artists are rebellious" and "Engineers are practical." Holland's Vocational Preference Inventory and much self-concept research attempt to draw out a person's vocational stereotypes and to show patterns among them (e.g., people who want to become military officers tend to dislike fashion designers). Such preconceptions become a problem when they limit the range or career alternatives a person can consider or explore with any enthusiasm—"If you're not a doctor, you're second rate," "There's the real world of business and the ivory towers of professors." Jessica, for example, may hesitate to investigate a career in writing because her parents have frequently commented on the lamentable political biases and lack of personal integrity "among all journalists." Where such stereotypes seem to be a barrier to career exploration, knowledge of how they are formed may help the counselor suggest to the client ways of altering irrational beliefs, emotional reactions, and prejudices.

BEHAVIORAL SELF-CONTROL

We now turn to the topic of self-control or self-management psychology. As a conceptual framework, self-control theory and techniques provide a number of promising insights into ways of helping persons solve and prevent many "problems of living," such as selecting a career and finding satisfaction in one's vocation. The selecting or changing of a career, as well as experiencing satisfaction in it, is more complicated than the personality-type/career-type matching or self-concept implementation studies suggest. An effective "career decider" must develop and sustain many diverse behaviors over time, many of which are less likely or less probable in terms of the person's usual way of doing things. Such behaviors are the means a person uses to engineer selection and satisfaction. Specifically, these behaviors involve analyzing the environment; committing oneself to take action and maintain action; identifying and altering faulty perceptions, beliefs, and attributions; trying out new ways of acting; and restructuring the environment to promote change and foster encouragement. Clearly such actions require a great deal of sustained effort and conscious attention. Indeed this demand for effort and attention is the way self-control has been traditionally conceived (James, 1890; Klausner, 1965).

Although the logical steps of making career decisions wisely have been articulated for some time (e.g., Krumboltz & Baker, 1973), controlled studies of how to implement those actions have not been carried out. How, for example, can a counselor help an adolescent learn and actually enact the sequence of behaviors used in seeking and processing information, clarifying short-term and long-term personal goals, and managing time in order to explore career options? What are the personal skills needed by a person to engage in the ongoing process involved in career decision making? We believe that self-control processes bear on these questions.

What Is Self-Control?

Behavioral self-control is becoming a popular topic in psychological theory and practice; recently it has begun to inspire much discussion and research. The number of published experimental case studies and controlled group experiments has soared. Several textbooks on self-control have appeared recently (e.g., Goldfried & Merbaum, 1973; Mahoney, 1974; Mahoney & Thoresen, 1974; Thoresen & Mahoney, 1974; Watson & Tharp, 1972), and the popular literature is also starting to reflect interest in how self-control theory can be used to solve common personal problems (e.g., Coates & Thoresen, 1977; Miller & Munoz, 1976; Mooney, 1974.[1]

Self-control can be defined as *learnable cognitive processes that a person uses to develop controlling actions which, in turn, function to alter factors influencing behavior* (Thoresen, 1976; Thoresen & Coates, 1976). This rather technical definition stresses something often unrecognized—namely, the distinction between a person learning self-controlling skills and a person using those skills to change his or her own behavior. Understanding the processes involved in acquiring these skills and in performing them requires different theoretical models and concepts.

The term behavior is used here to include internal, covert actions (e.g., positive self-statements, imagery rehearsal of external actions) as well as external, overt actions (e.g., speaking assertively to others, rearranging one's time schedule). Self-control is not viewed as a dichotomous category distinct from something called external control (cf. Rachlin, 1974) but rather as part of a dynamic continuum of controlling factors. Thus it is not a question of having or not having self-control, as if it were an enduring personality trait. Instead, it is a matter of how much and what kind of self-controlling behaviors a person can exercise in certain situations. The same person, for example, may exercise considerable self-control when it comes to alcoholic drinking but manage badly when faced with time pressures. Self-control, like personality, is much more of a "situation specific" phenomenon than is commonly recognized (Mischel, 1973; Mischel & Mischel, 1975).

In understanding self-control processes the notion of reciprocal influence is crucial. There is the recycling influence of the person's actions influencing his or her environment and, in turn, the person being influenced by that same environment. Thus neither the person nor the environment is autonomous (Bandura, 1974). Self-control should not be conceived of as some exclusive homunculus ("little man inside") that gets manifested in willpower or a drive to achieve (cf. Thoresen & Mahoney, 1974) nor should it be reduced strictly to a matter of external contingencies (self-reinforcement) that create the illusion of self-control (cf. Goldiamond, 1976; Thoresen & Wilbur, 1976). Instead, self-control should be viewed as a series of specific, cognitively mediated actions that a person uses to regulate and alter situations, including the cognitive environment, so that desired change takes place.

Major Concepts and Techniques

A tentative framework for teaching and learning self-control skills has been proposed which can provide a conceptual basis for experimental studies (Thoresen, 1976; Thoresen and Coates, 1976). The framework stresses four

[1]In addition to these articles and books, an introductory film on how self-control methods can be used to solve a variety of problems is available (Thoresen, 1976).

broad areas, recognizing that they are not independent from each other: commitment, awareness, restructuring environments, and evaluating consequences and standards. Table 2 presents these four areas along with some examples of questions relevant to each area. We shall briefly discuss each area as it relates to some career issues.

Table 2. Four major areas in teaching and learning self-control skills with some questions and tasks to consider

---

Commitment (Developing and Sustaining "Motivation")
a. Assess what you attribute your past and present behavior to.
b. Explore your beliefs and anticipations about your ability to change and the possible consequences.
c. Find out how often you engage in positive self-statements and receive encouraging comments from significant others.

Awareness (Observing One's Behavior)
a. Notice what you say to yourself about problem situations.
b. Determine under what circumstances you currently engage in the behavior you want to change.
c. Notice how frequently you currently engage in the behavior you want to change.

Restructuring Environments (Planning Situations and Environments)
a. Establish a supportive environment: teach family, friends and/or associates how you would like them to help.
b. Modify the stimuli or cues that prompt the behavior you want to change.
   external: Rearrange your physical environment.
   internal: Alter undesirable internal cues such as thoughts and images.
c. Develop a written contract which specifies goals, behavior needed to attain those goals, environmental planning, and specific consequences for success and failure.

Evaluating Consequences and Standards for Self-Evaluations (Assessing and Changing Current Reinforcement and Standards)
a. Assess how currently experienced consequences may be maintaining behavior to be changed.
b. Assess long-term goals; redesign goals into series of short-term sub-goals.
c. Use self-rewarding experiences.
   covert: Plan positive thoughts to follow successful actions.
   overt: Plan to give yourself or have someone give you a reward for success (e.g., playing golf on Saturday, a gift, and so on).
d. Use self-punishing experiences.
   covert: Plan negative thoughts and/or images to follow undesired actions immediately.
   overt: Withhold a selected pleasant activity (e.g., watching your favorite TV show) or take away something you have (e.g., fine yourself 10 points each time an undesirable behavior occurs).

Commitment. This first area includes the person's attitudes, beliefs, and conceptions—what might be called the cognitive ABC's—relevant to self-change. What, for example, does the client believe about his or her own abilities and skills in academic work? What are the client's self-attributions about his or her problem of constantly avoiding choices and shying away from new experiences? Does the person's conception of himself or herself as someone who "never really gets off the ground" relate to his or her getting involved actively in career-selection activities? The initial focus on commitment behaviors recognizes the need to clarify and make explicit what traditionally has been called motivation. Rather than conceptualizing motivation as a static prerequisite for change, we view it as developing and building commitment behaviors slowly over time. For example, helping clients recognize and alter irrational beliefs and distorted stereotypes of themselves and career areas serves as one step in creating commitment.

Awareness. Awareness is closely related to commitment. Gaining knowledge of one's actual behavior in specific situations often helps clarify and alter misperceptions and faulty beliefs (e.g., "I never . . ." or "I always . . ." statements can be modified by specific frequency data). The term *self-observation*, sometimes referred to as self-recording or self-monitoring, characterizes one way in which awareness can be translated into operational terms. The person learns to discriminate (notice), count, chart, and evaluate certain actions, some of which may be thoughts or images. For example, a client may notice and record the number of times she reads, writes, discusses, or thinks about three possible career options (e.g., medicine, psychiatric nursing, or social work). A dissatisfied middle-aged accountant who is starting to think about changing careers may observe the frequency and intensity of his tension headaches or depressing moods. A high school senior may establish a self-contract in which she agrees to spend at least 15 minutes each day on career alternatives. As part of her self-control program she observes and records the number of minutes spent each day on a chart posted in her bedroom by her desk. Systematically observing your own behaviors can provide the kind of data that fosters commitment and also sets the stage for knowing what to alter in the environment.

Restructuring environments. This strategy, sometimes referred to as stimulus or situational control, is concerned with physical, social, and cognitive events. As the examples in Table 2 suggest, the focus is on changing the particular features of the environment from hindering to helping persons in their efforts to change. Hence a procrastinating housewife, wanting to convert into action her often-expressed intentions of exploring part-time job possibilities, may alter her environment by placing a three-by-five index card by the telephone to cue her to call the Women's Career Center. A high school junior might negotiate a verbal (or written) self-contract with his counselor for reading at least twenty minutes each day about careers in forestry management, sporting-goods sales, and respiration therapy. Such a contract or agreement would specify positive as well as negative consequences for completing the task. It might also specify how the social and/or physical environment could be altered to help carry out the reading. Perhaps his older brother or father could be involved in prompting him to do the reading. An industrial business manager confronted with a disruptive stream of personnel problems may rearrange his work schedule to be in his office in the morning, a time when he finds it easiest to listen empathically and offer constructive suggestions. He might also learn to rearrange his own internal environment in potentially stressful situations by cueing himself subvocally with self-instruction to "relax," "remain calm," "take a deep breath."

Friends, spouses, and siblings, of course, represent the most significant features of a person's social environment. As Table 2 points out, these persons can learn to provide support and encouragement for self-change. "If you're not part of the solution, you're part of the problem" aptly captures the import of arranging the social environment to support self-change. The ongoing actions required of an effective career decider can be encouraged and maintained by systematically planning environments.

Evaluating consequences and standards. Much of what a person does and will do is influenced directly or indirectly by the effects or results of his or her actions. Consequences experienced immediately or anticipated in the future can be planned by the person to encourage self-change. An impressive variety of pleasant events can serve as positive consequences to increase certain actions while a host of negative or aversive experiences can provide discouraging consequences to reduce behavior. Table 2 suggests that consequences may be cognitive or external to the person.

Too often a client is routinely expected to labor long and hard in career-relevant actions without providing immediate step-by-step support and encouragement. The tedious tasks of, for example, gathering accurate and reliable information on career options is not likely to continue for long unless the person enjoys something in return for his or her efforts. The painstaking work of sifting and sorting through information on careers and carefully weighing it against personal values, experiences, and abilities will remain a rarely performed endeavor unless positive consequences are provided. Clearly, if clients are to learn to view career decisions as somewhat "tentative"—that is, as life-long inquiries in which one engages repeatedly over time—they must be taught how to arrange consequences so as to encourage and support their long-term efforts.

Current Limitations

Unfortunately, self-control theory has outstripped supporting data. Most controlled studies have been concerned with selected clinical problems of adults (e.g., obesity) or a limited range of children's problems (e.g., disruptive classroom behavior). Further, a preponderance of published reports have been analogue studies; college students have often been subjects in laboratory settings. To date no published studies using self-control processes with career behaviors have been reported. Still, existing data is at least promising. There is every reason to believe that self-control processes have direct and immediate relevance to theory and research in career decision making and vocational development.

Table 3 provides an example of how self-control processes have been used to establish a multicomponent intervention program for children and adolescents. The topic, weight reduction, is not directly germane to careers, yet many of the same components *could* be employed in a training system to teach career decision making.

Table 3. Self-control weight reduction program for children and adolescents

---

Observing Actions (Discriminating, Counting, Evaluating)
1. *Commitment/Cognitive Environment:* Contracts are established to promote adherence; weight-relevant cognitions and maladaptive self-thoughts are identified and modified through the use of self-instruction training. Self-attribution training to replace inappropriate belief systems and to build commitment to slow but steady reduction.
2. *Self-Monitoring:* Record quantity and quality of food consumed, eating situations, weight, selected cognitions, social behaviors.

Planning Environment
3. *Family Involvement:* Sessions conducted in the home, supplemented with appropriate reading material, modeling, and guided practice; specific steps outlined; contractual agreements and contingency arrangements negotiated.
   a. *Support:* Family trained in two specific procedures: offer praise for adherence to program objectives; never offer person food at or between meals. Child trained to identify and reinforce helpful family behaviors.
   b. *Stimulus Control:* Entire family establishes regular eating times and location; family reduces rate of eating, food served on smaller plates, food platters not kept on table.
   c. *Nutrition:* Meals prepared in accordance with protein, vitamin, and caloric needs of dieter; restricted foods kept out of the house or in inconspicuous places.
   d. *Negotiation-Skills Training:* Reduce family conflict; permit development and implementation of strategies to promote weight-loss program.
4. *Nutrition:* Child instructed in the basics of food metabolism and caloric values, importance of balanced diet; foods from various categories (highly recommended, recommended, restricted) identified; plans for eating these foods outlined; lists made and kept in conspicuous place; child assists with food-shopping responsibilities.
5. *Stimulus Control:* Child separates eating from other activities; eats more slowly; places high-calorie foods in inconspicuous places.
6. *Physical Exercises:* Child encouraged to participate in initially nonstrenuous and pleasurable exercise, perhaps combined with family or peer involvement programs.
7. *Social-Skills Training:* Training in appropriate social skills to reduce isolation, provide substitute activities, relieve boredom, depression, anxiety.

8. *Peer-Involvement Program:* Therapist meets with one or two peers identified by child; possible use of small counseling groups.
   a. *Peer Support:* Praise for progress and encouragement to continue in weight-loss program.
   b. *Stimulus Control:* Peers would avoid eating with client at inappropriate times and places; would not offer client food.
   c. *Tutoring, Modeling, and Buddy System:* Assist child in finding alternative activities during times of temptation; model appropriate behaviors.
9. *Relaxation Training:* Identify and learn to use activities to reduce stress; combine with cue-controlled relaxation.

Arranging Consequences
10. *Phase I—Training:* Exposure to film or live models demonstrating appropriate self-reinforcement for habit change; therapist reinforcement of child habit change; parent daily reinforcement of child habit change.
11. *Phase II—Self-Reinforcement:* Gradual transfer of reinforcement administration to child; reinforcement for matching therapist and parent evaluations; social praise; complete self-administration and evaluation of reinforcement.
   Maintenance: Maintain family and peer support, administration of self-reinforcement, use of cognitive environment; schedule meetings of lengthened intervals; focus client attention on specific strategies on a weekly basis during followup; phone calls, postcards, surprise meetings held with therapist or significant others on variable-interval schedule.
12. *Role Playing/Covert Rehearsal:* Practice alternative responses to difficult eating and interpersonal situations. Combine with abbreviated problem-solving training.

Adapted from *Childhood Obesity: Some Problems and Treatment Possibilities,* by T. J. Coates and C. E. Thoresen. Unpublished manuscript, Stanford University, 1975.

Using Self-Control Techniques with Jessica

Behavioral self-control methods relevant to Jessica's dilemma can be seen as an extension of the general social learning model of career decision making cited earlier (Krumboltz, Note 3). These techniques are directly linked to a major field of psychological theory and research (e.g., Bandura, 1969, 1975; Mischel, 1973; Thoresen & Mahoney, 1974) and, in this way, provide an ongoing basis for revision and improvement based on a broad range of scholarly work.

Jessica's attempt to develop a career orientation using a self-control program could be enhanced by improving her skills in the four areas described in Table 2. The counselor could help Jessica develop a general commitment to the decision-making process as well as more specific commitments to particular changes. Self-awareness in the form of both quantitative and qualitative information about past and present thoughts, feelings, and external actions might help Jessica establish the general objectives she would need to guide her career search. The information search itself, as well as her own efforts at self-discovery, could be encouraged and supported by environmental planning and restructuring. Additional support for these efforts could also come from scheduling various self-rewards. Of course the four major areas would not necessarily be pursued in counseling for all persons in the same sequence discussed here.

In general, the early focus in counseling would center heavily on issues of self-awareness and commitment, while later emphasis would tend to shift to specific techniques for achieving established goals, such as task approach skills, environmental structuring, and self-reward methods. However, as long as counseling continues, new awareness and commitments would tend to emerge. Thus counseling would have to remain a flexible process, calling for tentativeness and timing by the counselor. In Table 4, we present some specific self-control actions that Jessica might take in her efforts to select a career. These examples are only suggestive, yet they illustrate how self-control could be used.

Table 4. Jessica's use of self-control techniques: Some possible examples

---

I. *Commitment*
   A. Jessica makes general commitment to career decision making process.
      1. Writes brief, vivid description of:
         a. Life as it will probably be if she makes no decision at all.
         b. Life as it could possibly be if she makes a wise choice.
      2. Discusses descriptions with counselor.
      3. Writes self-contract to explore:
         a. What she enjoys and dislikes most about her present life (classes, activities, subjects, and so on).
         b. What things she does best and what she does least well.
         c. What things she has enjoyed in the past and what achievements have been most meaningful.
         d. What her career-relevant skills and personal qualities are, as well as specific habits or behaviors that may hinder an attempt to decide wisely.
   B. Jessica makes specific commitments (after finding that she has certain problems):
      1. To reduce fear of asking professors for help in getting information about careers.
      2. To stop procrastinating; spend more time in library reading relevant books on journalism.
      3. To change her negative stereotypes about writers.
      4. To learn to express her views more effectively when working with males.

II. *Awareness*
   A. Jessica self-observes her past and current career-relevant thoughts, feelings, and external actions.
      1. Writes a work autobiography describing past activities, their outcomes, and her personal feelings about them.
      2. Observes systematically for two weeks her own thoughts and feelings about when she is happiest and when most depressed.
      3. Observes herself coming to counseling sessions unprepared and embar-

rassed because she was afraid to request an appointment with a journalism professor.

III. *Restructuring Environments*
  A. Jessica arranges her external environment to support her career search and self-change efforts.
    1. Arranges to meet once a week with several other female students to discuss what they have learned about themselves and their career interests during the past week.
    2. Plans to spend 30 minutes per day at a particular desk in library reading room researching careers.
    3. Places a stimulus cue (card) in each of her notebooks as reminders to research careers in library.
    4. Arranges (with help of counselor) to observe models of effectiveness, self-assertion, and interview behaviors.
    5. Plans to increase time spent with one of her more assertive female friends.
  B. Jessica arranges her internal environment to support her efforts.
    1. Makes a list of "nervous" and "depressive" thoughts about herself and the future.
    2. Writes a counterstatement for each thought and rehearses these new thoughts twice a day for 10 minutes each time.
    3. Learns deep muscle-relaxation skills (with help from her counselor) and practices them twice daily for about 30 minutes each time.
    4. Uses relaxation skills just prior to approaching professors for information.
    5. Makes a list of things about journalism that she admires and each day devotes time to these thoughts while doing something she enjoys.

IV. *Evaluating Consequences and Standards*
  A. Jessica examines how current consequences maintain present behavior.
    1. Notes how talking about business career is more socially encouraged than talking about law or journalism.
    2. Discusses with counselor how avoidance of professors is reinforced since it reduces tension and nervous feeling.
    3. Recognizes that social support and encouragement from female peers (weekly discussion group) plays important role in doing the "less likely" and more effortful behaviors, such as reading and thinking about career alternatives.
  B. Jessica arranges positive consequences for accomplishing desired changes.
    1. Agrees to give herself five points each day for 30 minutes of career reading toward a new back-pack for summer camping (150 points needed).
    2. Buys a cup of her favorite Viennese Mocha at the campus coffee shop each time after talking to a professor about her interests.
    3. Plays a favorite record while she relaxes or thinks positive thoughts about her future; immediately removes the records and leaves the room if negative thoughts intrude.
  C. Jessica arranges negative consequences for undesired thoughts and actions.
    1. Imagines herself receiving a rejection notice from a graduate school every time she finds herself procrastinating.
    2. Arranges to contribute $1.00 to her most hated political cause whenever she fails to arrange her weekly appointment with a professor.

SOME NEEDED RESEARCH

Let's look at some research needs mentioned earlier. First, we need to know more about how to help people make career changes throughout their lives. Career researchers should devote more attention to people who are past their late teens and early twenties. Within a cognitive social learning framework, we have suggested that career selection requires the learning and using of certain cognitive and social skills. Seldom do persons naturally acquire such skills. Indeed, they may not know they need them until they start looking for work. The waste in human hopes and counselor effort might be prevented if people were taught how to make and engineer decisions earlier in their lives. In addition to research with older groups (career changers) investigations are needed of methods to teach decision skills to children in the primary grades (e.g., Russell & Thoresen, 1976; Spivack & Shure, 1974). "Later and earlier" might well be a watchword for selecting age groups for future studies.

Second, we have called attention to the low yields for counseling practice from current research on vast student populations. Almost all career research is vulnerable to the criticisms that Eisner (1972) has leveled against research in education:

1. Failure to distinguish between statistical and practical (e.g., educational) significance.
2. Tendency to ask only those questions that fit a particular research paradigm (e.g, correlational).
3. Neglect of long-term changes and other effects.
4. Artificial focus on the person apart from how that person acts in the natural environment.
5. Brevity or superficiality of treatment interventions.

These considerations and others mentioned earlier lead us to argue for intensive research designs: controlled descriptive and experimental case studies of single persons over time—that is, time-series research (Thoresen, in press). Unlike the older, clinical-case method, intensive designs meet the scientific criteria of systematic observation and rigorous instrumentation techniques. Such studies can also satisfy the challenges to the internal and external validity of experiments as elaborated by Campbell and Stanley (1966). Indeed, intensive designs of one or a few cases well surpass many of the presumed advantages of comparative group experiments and correlational-survey designs (cf. Thoresen, in press).

More carefully planned mixed and stratified group designs are also needed, along with greater attention to person/environment relationships. Specifically, we would like to see more longitudinal studies of individual school children and adult career changers in which several carefully chosen cognitive and social variables are systematically explored. Data from such studies could provide the base from which hypotheses could be generated and then tested using mixed factorial designs and regression analyses. The major objective would be to get closer to the personal, anecdotal reality of clients, to reduce stereotypical notions based on group designs, and to build our theories out of these encounters in a systematic way. As we learn more about the characteristics and behavior patterns of individuals in specific "real-life" situations, we may be able to develop more lasting and valid generalizations (Cronbach, 1975).

Some questions about self-control techniques that merit investigation include the following:

Commitment
— Do persons who view themselves as capable of making changes in their environment engage in decision making more readily than those who see themselves as less capable?
— How can the "change of choice" or delay-of-gratification problem (decay in power of delayed but larger reward versus smaller, more available ones) be solved?
— What are effective ways of altering beliefs about future consequences and their relation to taking certain actions ("behavior-outcome rules")?
— What is the difference in outcomes between a verbal and a written commitment (self-contract) with and without a support person involved?
— What commitment-sustaining methods are effective during the maintenance and personal-progress phases after formal training has been completed?

Awareness
— What techniques are most effective for teaching people (especially children) to observe in a systematic fashion what they think, feel, or do on a daily basis over time?
— How much do self-observing techniques contribute to self-change (e.g., will systematic observing of the number of times a person makes a decision over several days help a person become more decisive about his or her career)?
— How do increases in conscious awareness influence commitment behaviors as well as the experience of conflict between alternative actions and effort?

Restructuring Environments
— How can observational (social modeling) learning and guided practice with performance aids be used to teach children to make explicit decisions both at home and in school?
— What kinds of physical- and social-stimulus methods (e.g., cueing) work best for people of different ages, cultures, or work/living settings?

— How can social-support systems (e.g., peers) be utilized to encourage and maintain career-choice activities in different settings and at different ages?

Evaluating Consequences and Standards
— What patterning of self-rewards and/or self-punishments is most effective?
— Can the approach/avoidance paradigm be used to help clients better understand how conflicting consequences maintain their behavior (often without their awareness)?
— What is the relative efficacy of tangible (material) as opposed to intangible consequences used positively and negatively?
— Can excessively high or "unrealistic" goals and self-standards be reduced by using mini-goals and explicit criteria for short-term tasks?

As can be seen, the questions vary from the general to the rather specific. The specificity of our questions depends on how the information will be used in a given instance.

We believe the best long-term approach would be to develop multi-component educational programs to teach self-control skills in career decision making in specific settings or to certain client groups (e.g., elementary schools, adult career changers). These programs could be evaluated in terms of changes in specific client behaviors. Initially, we would try to discover whether the total ensemble of techniques in the self-control training program had a significant effect in a personal as well as quantitative sense. If the program achieved promising results, the next step would be to assess the relative merits of its various components by means of carefully planned factorial designs.

Career *choice* is a deceptive metaphor: it calls to mind a single moment of decision rather than an ongoing process. For many, counseling for career decisions means helping someone decide where to get hired. In some ways we have "impaled ourselves on an inadequate construct," to cite George Kelly's (1955) apt phrase. Clearly, it is time to take a much broader view of the career problem. To paraphrase some provocative work in the philosophy of science (Kuhn, 1970; Popper, 1972), we have some real "troubles" to deal with in the career area and our scientific puzzles—our conventional research methods—are not well designed to solve them. Instead we seem locked in to using our puzzles to resolve "problems"—that is, situations known to be solvable by using certain puzzles. The matching game, such as correlating personality types with job titles, may seem like the best game in town but at the very least it shouldn't be the only one.

We face the challenging task of teaching people how to become better architects of their lives—that's a genuine trouble we are just beginning to fathom. Responsibility to our clients includes initiating them into the builder's art—those survival skills found useful in fashioning a way of life of which work is a significant part. It is as if we were preparing people to build their own houses in a time of rapid change; teaching them how to create practical and pleasing means of shelter that would be durable yet flexible to accommodate changing needs. We believe that cognitive social learning theory and self-control research can provide the materials from which sturdy careers can be built.

REFERENCE NOTES

1. Coates, T. J., & Thoresen, C. E. *Childhood obesity: Some problems and treatment possibilities.* Unpublished manuscript, Stanford University, 1975.
2. Dayton, C. M., & Uhl, N. P. *Relationship between Holland Vocational Preference Inventory scores and performance measures of high school students.* Cooperative Research No. 5-0581-2-12-1. College Park, Md.: Research and Demonstration Center, University of Maryland, 1966.
3. Krumboltz, J. D. A social learning theory of career decision-making. In A. Mitchell, G. Jones, & J. Krumboltz (Eds.), Final Report No. NIE-C-74-0134, *A social learning theory of career decision making.* Palo Alto, Calif.: American Institutes for Research, 1975.
4. Mitchell, A. M., Jones, G. B., & Krumboltz, J. D. (Eds.), Final Report No. NIE-C-74-0134, *A social learning theory of career decision making.* Palo Alto, Calif.: American Institutes for Research, 1975.

REFERENCES

Atkinson, J. W., & Feather, N. T. *A theory of achievement motivation.* New York: Wiley, 1966.

Bailey, L., & Stadt, R. *Career education: New approaches to human development.* Bloomington, Ill.: McKnight, 1973.

Bandura, A. *Principles of behavior modification.* New York: Holt, Rinehart & Winston, 1969.

Bandura, A. Behavior theory and the models of man. *American Psychologist,* 1974, *29,* 859-869.

Bandura, A. *Social learning theory.* Englewood Cliffs, N. J.: Prentice-Hall, 1975.

Bem, D. Self-perception theory. In L. Berkowitz (Ed.), *Advances in experimental social psychology* (Vol. 6). New York: Academic Press, 1972. Pp. 1-62.

Bernard, C. *An introduction to the study of experimental medicine.* New York: Dover, 1957. (Original published, 1865.)

Block, J. Some reasons for the apparent inconsistency of personality. *Psychological Bulletin,* 1968, *70,* 210-212.

Borow, H. (Ed.). *Career guidance for a new age.* Boston: Houghton Mifflin, 1973.

Campbell, D. P. *Manual for the Strong-Campbell Interest Inventory, +325* (merged form). Stanford, Calif.: Stanford University Press, 1974.

Campbell, D. T., & Stanley, J. C. *Experimental and quasi-experimental designs for research.* Chicago: Rand McNally, 1966.

Coates, T. J., & Thoresen, C. E. *How to sleep better: A drug-free program for overcoming insomnia.* Englewood Cliffs, N. J.: Prentice-Hall, 1977.

Crites, J. O. *Vocational psychology.* New York: McGraw-Hill, 1969.

Cronbach, J. J. Beyond the two disciplines of scientific psychology. *American Psychologist,* 1975, *30,* 116-127.

Dolliver, R. H. Strong Vocational Interest Blank versus expressed vocational interests: A review. *Psychological Bulletin*, 1969, *72*, 95-107.

Eisner, E. W. Emerging models for educational evaluation. *School Review*, 1972, *80*, 573-590.

Feibleman, J. K. *Scientific method.* Hague: Martinus Nijhoff, 1972.

Folsom, C., Jr. *The validity of Holland's theory of vocational choice.* Unpublished doctoral dissertation, University of Maine, 1971. No. 72-5626.

Goldfried, M. R., & Goldfried, A. P. Cognitive change methods. In F. H. Kanfer & A. P. Goldstein (Eds.), *Helping people change.* New York: Pergamon Press, 1976.

Goldfried, M. R., & Merbaum, M. (Eds.). *Behavior change through self-control.* New York: Holt, Rinehart & Winston, 1973.

Goldiamond, I. Self-reinforcement. *Journal of Applied Behavior Analysis*, 1976, *6*, 509-514.

Goldman, L. *Using tests in counseling.* New York: Appleton-Century-Crofts, 1961.

Greenhaus, J. H. Self-esteem as an influence on occupational choice and occupational satisfaction. *Journal of Vocational Behavior*, 1971, *1*, 75-83.

Hannum, J. W., Thoresen, C. E., & Hubbard, D. A behavioral study of esteem with elementary teachers. In M. J. Mahoney & C. E. Thoresen, (Eds.), *Self-control: Power to the person.* Monterey: Brooks/Cole, 1974. Pp. 144-155.

Hauselman, A. J. *Personality and the choice of undergraduate major: A test of Holland's theory.* Unpublished doctoral dissertation, University of Kentucky, 1971. No. 72-9397.

Heckhausen, H. Achievement motive research: Current problems and some contributions towards a general theory of motivation. In W. J. Arnold (Ed.), *Nebraska symposium on motivation.* Lincoln: University of Nebraska Press, 1968. Pp. 103-174.

Helms, S. T., & Williams, G. D. *An experimental study of the reactions of high school students to simulated jobs.* (Research Report No. 161.) Baltimore: Center for Social Organization of Schools, Johns Hopkins University, 1973. (ERIC Document Reproduction Service No. ED 087-882.)

Holland, J. L. A personality inventory employing occupational titles. *Journal of Applied Psychology*, 1958, *42*, 336-342.

Holland, J. L. Explorations of a theory of vocational choice: VI. A longitudinal study using a sample of typical college students. *Journal of Applied Psychology*, 1968, *52*, 1-37.

Holland, J. L. *Making vocational choices: A theory of careers.* Englewood Cliffs, N. J.: Prentice-Hall, 1973.

Holland, J. L. *The occupations finder.* Palo Alto, Calif.: Consulting Psychologists Press, 1974.

Holland, J. L. *Manual for the Vocational Preference Inventory.* Palo Alto, Calif.: Consulting Psychologists Press, 1975.

Holland, J. L., & Gottfredson, G. D. *Using a typology of persons and environments to explain careers: Some extensions and clarifications.* (Research Report No. 204.) Baltimore: Center for Social Organization of Schools, Johns Hopkins University, 1975.

Holland, J. L., & Lutz, S. W. The predictive value of a student's choice of vocation. *Personnel and Guidance Journal*, 1968, *46*, 428-436.

Holland, J. L., Sorensen, A. B., Clark, J. P., Nafziger, D. H., & Blum, Z. D. Applying an occupational classification to a representative sample of work histories. *Journal of Applied Psychology*, 1973, *58*, 34-41.

Hughes, H. M., Jr. Vocational choice, level and consistency: An investigation of Holland's theory on an employed sample. *Journal of Vocational Behavior*, 1972, *2*(4), 377-388.

Hunt, R. A. Self and other semantic concepts in relation to choice of a vocation. *Journal of Applied Psychology*, 1967, *51*, 242-246.

Insel, P. M., & Moos, R. H. Psychological environments: Expanding the scope of human ecology. *American Psychologist*, 1974, *29*, 179-188.

James, W. *The principles of psychology*. New York: Holt, 1890.

Jones, E. E., Gergen, K. J., & Davis, K. E. Some determinants of reactions to being approved or disapproved as a person. *Psychological Monographs*, 1962, Whole No. 521.

Kaplan, A. *The conduct of inquiry: Methodology for behavioral science*. Scranton, Penn.: Chandler, 1964.

Kelly, G. A. *The psychology of personal constructs*. New York: W. W. Norton, 1955.

Klausner, S. Z. (Ed.). *The quest for self-control*. New York: Free Press, 1965.

Kogan, N., & Wallach, M. A. *Risk taking: A study in cognition and personality*. New York: Holt, Rinehart & Winston, 1964.

Krumboltz, J. D., & Baker, R. D. Behavioral counseling for vocational decisions. In H. Borow (Ed.), *Career guidance for a new age*. Boston: Houghton Mifflin, 1973.

Krumboltz, J. D., with Mitchell, A. M., & Jones, G. B. A social learning theory of career selection. *The Counseling Psychologist*, 1976, *6*(1), 71-73.

Krumboltz, J. D., & Thoresen, C. E. (Eds.). *Behavioral counseling: Cases and techniques*. New York: Holt, Rinehart & Winston, 1969.

Krumboltz, J. D., & Thoresen, C. E. (Eds.). *Counseling methods*. New York: Holt, Rinehart & Winston, 1976.

Kuhn, T. S. *The structure of scientific revolutions*. Chicago: University of Chicago Press, 1970.

Lackenmeyer, C. W. Experimentation—misunderstood methodology in psychological and social-psychological research. *American Psychologist*, 1970, *25*, 617-624.

Lackey, A. An annotated bibliography for Holland's theory: The self-directed search, and the vocational preference inventory (1972-1975). *JSAS Catalog of Selected Documents in Psychology*, 1975, *5*, 352.

Mahoney, M. J. *Cognition and behavior modification*. Boston: Ballinger, 1974.

Mahoney, M. J. *The scientist*. Boston: Ballinger, 1976.

Mahoney, M. J., & Thoresen, C. E. *Self-control: Power to the person*. Monterey, Calif.: Brooks/Cole, 1974.

Mansfield, R. Self-esteem, self-perceived abilities, and vocational choice. *Journal of Counseling Psychology*, 1973, *3*, 431-433.

Meehl, P. E. Theory testing in psychology and physics: A methodological paradox. *Philosophy of Science*, 1967, *34*, 103-115.

Meichenbaum, D. *Cognitive behavior modification*. Morristown, N. J.: General Learning Press, 1974.

Miller, W., & Munoz, R. *How to control your drinking*. Englewood Cliffs, N. J.: Prentice-Hall, 1976.

Mischel, W. *Personality and assessment*. New York: Wiley, 1968.

Mischel, W. Toward a cognitive social learning reconceptualization of personality. *Psychological Review*, 1973, *80*, 252-283.

Mischel, W., & Masters, J. C. Effects of probability of reward attainment on responses to frustration. *Journal of Personality and Social Psychology*, 1966, *3*, 390-396.

Mischel, W., & Mischel, H. A cognitive social learning approach to morality and self-behavior. In T. Lickman (Ed.), *Morality: A handbook of moral behavior*. New York: Holt, Rinehart & Winston, 1975.

Mooney, M. Willpower is a dirty word. *Woman's Day*, October, 1974. P. 72 *ff.*

Osipow, S. H. *Theories of career development*. New York: Appleton-Century-Crofts, 1968.

Parsons, G. E., & Wigtil, J. V. Occupational mobility as measured by Holland's theory of career selection. *Journal of Vocational Behavior*, 1974, *5*, 321-330.

Platt, T. Strong inference. *Science*, 1964, *146*, 347-353.

Popper, K. R. *Objective knowledge*. London: Oxford University Press, 1972.

Rachlin, H. Self-control. *Behaviorism*, 1974, *3*, 94-107.

Rotter, J. B. *Social learning and clinical psychology*. Englewood Cliffs, N. J.: Prentice-Hall, 1954.

Russell, M. L., & Thoresen, C. E. Teaching decision-making skills to children. In J. D. Krumboltz & C. E. Thoresen (Eds.), *Counseling methods*. New York: Holt, Rinehart & Winston, 1976. Pp. 377-383.

Spivack, G., & Shure, H. B. *Social adjustment of young children: A cognitive approach to solving real-life problems*. San Francisco: Jossey-Bass, 1974.

Super, D. E. *Career development: Self-concept theory: Essays in vocational development*. New York: College Entrance Examination Board, 1963.

Super, D. E. Vocational theory: Persons, positions, and processes. *The Counseling Psychologist*, 1969, *1*, 2-9.

Terkel, S. *Working: People talk about what they do all day and how they feel about what they do*. New York: Pantheon Books, 1974.

Thoresen, C. E. Relevance and research in counseling. *Review of Educational Research*, 1969, *39*, 263-281.

Thoresen, C. E. Behavioral means and humanistic ends. In C. E. Thoresen (Ed.), *Behavioral modification in education*. 72nd Yearbook of the National Society for the Study of Education. Chicago: University of Chicago Press, 1973. (a)

Thoresen, C. E. The healthy personality as a sick trait. *The Counseling Psychologist*, 1973, *4*, 51-55. (b)

Thoresen, C. E. *Self-control: Learning how to C.A.R.E. for yourself*. Madison, Wisconsin: Counseling Films, Box 1047, 1976. (Film)

Thoresen, C. E. *Let's get intensive: Single case research*. Englewood Cliffs, N. J.: Prentice-Hall, in press.

Thoresen, C. E., & Coates, T. J. Behavioral self-control: Some clinical concerns. In M. Hersen, R. Eisler, & P. Miller (Eds.), *Progress in behavior modification* (Vol. 2). New York: Academic Press, 1976. Pp. 301-352.

Thoresen, C. E., & Mahoney, M. J. *Behavioral self-control*. New York: Holt, Rinehart & Winston, 1974.

Thoresen, C. E., & Mehrens, W. A. Decision theory and vocational counseling: Important concepts and questions. *Personnel and Guidance Journal*, 1967, *46*, 165-172.

Thoresen, C. E., & Wilbur, C. S. Some encouraging thoughts about self-reinforcement. *Journal of Applied Behavior Analysis*, 1976, *6*, 518-520.

Watson, D. L., & Tharp, R. G. *Self-directed behavior: Self-modification for personal adjustment*. Monterey, Calif.: Brooks/Cole, 1972.

Werner, W. E. *A study of Holland's theory of vocational choice as it applies to vocational high school students.* Unpublished doctoral dissertation, State University of New York at Buffalo, 1969.

Wiggins, J. D. The relation of job satisfaction to vocational preferences among teachers of the educable mentally retarded. *Journal of Vocational Behavior,* 1976, *8,* 13-18.

Yabroff, W. Learning decision-making. In J. D. Krumboltz & C. E. Thoresen (Eds.), *Behavioral counseling: Cases and techniques.* New York: Holt, Rinehart & Winston, 1969.

Ziegler, D. J. Self-concept, occupational member concept, and occupational interest area relationships in male college students. *Journal of Counseling Psychology,* 1970, *17,* 133-136.

RESEARCH PRIORITIES AND RESOURCES IN CAREER DECISION MAKING

9

G. BRIAN JONES
STEVEN M. JUNG
American Institutes for Research

The social learning theory and its propositions as outlined by Krumboltz (Chapter 5 of this text) suggest a number of research questions that could be addressed to test this theory and expand the body of knowledge on career decision making (CDM). The research and development issues reviewed in the first section below build on these questions. They were derived not only from this theory and its propositions but also from diverse input gathered from four sources.

First, an extensive literature review was conducted. Second, four workshops were presented for persons who had principal interests and activities in CDM theory, research, program development and practice within the fields of economics, sociology, psychology, guidance, and education. Third, a conference was held to consider key CDM issues in order to provide input to the National Institute for Education for further research and development in this area. Fourth, the data bases collected and reviewed for the Careers Research Data Set Index, summarized in the second section of this article, were examined.

The research priorities suggested below were selected to meet the following purposes:

> To reflect a comprehensive perspective of CDM that embraces contributions from the fields of psychology, economics, sociology, counseling and guidance, education, and futurism.

The work described in this article was carried out by the American Institutes for Research (AIR) under contract with the National Institute for Education (NIE), United States Department of Health, Education and Welfare. Points of view or opinions stated do not represent NIE position or policy. The authors appreciatively acknowledge both the leadership of AIR's Dr. Anita M. Mitchell and NIE's Dr. Ivan Charner throughout the above study and their input to the documents on which this article is based.

To focus on both direct interventions (for influencing the career decision maker) and indirect interventions (for influencing environmental conditions) that can influence career preferences, skills, and entries.

To emphasize both the individual and societal benefits of such interventions.

To insure that each priority's implementation would produce not only descriptive data adding to the understanding of CDM but also prescriptive evidence documenting how CDM can be improved from the individual and societal viewpoints.

To incorporate research and development issues that ask questions about short-term and long-term effects on and of CDM.

To include a rigorous testing and practical investigation of the social learning theory of CDM.

To incorporate a replication of constructs operationalized by other theories which ultimately might be shown to expand the social learning theory or to contradict it.

RECOMMENDED RESEARCH AND DEVELOPMENT PRIORITIES

Priority Issue 1. The social learning theory proposes that there are four types of learning experiences that have a positive influence, and four more that have negative influence, on the individual's acquisition of educational and occupational preferences. How valid are these predictions for the population in general? How valid are they for important target groups such as women, ethnic minorities, and adults experiencing career changes? Are other influencers more potent than one or more of these?

Since this theory focuses on causal relationships between an individual's experiences and the consequences of those experiences (i.e., products or outcomes such as preferences), empirical evidence substantiating such cause/effect interactions has to be produced for the theory to be supported. Krumboltz (Chapter 5 of this text) identified in his first eight propositions four factors that positively influence, and four more that have a negative influence on, preferences for a course, occupation, or field of work. The literature lends some support to these propositions, but limitations, including gaps, in the evidence were apparent. More clearcut support is required.

These eight propositions dealing with educational and occupational preferences can be subjected to empirical tests. The interactions between preferences and independent variables must be validated not only for the general population but also for significant target groups experiencing crucial CDM needs. Research evidence documenting such interactions would provide answers to questions such as: What specific learning experiences will increase the probability that any given course of study, occupation, or field of work will be stated as a preference by women and representatives of specific ethnic minority groups? Does a pattern of grades received in school indicate that the differential reinforcement of academic marks influences subsequent educational and occupational preferences? At a high school career day, what features about the presentations on each occupation lead students to express interest or disinterest in an occupation?

Priority Issue 2. The social learning theory also postulates that six types of learning conditions and events influence the individual's acquisition of CDM-related cognitive and performance skills and emotional responses associated with those skills. Once again, are these predictions valid for the population in general? Do they hold for target groups such as women, ethnic minorities, and persons making mid-career changes? Are other influencers more powerful than these?

A second construct central to this theory is the TAS, task approach skill. This construct is operationalized by skills such as those involved in career planning, self-observing, goal setting, information seeking, using decision-making methods, and using mediating and thought processes. Since a literature review provides only partial support for the six propositions discussing such skills, research focused on them is required.

Investigating the interactions of the six independent variables listed in the Krumboltz article (Chapter 5 of this text) and CDM skills and feelings will not only test an important second part of this theory but also answer pertinent questions such as: What types of learning experiences cause people to develop the skills and feelings by which they want to and are able to expose themselves to a greater number of educational or occupational alternatives in contrast to limiting the alternatives they explore? To what extent does schooling punish or not positively reinforce students for developing their CDM skills? How do individuals best gain knowledge about the options available, about how to use predictive data, about ways of anticipating contingencies that might affect plans, and about techniques for "putting it all together" in order to set goals and develop plans?

Priority Issue 3. An individual's actual entry into or avoidance of an educational or occupational option is predicted by this social learning theory to be a function of at least five types of factors. Is this prediction valid for the general population? For selected target groups? Are other factors more influential?

A full-fledged test of this theory also must investigate hypotheses derived from the five propositions that focus on these factors. Research tailored to this issue will provide responses to questions such as: Are there patterns of learning experiences that characterize people who are employed in each occupation? To what extent does the quality of the relationship between a child and her/his same-sexed parent influence the degree to which the child selects the same occupation as that parent? How do the occupational choices of an individual's siblings, parents, relatives, and friends affect her/his selection of the same or different occupations?

Priority Issue 4. The social learning theory of CDM stresses the significant role that planned and unplanned environmental (e.g., social, cultural, economic, or political) conditions and events play as "input" influencers of career decisions. What are the social and cultural barriers and constraints that inhibit the CDM of individuals in general, as well as the CDM of persons in important target groups such as women, ethnic minorities, and adults undergoing mid-career changes? What are the facilitators? How can these constraints be removed, thus facilitating CDM that benefits both the individual and society? How can the facilitators be reinforced?

An individual has the freedom over her/his CDM only to the extent that s/he can control the influence of environmental factors. Sometimes such conditions and events are unplanned so that no preparation on the part of the individual decision maker is possible and the range of decision alternatives is controlled by these forces external to the individual. In other situations, there are predictable factors that no one person can change or control in any way. In such settings, the decision alternatives are limited by these forces that curtail individual freedom and produce feelings of powerlessness.

A significant category of such planned and chance factors entails those that are embedded in the social and cultural environment in which the individual grows up and currently exists. Examples of this category of influencers include: (a) factors involved with a person's socioeconomic status which limit the number and nature of the social role models to which s/he has access, (b) controls exerted by incumbents of certain occupations so that the aspirant's freedom is curtailed by the inaccessibility of necessary educational and occupational information (e.g., experiences that help career decision makers acquire a feel for what an occupational structure and a specific job are really like), (c) sex role stereotypes that are reflected in occupational materials or that exclude certain people from identifiable training or job possibilities, and (d) racial stereotypes and perceptions held by members of ethnic minority groups as reflected in national policies, discriminatory policies, and subtle practices of major businesses and industries.

The effects social and cultural constraints and facilitators have on CDM need to be documented so that those that are modifiable can be changed to benefit both individual and societal outcomes. For those barriers that are not so amenable to change, the freedom of the decision maker can be increased if s/he is helped to be aware of these constraints and to function effectively in spite of them.

Priority Issue 5. What are the economic and political barriers and constraints that inhibit the CDM of individuals in general and of the target-group members noted in Issue 4? What are the facilitators? How can the effects of these inhibitors be reduced so that CDM can be facilitated to benefit both the individual and society? How can the facilitators be reinforced?

Here the impediments and facilitators are of an economic and political, rather than a social and cultural, nature. Perhaps this category of planned and unplanned environmental influencers contains more explicit, and less subtle, variables. However, their impact on CDM seems no less powerful.

Examples of economic and political factors include: (a) labor laws, licensing practices, certification requirements, and union rules that eliminate certain applicants from education, training, or job options; (b) relatively unexpected and uncontrollable economic trends that decrease certain job opportunities and increase unemployment rates such as during times of recession or depression; (c) pricing mechanisms that produce high training costs so that certain training applicants are excluded; (d) unavailability of labor-market information so that the career decider must make selections on inadequate data; (e) the similar inaccessibility of information on the costs (e.g., foregone earnings) and benefits of education and training; and (f) the use of leisure time and the impact this has on CDM as both a human capital-investment factor and a consumption variable.

If economic and political barriers and supports can be identified for people in general, and target groups in particular, several types of interventions could be researched. One type could explore alternative ways to remove such impediments, while another could try to help the career decision maker "make it" in spite of barriers. Still another could investigate strategies for making the supports even more facilitating than they currently are.

Priority Issue 6. What are the educational conditions and events that constrain the CDM of individuals in general and of the target group members listed in Issue 4? What are the factors that support CDM? How can these conditions and events be modified to improve each individual's CDM so that s/he and society benefit?

School, training program, and college and university variables are separately identified here only to highlight the important impact that educational institutions have on CDM. Research conducted on such variables would investigate the CDM influence of: (a) tracking systems that limit an individual's options in preschool as well as in elementary and secondary schools; (b) teacher and counselor preferences, values, and CDM skills that shape students' decisions; (c) the lack of conformity and the lowering of local, state, and national standards for education and training so that students graduate without achieving minimal standards of competence; (d) aspects of school organization, climate, and atmosphere that support, as well as those that do not support, student acquisition and practice of decision-making skills; and (e) positive and negative effects that compulsory-schooling regulations have on CDM.

Priority Issue 7. The social learning theory of CDM emphasizes not only the impact that past and current conditions and events have on CDM, but also the effects the individual's awareness of future conditions (short- and long-term) can have on her/his career preferences, skills, feelings, selections, and subsequent actions. How can future projections be most efficiently and accurately developed for the individual to use in her/his CDM? What are the most effective methods for communicating these projections both to career deciders and to social institutions that influence CDM?

If it is true that the future will be increasingly unpredictable and that career decisions made within one set of future conditions will become completely inappropriate in another, it can be hypothesized that the individual's CDM would be improved if s/he knew what her/his life would be like in several possible futures. This statement begs the question about whether plausible, alternative future projections can be made accurately and efficiently. To provide career deciders with future information necessitates that procedures be established for monitoring current trends, that strategies are available or can be developed for projecting future trends with the emphasis on CDM, that effective methods can be implemented to disseminate such information to career deciders so that the dynamism of change is reflected, and that feedback mechanisms can be employed to improve the above information-collection and -utilization process. Futures studies constitute a virgin area for CDM research and development.

Priority Issue 8. As stated in Issues 1 through 3, this theory concentrates on three consequences (or outcomes) of CDM learning experiences: preferences, task approach skills and related emotional responses, and selections and subsequent actions. What CDM skills can be identified and substantiated?

While Issue 2 deals with the impact of personal and environmental influencers on the individual's CDM skills, it does not attend to the specific nature of those skills. The literature revealed that little empirical evidence is available on either comprehensive models of CDM or specific CDM skills and competencies and career planning, development, selection, and action tasks to which they relate. Most of the available information is based on expert opinion using generalizations adapted from studies of industrial, political, and military problem solving. Many CDM references seem to imply that there is a model of CDM rather than alternate approaches that might be efficacious for different decision makers. The model that is frequently recommended is a derivative of the scientific method and thus tends to emphasize a highly rational, logical, step-by-step approach to decision making. Not everyone agrees that career decisions are, or should be, made that way. Descriptive research is needed to investigate these speculations. Operational strategies and identifiable characteristics of successful decision makers must be explored.

Priority Issue 9. If descriptive data collected for Issue 8 substantiate the existence of CDM skills and related responses, prescriptive research should experimentally investigate the impact of direct and indirect interventions aimed at helping the individual acquire, practice, and use such skills and responses. What are the anticipated and side effects of teaching these skills?

A basic assumption of the CDM theory proposed here is that decision-making skills are learned and can be modified through the application of learning principles. A literature review indicated that programmatic attempts have been made to help people acquire and practice CDM skills. However, it also accentuated the fact that no significant evaluative-research activities have been conducted to provide solid data on the impact of these programs. There is a need for constructing instruments appropriate for such research, developing evaluation designs and procedures employing these techniques, and conducting actual evaluation studies that produce information determining at least the cost/effectiveness of specific programs and perhaps even the cost/efficiency of alternate, comparable approaches.

SURVEY OF RESEARCH RESOURCES

Research to contribute partial answers to questions such as those outlined in the above priority issues will no doubt be carried out at numerous sites and under numerous sponsorships in the future. Unfortunately, there is a common tendency under such circumstances to gather new data specific to each new research effort. A major consideration for new research efforts should always be data produced by similar research efforts in the past. Even though the existing data may not be exactly suitable to the investigation of new hypotheses, modern data-analysis techniques offer opportunities for potentially productive pilot studies and other reexamination.

For a number of practical reasons, secondary reanalyses of existing data are rarely performed; a few reasons are mentioned here. In general, it is difficult for researchers to obtain support for such analyses from conventional funding sources. More often than not, the professional "incentives" among researchers (e.g., peer recognition, journal publications, elevation in rank) accrue to the initiator, the theoretician, the responsible investigator of large-scale data-collection efforts. The occasional researcher who does attempt secondary reanalyses is often frustrated by lack of cooperation at the initial source, lack of documentation sufficient to permit adequate interpretation of analysis results, and multiple, uncontrolled rival hypotheses.

Major funding sources can set policies which encourage consideration of secondary reanalysis as a first step in any systematic CDM-research efforts. They should do so. Meaningful secondary reanalyses will generally take the form of pilot studies, cross-validations, and utilizations of previously unused data-analysis techniques. Several such meaningful reanalyses of national data resources, such as those to be described subsequently, should be funded initially. Apart from their substantive impact, these studies should be performed as models of appropriate reanalysis techniques and procedures for the benefit of other researchers. In reports of these studies, as much attention should be given to explaining the methodology used as in describing the results and conclusions.

A prerequisite for the use of existing data is some mechanism for sharing among career researchers an awareness of and an opportunity to explore these data. In the NIE project on which this and the Krumboltz article (Chapter 5 of this text) were based, an attempt was made to compile a comprehensive international index of data sets which are potentially relevant to careers research and are routinely available for acquisition and use by careers researchers. This Careers Research Data Set Index (CRDSI) was supplemented by the actual acquisition of ten selected data sets to comprise a Careers Research Data Bank (CRDB) for the NIE. The staff of NIE's Career

Education Task Force will disseminate information to interested researchers about the CRDSI and will make available copies of the CRDB data sets and associated documentation.

The Careers Research Data Set Index (CRDSI)

The CRDSI is an on-line computer-based index containing information about 95 separate machine-readable data sets.[1] Available information includes: name; date of initial collection; current location of data; name, title, and phone number of contact person at current location; name of responsible investigator(s) for the research program that generated the data; number of publications available; an access category describing the conditions of access to the data set; characteristics of the study sample, including number of subjects, number of observations on these subjects, subject's country and region (within the USA) of residence, age, educational level, sex, race, and religion; an abstract; condition of the data, including tape format, availability of codebook and/or questionnaire, and fee; and categories of career decisions and decision influencers about which data were collected.

The Index permits keyword searches to be performed using various aspects of the above information; procedures for carrying out such searches may be obtained from NIE or from the authors. The index also permits generation of hard-copy printouts based on any aspect or combination of aspects of the above information. To date, printouts have been generated for categories of career decisions and categories of decision influencers about which data were collected.

The Careers Research Data Bank (CRDB)

The CRDB is composed of ten data sets (listed in Table 1) selected from among the 95 included in the CRDSI. The selection process was designed to insure that the CRDB data sets possess high potential for reexamination and secondary analysis. All data sets reside on magnetic computer tape in a standard recording mode (9 track, 1600 BPI density, EBCDIC character set, odd parity) with IBM standard labels. Standardized documentation for all sets includes codebooks and marginal-frequency distributions where available.

Because evidence of accessibility and at least minimal documentation were required before a data set was included in the CRDSI, it may be assumed that listed data sets represent good candidates for secondary reanalysis. The CRDB data sets are comprehensive and possess generally excellent documentation packages, and funding sources should give them preference for in-house and contracted reanalyses such as those suggested above.

---

[1]A listing of the 95 data sets is available upon request from the author, P. O. Box 1113, Palo Alto, California 94302.

Table 1. Data sets accepted for Careers Research Data Bank

1. Study of Students of Public and Proprietary Vocational Training Programs, American Institutes for Research (AIR).
2. Study of Alumni of Public and Proprietary Vocational Training Programs, AIR.
3. Project TALENT, One Year/Five Year/Eleven Year Follow-Up, Public Use Sample, AIR.
4. Assessment of Career Development and Career Planning Program, Grades 8-11 Students, National Norm Group, American College Testing Program, Iowa City.
5. Career Planning Program, Grades 12-13 Students, National Norm Group, American College Testing Program, Iowa City.
6. Study of High School Graduates of 1965, Oakland Public Schools, COMSIS.
7. A Longitudinal Study of Career Plans and Experiences of June 1961 College Graduates, 1968 Follow-Up Sample, National Opinion Research Center, Chicago.
8. Explorations in Equality of Opportunity, University of North Carolina.
9. Careers Study, Stage III: 1960 Graduates, University of Essex, England.
10. School to College—Opportunities for Post High School Education (SCOPE), International Data Library and Reference Service, Survey Research Center, University of California, Berkeley (four tape reels, one each for California, Illinois, Massachusetts, and North Carolina).

Finally, all career researchers would do well to honor in practice this observation by Caleb Calton, an 18th century English clergyman.

> If we can advance propositions both true and new, these are our own by right of discovery; and if we can repeat what is old, more briefly and brightly than others, this also becomes our own.

REFERENCE

Krumboltz, J. D. A social learning theory of career selection. *The Counseling Psychologist*, 1976, 6(1), 71-81.

A CONCEPTUAL FRAMEWORK FOR CAREER AWARENESS IN CAREER DECISION MAKING

10

ROBERT WISE
IVAN CHARNER
MARY LOU RANDOUR
National Institute of Education

I. INTRODUCTION

A program of educational research and development for career development must address two goals if it is to be fully conceived. First, it must seek to understand the process of career development and the contribution of educational experiences to career development. Second, it must seek to identify and provide educational opportunities that encourage the best possible career development of each and every individual. It is readily apparent that progress is being made toward both of these goals at present, yet no one could deny that further progress is needed.

Along with topics such as exploration, preparation, and career access, career awareness is understood as a fundamental construct in the literatures on career development and decision making and the relationship between education and work. Career awareness is fundamental in that it is seen as the basis for making choices that affect the direction of a person's career. The productivity and usefulness of this construct for research-and-development efforts would be well served by a conceptual framework which clarifies the important aspects of career awareness in career decision making and which sets these aspects in their proper relationship to each other and to their antecedents and consequences.

An earlier version of this paper was presented at the annual meeting of the American Educational Research Association in San Francisco, April 1976. It has been revised on the basis of comments made at that meeting and critical readings by others. This paper was written by the staff of the Career Awareness Division of the Institute's Education and Work Group and is used in performing Division functions. As it is already in the public domain, this article is not subject to the copyright of *The Counseling Psychologist* or Brooks/Cole Publishing Company.

This article presents a conceptual framework that is intended as a basis for research and development.[1] Such a framework will be successful to the extent that it joins the varying and incomplete notions appearing in the literature on career awareness and to the extent that it identifies what is important for a fuller understanding of career awareness in the career decision making process. The authors have tried to develop a framework which on the one hand reflects the richness of the career awareness concept without being overly complex and on the other hand achieves clarity without being simplistic. In the remainder of this section, the major parts of the framework will be briefly introduced.

The basic structure of the conceptual framework is presented in Figure 1. As this figure shows, the framework has four major parts, and these parts are related as antecedents and consequences to each other. The four parts are the

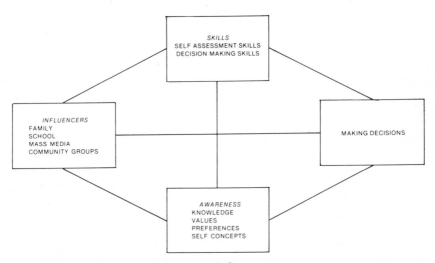

Figure 1. A framework for career awareness.

institutional influencers on career awareness and career choice, the concept of career awareness, the skills of self-assessment and decision making, and the making of actual decisions in career-forming situations. Put as simply as possible, the framework first conceives career awareness to be the inventory of knowledge, values, preferences, and self-concepts which an individual draws

[1]This framework was developed for purposes of planning research-and-development programs. As such, it serves primarily to organize discourse about its particular subject. It is not offered as a theory of the development of career awareness nor as a model of the dynamics of career decision making. However, it is intended that this framework be compatible with theories of career development and with models of economic, labor market, and other systems that affect career development.

on in the course of making career-related choices. Further, an individual can make use of certain skills to assess his or her own awareness and competencies and to identify and assess career opportunities. These skills, along with career awareness, are the resources on which the individual relies when faced with choosing among alternatives in career-forming situations. Finally, career awareness, the skills of assessment and decision making, and actual decision making are all influenced by a variety of social institutions, primary of which are family, school, community groups, and the mass media. In sum, Figure 1 presents three sorts of antecedents to the making of career-related decisions: social influencers, the four aspects of career awareness, and the skills of self-assessment and career decision making. Sections II, III, IV, and V of this article discuss these three parts of the framework and how each is related to the making of career-related decisions.

Sections II and III together present a conceptualization of career awareness. To be fully formed, a conceptualization of career awareness should address two related subjects. First, it should characterize the object of awareness—that is, what one is to be aware of. In the case of career awareness, the object is work. Toward this end, Section II discusses three major dimensions of work: the routines of work, the requisites of work, and the returns of work. We do not offer a definition of work in the sense of drawing a line between what is work and what is not. Rather, we have tried to identify those important qualities of work that would allow a meaningful discussion of what constitutes being aware of work. We also have tried to develop a broad view of the nature of work, not limiting it to that which adults do to earn a living.

The other subject of career awareness is the self. Section III describes the qualities of self that are involved in being aware of work. It is obvious from reading research-and-development literature that career awareness is a dynamic and multifaceted concept. This complexity led us to identify four major aspects of awareness—that is, four ways in which an individual can show an awareness of the dimensions of work. These four aspects of awareness are knowledge, values, preferences, and self-concepts. It is when these qualities of self are directed toward the dimensions of work that we can specify what constitutes career awareness. Section III discusses these four aspects of awareness, how each attends to the dimensions of work, and how they are interrelated.

Section IV continues the discussion of the self as a subject in career awareness by presenting two sets of "skills" involved in making career-related choices. One set of skills is that of self-assessment—specifically, the skills involved in assessing one's stock of knowledge, values, preferences, and self-concepts in relation to some type of work or work setting. The other skills are those used to identify and assess career opportunities. The assessments derived from applying these two sets of skills provide the basis for decisions. Thus, it is the combination of self-assessment and the assessment of career-related options that constitutes the actual career decision making process. Section IV describes these two sets of skills in terms of the types of questions that one can ask in a particular decision situation.

Section V turns away from the subjects of work and self to discuss the four major types of institutional influencers than can affect how an individual thinks about work and self and what skills he or she is able to use in making career-related decisions. This section presents some of the basic features of family, school, community groups, and mass media and discusses their participation in the processes of instruction and socialization. The underlying premise here is that there are many factors affecting one's awareness, skills, and decisions.

II. DIMENSIONS OF WORK

The term *work* is used in many different contexts. There is office work, housework, schoolwork, clockwork, and the devil's work. We go to work, work on the lawn, and hope things work out. Work is a topic for labor economists, sociologists, career-development researchers, industrial psychologists, career counselors, teachers, and career educators. There are a variety of words that refer to work: job, employment, position, occupation, vocation, career, labor; and there are words that suggest opposites of work: leisure, play, relaxation, avocation, unemployment. Reviews of terms associated with work have suggested that there are no standard definitions for these various terms and that there are no common understandings about how we are to distinguish among them.

One way to address the concept of work would be to take the above family of terms and their opposites as the basic terms in our framework and attempt to define each in some precise way. This setting out of definitions has been tried in the past, and distinctions have been made, for example, between work and labor or work and play. In developing this framework, we have not taken this approach. Terms for work have developed in a variety of social and institutional contexts, and as a result they have rich and overlapping connotations. Thus, it would be a difficult task to differentiate among these terms without appearing somewhat arbitrary. But more importantly, making distinctions between what is work and what is not work may not lead to the most useful basis for understanding what is significant about work. A field advances on several fronts simultaneously and the language of the field evolves from the sifting and sorting of questions and findings from theory and research in the field. The primary terms that are nominated for a place in a conceptual framework should be ones that facilitate the identification of significant problems and questions that the field can address.

Rather than attempt to develop a precise definition for the term *work* and its relatives, the approach we have taken is to identify what seem to be primary dimensions of work: routines, requisites, and returns. These dimensions of work are based on a study by Temme (1975) and are listed in Table 1. These three categories refer respectively to what constitutes the *activities* of work, what is *required* to be able to perform those activities, and what *benefits* can be derived from doing those activities. They can be used to describe any particular instance of work, and they can be used to compare and contrast instances of work. It should also be noted that these three dimensions do not limit work to those activities that are performed in the "labor market" by adults. Playing baseball, writing a composition, and taking care of pets—if they can be characterized as having routines, requisites, and returns—are examples of work by this framework.

Table 1. The dimensions of work

Routines	*Requisites*	*Returns*
content	proficiencies	earnings
functions	physical conditions	prestige
	market	power
	social	autonomy
		associations
		social benefit
		personal growth

Before discussing each dimension in turn, it will be useful to set out the meaning of a few work-related terms that we use in this framework. The particular terms we find useful to define for this discussion are *work position*, *job*, *occupation*, and *career*. These are defined as follows:

> *Work position:* a set of work activities that can be performed by an individual.
> *Job:* a work position, commonly used as the basic unit of work in an organization and commonly associated with earning a living.
> *Occupation:* a category of work positions, usually jobs, that have been characterized as having similar routines, requisites, and returns.
> *Career:* the work positions, identified by job or occupational labels, that an individual holds in a lifetime.

The Routines of Work

This dimension refers to the activities of work—that is, what some instance of work is about or what is involved in performing the work. There are two sub-dimensions along which the activities of work can be described: the *content* of work and the *function* performed on that content. Each of these sub-dimensions has appeared in various classifications of types of work. An example of a work classification based primarily on content categories is the U. S. Office of Education's 15 occupational clusters. The *Dictionary of Occupational Titles'* (U. S. Dept. of Labor, 1965) scheme of 144 worker-trait groups is an example of a classification which includes a description of work functions to be performed. The most desirable classification of work routines would describe work activities in terms of both content and function. In this regard, the *Dictionary of Occupational Titles'* "Data-People-Things" classification scheme seems to be a well-developed system for classifying work activities in this way. Briefly, according to this scheme, every type of work involves, to one degree or another, three types of content:

Data (information, knowledge, and conceptions, related to data, people, or things, obtained by observation, investigation, interpretation, visualization, mental creation; take the form of numbers, words, symbols; other data are ideas, concepts, oral verbalization),

People (human beings; also animals dealt with on an individual basis as if they were human), and

Things (inanimate objects as distinguished from human beings, substances, or materials; machines, tools, equipment; products; a thing is tangible and has shape, form, and other physical characteristics).

For each of these three contents, the *Dictionary of Occupational Titles'* scheme then lists work functions and orders these functions in terms of their level of complexity as follows:

Data	*People*	*Things*
Synthesizing	Mentoring	Setting-Up
Coordinating	Negotiating	Precision Working
Analyzing	Instructing	Operating
Compiling	Supervising	Driving-Operation
Computing	Diverting	Manipulating
Copying	Persuading	Tending
Comparing	Speaking-Signaling	Feeding-Offbearing
	Serving	Handling

This scheme allows us to describe types of work situations in terms of the mental, interpersonal, and physical activities that are involved and also to compare different types of work in these terms. It assumes that all three types of activities can be found in most work. Any classification scheme, by intent, brings into the foreground certain features of work activities and pushes into the background other features. The "Data-People-Things" scheme is one way to describe the routines of work so that their central features can be identified and compared.

The Requisites of Work

A work requisite is any ability level or physical or social condition of work which functions to *constrain* the eligibility of an individual to perform some specific work activity. Requisites can derive from either the work routine itself or its setting or from market or social criteria applied in the selection process for a work position.

A given work activity requires certain capacities or skills to be used at some level of *proficiency*. Further, the level of proficiency for the same work routine may vary from one institution to another, and from one work setting to another. To the extent that many jobs require basic reading, computation, communication, and reasoning skills, it is useful to distinguish between at least two general types of proficiency requisites:

> *General educational requisites:* literacy, social, and reasoning skills that are necessary to be a productive individual in most work settings.
>
> *Specific work requisites:* the particular capacities, skills, and proficiencies needed to perform some specified work routine.

A second type of requisite reflects the *physical conditions* of the work place. Some work requires being isolated from other people for long periods of time, while other work requires that a person work continuously in a relatively public setting. Some work requires regular exposure to the elements, while other work keeps one cut off from the natural climate. These conditions and others may in some cases be formally stated requisites of a work position or else be so commonly known that no special acknowledgement is given to them as requisites.

Two additional types of requisites are not found in the nature of the work or the physical conditions of the work but in the processes of recruitment and selection for jobs. They reflect the *labor market*—that is, the supply and demand for individuals with certain credentials or degrees—and the *social desirability* of certain worker traits unrelated to the work routines, such as gender and ethnicity. Even when the routines of the work remain constant over time, these requisites change as a function of the changing supply of qualified applicants or as a result of social pressure to adjust past hiring practices to accommodate different social groups. A job which once required a master's degree may now require a doctorate. Being a white male may enhance or detract from one's eligibility for certain positions today.

The first two types of requisites identified above can be referred to as structural requisites—that is, requisites that pertain to the structure inherent in routines or conditions of the work. The latter two types are market and social requisites that vary with the economy and changing social expectations. Whether a requirement is structural or market/social, it functions to constrain who can qualify to perform the work.

The Returns of Work

Returns are the benefits and rewards that one can accrue as a consequence of performing a work routine. Seven types of returns that can be used to differentiate various types of work are as follows:

Earnings: the rate at which a person is paid for time spent working, including direct pay and fringe benefits.

Prestige: the social esteem accorded to an incumbent of a work position by virtue of holding the position.

Power: the influence over the behavior of other persons which derives from holding a work position.

Autonomy: the freedom to control how one conducts one's own work.

Associations: the type and quality of interpersonal relationships that can be formed as a result of holding a work position.

Social benefit: the opportunity to contribute to the benefit of others or to the public good.

Personal growth: the opportunity to improve one's proficiencies or develop new capacities.

All of these returns can function as satisfactions derived from work, which means that they can function as incentives or motivations for individuals to perform the work. Whether a particular return acts as a reward in a particular setting will depend on the worker. However, it is possible to generalize across particular settings and workers and refer to average levels of each return for a given work activity.

III. ASPECTS OF CAREER AWARENESS

The focus we have taken considers career awareness to be composed of four aspects which participate in a dynamic and interactive way. The four aspects are knowledge, values, preferences, and self-concepts. In this section, these four aspects of career awareness are discussed along with their relationships with each other and with the dimensions of work. Figure 2 shows how the four aspects of career awareness interact with one another.

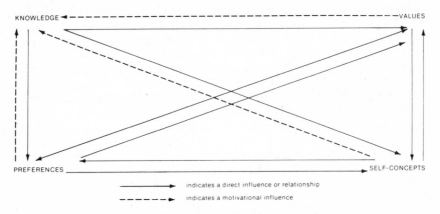

Figure 2. The aspects of career awareness.

Knowledge

By *knowledge* we mean factual information about work and self. This information can fall into three categories. First, knowledge of work can refer to routines, requisites, and returns of work-in-general and can include information about the dimensions of specific work positions. In addition to general and specific knowledge of work, information about the wide array of antecedents to and consequences of work can also be thought of as knowledge of work. This second type of knowledge includes knowledge of strategies people use to gain access to positions, knowledge of the lifestyles of individuals in various occupations, and a knowledge of how the labor market functions. Knowledge of self, as a third type of knowledge, includes knowledge of one's personal interests, values, and abilities.

As portrayed in Figure 2, knowledge has an important relationship with the other aspects of awareness. The solid arrows pointing from knowledge to the other aspects signify the potential of knowledge to directly affect the other aspects. Specifically, we would argue, increased knowledge about work could directly affect (a) preference for a work activity, (b) the value placed on a work activity, and (c) one's self-concept with regard to a work activity. The relationships of the other aspects to knowledge, however, can only be of an indirect nature (dotted arrows). Values, preferences, and self-concepts can motivate an individual to acquire more knowledge, but they cannot provide additional knowledge themselves.

Values

Value refers to the notion that an object such as a routine, requisite, or return has worth. Values are distinguishable by the commitment placed on the object in question; that is, a value represents a commitment to an object because it is good, right, or something one ought to do or believe as opposed to a simple "feeling of attraction" for the object. As Bloom, Hastings, and Madus (1971) suggest, a value is a social product which has been internalized and has come to be used as one's own criterion for judgement or action. From Figure 2 we see values having the potential to directly affect preferences and self-concept, and having the potential to motivate knowledge acquisition.

Two points of clarification should be made in this discussion of values. First, it is possible to separate *knowing* the common values one's group places on routines, requisites, and returns of work from *having* one's own work values. Second, one can distinguish between valuing the specifics of work and valuing work-in-general. Work values that are specific involve commitments to particular routines, requisites, or returns of work. Values toward work-in-general refers to those values which are not related to any of the dimensions of work but rather reflect the "work ethic" and how we should approach working.

Preferences

Preference refers to that set of routines, requisites, and returns of work which are aspired to or liked or for which one has an interest. In varying degrees, aspiration, liking, and interest are synonyms for one's preference for education/training, occupations, activities, and lifestyles. They all involve a "feeling of attraction" that an individual has for the work activity, requisite, or return in question. These feelings of attraction for aspects of work are sometimes labeled "ideal" (aspiration) and "real" (expectation). The distinction here is between an ideal preference, for which the individual *does not* take into consideration an array of personal, institutional, and social influences and real preferences for which these influences *are* taken into consideration.

In the array of work-related preferences, the distinction between an occupational preference and an activity preference is important. An occupational preference is a preference for a job or occupational category (engineer), while an activity preference represents interest in some part of the routines of work (solving math problems). What emerges is a difference between a preference for the defining set of routines, requisites, and returns associated with an occupation and a preference for activities. This distinction allows us to talk, for example, about the work interests of children without assuming that they have occupational preferences.

In relation to the other aspects of career awareness (see Figure 2), we see preferences as a potential motivator of knowledge acquisition and as having the potential to be directly related to values and self-concept. In addition, preferences can affect and be affected by the performance of an activity. It has often been assumed that interests or preferences positively affect performance, yet the research in this area has shown that successful performance of an activity can result in increased interest in that activity (see Osipow, Note 1). Thus performance may in fact shape interests as well as interests affecting performance.

Self-Concepts

Self-concept refers to the belief held about an ability one has and about how successful one would be at an activity involving that ability. Because each of us has many abilities, we each have many self-concepts. The sum of one's positive and negative self-concepts is one's self-esteem. Self-esteem reflects a generalized feeling one has about self. Self-concept can refer to the feelings one has about proficiencies with regard to specific work activities or skill requisites and can represent one part of the wide array of pieces that result in an individual's feelings about his or her generalized self-esteem.

Self-concept has been linked to educational and occupational success (see Banks, 1972). Self-concept, therefore, emerges as an important element of career awareness not only in its relation to the other elements but also in its impact on success in the routines and activities of education, work, and other life roles.

A self-concept is the comparing of one's self; that is, how one feels about performing a certain task is a function of the institution or individuals one uses for comparison. As with values and preferences, we see self-concepts as having the potential to directly affect all of the other aspects except knowledge (refer to Figure 2); self-concepts can potentially serve to motivate the acquisition of knowledge.

A Career-Awareness Matrix

Above, we have defined the four aspects of career awareness and explained how they relate to each other. We have tried to be sensitive to the complexities of these aspects of awareness both as separate constructs and especially as they interact. By crossing the four aspects of awareness with the three dimensions of work, a matrix of career awareness is created, as shown in Table 2. This matrix distinguishes twelve possible facets of career awareness. Specifically, one can have knowledge of the routines, requisites, and returns of work; one can value them; one can have preferences among them; and one can have self-concepts about routines and some of the requisites of work. Since self-concepts have to do with abilities and performance, one cannot have self-concepts with respect to market and social requisites (which are defined as work constraints not related to ability or performance) or work returns (which are defined as consequences of work performed). In sum, there are eleven facets of career awareness. These facets and their interactions form one's career awareness and have important consequences for one's career and life development.

IV. SELF-ASSESSMENT AND DECISION-MAKING SKILLS

Self-Assessment Skills

The knowledge, values, preferences, and self-concepts one has in relation to the dimensions of work are important, but the ability to assess what one knows or how one feels about the routines, requisites, and returns of work is also important. To assess personal attributes one uses self-assessment skills. These skills involve the ability to ask and answer questions about how one perceives oneself in terms of the matrix of career awareness. The two types of situations which require self-assessment are those in which one is concerned with *searching* for new opportunities for work, exploration, or self-development and those that arise when one is faced with *deciding* among career-related alternatives. Table 3 presents the types of questions that can be asked when one is either searching or deciding. In assessing values toward

Table 2. The career-awareness matrix

Aspects of Career Awareness	Dimensions of Work		
	Routines	Requisites	Returns
Knowledge	X	X	X
Values	X	X	X
Preferences	X	X	X
Self-Concepts	X	X	

Table 3. Self-awareness skills

Aspects of Career Awareness	Self-Awareness Skills	
	Searching	For Deciding
Knowledge	What do I know?	Do I know enough?
Values	What is important to me?	How important is this to me?
Preferences	What do I like?	How much do I like this?
Self-Concepts	What do I do well?	How good am I at this?

work returns, for instance, in order to locate a more satisfying job, the individual would answer the question "What returns are important to me?" (a search question). When faced with an opportunity to apply for a particular job, the question to be asked is "How important to me is the prestige this job offers?" (a decision question). Self-assessment skills, as described here, involve the separate assessment of each of one's personal attributes as needed in career-forming situations.

Decision-Making Skills

Decision-making skills come into play when one has to consider options. One important skill in this regard involves balancing the four aspects of career awareness for the purpose of making a particular decision; that is, the assessment of the comparative importance of the four aspects of career awareness in a particular decision situation is a decision-making skill. In addition to this skill, a number of others can be identified. Again, we shall describe the types of questions one would ask in using these decision-making skills. Table 4 presents the types of questions that can be asked in order to arrive at a decision on one course of action over another. For any given decision situation the individual may use any or all of these skills.

Table 4. Career decision-making skills

Decision-Making Skills	Questions to be Answered
Clarifying Goals	What do I want to achieve?
	When do I want to achieve it?
Gathering Information	What information do I need to have?
	How can I get more information?
Anticipating the Future	What social and economic changes may occur in the future?
Interpreting Experiences	What have I done that relates to my options?
	What does my experience suggest I might look for?
Identifying Opportunities	What options have I been given?
	What options can I imagine?
Assessing Opportunities	What are the benefits and costs of my options, for myself and others?
	What are my chances of succeeding with my options?

The nature of the specific situation for a particular person dictates the unique configuration of decision-making skills that may be employed. In making a decision about participation in a school science-fair competition, for instance, the individual could answer the following questions: "Why would I want to participate in the science fair?" (clarifying goals); "What are the rules for participating in the competition?" (gathering information); "Which of my hobbies or courses I have taken can help me prepare a project?" (interpreting experiences); "Do I have the time to prepare a project?" (assessing opportunities); and "What could happen if I win the competition?" (anticipating the future).

Self-assessment and decision-making skills can be called upon at any point in an individual's career, and, as society becomes more complex, situations of choice occur more frequently. The career-development process and the series of career choices by which it can be characterized should ideally proceed on the basis of finding a satisfying mix among the multiple roles an individual can assume. Self-assessment and decision-making skills increase in importance as the frequency and significance of career-related decisions increase.

V. INSTITUTIONAL INFLUENCERS

This section presents a discussion of the four major institutions that can influence the development of career awareness and the acquisition of skills in the career decision-making process. These four institutions are *family, school, mass media*, and *community groups*. The discussion will briefly describe how these institutions can influence the development of career awareness and what conditions affect their influence.

We assume that, of the four institutional influencers, family and school need no clarification here. On the other hand, it seems necessary to discuss what is meant by mass media and community groups. Mass media are all those printed and electronic means of communication that reach large groups of people and include television, radio, film, newspapers, magazines, and advertisements. Community groups include all formal groups in a community, such as churches, Girl Scouts, Elks; informal, spontaneous associations, such as play groups and peer groups; and groups of workers as they are represented by individuals working in the community, such as letter carriers and homemakers.

Functions

The four institutions—family, school, mass media, and community groups—function as influencers in two ways: they can instruct and they can socialize. Each institution has agents which can perform these instructional and socialization functions. This view of institutional functions is derived from Spady's (1973) work on the functions of schooling. The instructional function can be seen as both an intentional and an unintentional process. Whether intended or unintended, the consequences of instruction for an individual are increased knowledge and competence. Socialization, on the other hand, is a process that more directly influences the affective development of an individual and is one which transmits the attitudes, beliefs, expectations, and values that a person needs for success in social roles.

At any particular developmental stage of an individual, one influencer may be more powerful than another, and, for a given influencer, one function may predominate over the other. For example, during infancy and early childhood it is primarily the family which both instructs and socializes. The school and mass media enter the development process a little later. During childhood and adolescence the family may decline in importance or at least share its potency and functions with the other influencers. Schools and community groups become more influential during adolescence and can maintain their influence into adulthood. At what age the mass media's influence is most prominent is not clear, but its relevancy probably varies not only with an individual's age but also with her or his culture.

Dynamics

There are a number of conditions which can affect the potency of each institution as an influencer and whether the instruction or socialization function is primary for an institution. Some of these conditions are age and culture of the individual, the availability of the institution to the individual, and the individual's participation in it. Age has a bearing on one's personal associations and on the importance of various institutional agents. For example, during adolescence one's peers play a more prominent role in socialization than they do in early childhood. Similarly, the effect of an institutional influencer may vary because of differences in values, norms, and expectations of cultural groups. For example, in cultures in which academic achievement is valued, schools may have more salience for an individual than do peers.

In addition, availability and participation are necessary conditions for an institution to be influential. While almost everyone is a member of a family, the availability of the other influencers varies. A girls' club or certain examples of media, such as the *Village Voice*, may not be available in every community. Not only must the institution be available but also one must participate in its activities in order to be influenced.

An important thing to note about the four influencers is that they are interrelated. One way in which they are interrelated is through institutional interaction. For example, the family is affected by and uses the mass media, while the content of the mass media is framed, in part, by the demands of family, school, and community groups. Such interactions allow an institution to have both a direct influence on an individual and an indirect influence through another institution in which the individual participates. A second way in which the influencers are interrelated is through the sharing of agents across institutions; that is, the same institutional agent may perform an instructional or socialization function in any of the four institutions. A person may be a parent, a member of the school board, and a Girl Scout leader; that is, one person can act in three agent roles.

Types of Agents

How the instruction and socialization functions are carried out should be briefly noted. Instruction can be an important responsibility of the family, school, community groups, and mass media because of its direct effect on knowledge acquisition and skill training and its more subtle effects on values, preferences, and self-concepts. Teachers, parents, and peers act as instructional agents by providing a person with an opportunity to perform a task, to succeed or fail at it, and to be reinforced for success or discouraged by failure.

Agents of socialization are more difficult to conceptualize. They have been defined as *generalized other* (Mead, 1934), *reference groups* (Hyman & Singer, 1968), *role models, reference individuals* (Merton, 1965), and *significant others* (Sullivan, 1947). Sometimes these socialization agents are collectivities, such as generalized others and reference groups, and other times they are individuals, such as a role model or significant other. Individual socialization agents are more likely than groups to interact directly and to have a close and personal relationship with a person. Distinguished from the above socialization agents is the *symbolic model* (Bandura, 1971), which is a constructed or portrayed image of a person with whom there is no interaction. One comes under the influence of a socialization agent either because of membership in the group (such as the family) or because one selects the agent, as in the case of a role model. Little is known, however, about why one agent or group is selected over another. For example, Joe Namath may be selected as a symbolic model by some and Eric Sevareid by others. Whether individual or group, real or fictitious, imposed or selected, a socialization agent provides opportunities for an individual to acquire norms, values, and expectations, to make judgments, and to learn roles.

Through these instruction and socialization processes, institutions influence the development of preferences, values, and self-concepts and motivate the acquisition of knowledge. If we are to provide individuals with the knowledge, skills, and competencies necessary to choose, enter, and progress in work that is beneficial to themselves and others, we must understand these institutional influencers, the aspects of career awareness, and the skills of self-assessment and decision making as they relate to an individual's work throughout a lifetime. We have attempted to build a four-part conceptual framework of career awareness in the belief that career awareness is a fundamental aspect of career development and of the relationship between education and work.

REFERENCE NOTE

1. Osipow, S. *Career choices: Learning about interests and intervening in their development.* Paper presented at a Conference on Career Decision-Making, New York, 1975.

REFERENCES

Bandura, A. Analysis of modeling processes. In A. Bandura (Ed.), *Psychological modeling: Conflicting theories.* Chicago: Aldine-Atherton, 1971. Pp. 1-62.

Banks, J. (Ed.). *Black self-concept.* New York: McGraw-Hill, 1972.

Bloom, B., Hastings, T., & Madus, G. *Handbook on formative and summative evaluation of student learning.* New York: McGraw-Hill, 1971.

Hyman, H., & Singer, E. *Readings in reference group theory and research.* New York: Free Press, 1968.

Mead, G. *Mind, self, and society.* Chicago: University of Chicago Press, 1934.

Merton, R. *Social theory and social structure.* New York: Free Press, 1965.

Osipow, S. Success and preference: A replication and extension. *Journal of Applied Psychology,* 1972, *56,* 179-180.

Spady, W. G. Mastery learning: Its sociological implications. In J. Block (Ed.), *Schools, society, and mastery learning.* New York: Holt, Rinehart & Winston, 1973. Pp. 91-116.

Sullivan, H. *Conception of modern psychiatry.* Washington, D. C.: White Psychiatric Foundation, 1947.

Temme, L. *Occupation: Meanings and measures.* Washington, D. C.: Bureau of Social Science Research, 1975.

United States Department of Labor. *Dictionary of occupational titles* (3rd ed.). Washington, D. C.: U. S. Government Printing Office, 1965.

A COGNITIVE-DEVELOPMENTAL MODEL OF CAREER DEVELOPMENT— AN ADAPTATION OF THE PERRY SCHEME

11

L. LEE KNEFELKAMP
RON SLEPITZA
University of Maryland

The development of the career model presented in this article is best understood within the context of the assumptions that underlie the work. Briefly, those assumptions are:

1. One of the primary identity issues of the college student and young adult is career development—the process of career choice and decision making as it relates to one's concept of self.

2. The field of career development and the concepts of career development have continually expanded to encompass new contributions in the ways career development has been viewed. That expansion has resulted in an increased awareness and appreciation of the complexities of career development as a process and the need to focus on process elements in career counseling.

3. Career development has always had the individual as a primary focus. The career counselor has needed to understand the individual's needs, abilities, interests, personality types, and identity factors if appropriate career-development work was to take place.

4. It is now appropriate to expand the definition of process in career development and to add an additional individual-difference factor for the counselor to consider—that of the level of cognitive complexity with which the student approaches the career-development task.

The authors would like to acknowledge the contributions of Carole C. Widick and Steven Stulck of Ohio State University for the data presented in the "Ohio State Project" section.

Career-development models have often considered the importance of process—whether process was viewed in relation to decision making (Ginzberg, Ginsburg, Axelrod, & Herma, 1951; Tiedeman & O'Hara, 1963) or with reference to the developmental process over the life span (Super, 1957). These views of process, however, do not specify the *cognitive* processes used by individuals in organizing, integrating, and utilizing career-related information and activities. Jepsen (1974) has suggested that a next logical step for the field would be the utilization of the stage concept from cognitive-developmental psychology.

Such cognitive models (Piaget, 1952; Kohlberg, 1969; Perry, 1970) assume that stages or levels of development are sequential and hierarchical in nature and that they represent qualitative differences in the ways individuals approach the same task or issue (Rest, 1973). Thus, level of cognitive processing becomes an important variable for the counselor to consider when presenting career information and decision-making models.

5. A cognitive-developmental career model would be descriptive of the student but would have implications for how to promote developmental growth along the continuum of the model (Rest, 1973; Widick, Knefelkamp, & Parker, 1975).

6. A simple overlay of an existing cognitive model would not be sufficient. A new or adapted model is necessary that is specific to career development as an identity issue.

With the above assumptions as a base, the authors turned to the theoretical work of William Perry (1970) for a cognitive model that was relevant to college students and their identity issues. Based upon research conducted with Harvard undergraduates, Perry and his associates have derived a cognitive-stage framework focusing upon intellectual/ethical development. Nine positions or stages, each representing a qualitatively different mode of thinking about the nature of knowledge, comprise the Perry model. The stages tend to be reflected in the students' perceptions of the teacher's role and their own role as learners. The nine positions may be grouped into three more abstract categories of dualism, relativism, and commitment within relativism.

While the Perry scheme was created by design to describe the development of a student's reasoning about knowledge, it is also feasible that such a scheme can be viewed as a general process model. As such, it may provide a descriptive framework for viewing the development of an individual's reasoning about many aspects of the world. Support for this idea has been provided by Harvey, Hunt, and Schroder (1961) in their cognitive-developmental model of "conceptual systems." In this model, an individual has many conceptual systems or cognitive structures for a variety of "content" areas, for example, knowledge, values, and significant others. Harvey, Hunt, and Schroder asserted that each conceptual system of an individual progresses through a sequence of developmental stages. It is my contention that individuals have a conceptual system for career, career counseling, and career decision making and that the Perry scheme can be adapted to the development of an individual's thinking about these important areas.

THE NEW MODEL

Areas of Qualitative Change

In the creation of the career model, we have relied most heavily upon the conceptual contribution of Perry (1970). However Rest (1973), Kohlberg (1969), Harvey, Hunt and Schroder (1961), and Loevinger and Wessler (1970) have also provided us with empirical support for the existence of a series of qualitative changes that make up a developmental sequence. Results of our interview data and instrument responses led us to emphasize nine areas of qualitative change. Briefly they are:

1. *Locus of Control*—the source to which students turn to define themselves and their environment. We found that students progress from a position of control based upon external factors (e.g., parental admonitions, job-market pressures, or results of assessment instruments) to a position where information is processed predominantly through their own internal reference points.

2. *Analysis*—the ability of the individual to see a subject in its diverse perspectives, breaking down the subject into its component parts. As students develop their analytic ability, they increasingly become able to see cause-and-effect relationships.

3. *Synthesis*—the ability of the individual to integrate the diverse components of a subject into a complex whole. Being more complex than analysis, students did not exhibit this factor until they were rather cognitively mature (Stages 6 and 7) in their approach to the world.

4. *Semantic Structure*—refers specifically to the nature of the verbs and qualifiers used by students in their written and spoken expressions. In this regard, students progress from a semantic structure characterized by absolutes to a more open semantic structure that allows for greater alternatives and greater use of qualifiers and modifiers.

5. *Self-Processing*—the ability to examine oneself and be cognizant of one's defining factors. In its emergence and development, this variable closely parallels that of analysis.

6. *Openness to Alternative Perspectives*—the extent to which the individual is aware of and recognizes the legitimacy of other points of view and possible explanations, even if the student differs with that perspective.

7. *Ability to Assume Responsibility*—the willingness of the student to accept the consequences of actions or decisions made, regardless of unknown and unforeseen interfering factors.

8. *Ability to Take on New Roles*—the ability of students to expand their repertoire of abilities and behaviors within the context of new role or activity demands. The student moves from a position of not seeking new role or

activity opportunities, to a seeking and mastery of them, to an ability to confidently look forward to new opportunities for self within new roles; expansion of old roles and new activities increases as role-taking increases.

9. *Ability to Take Risks with Self*—closely related to role-taking ability, this area refers to the individual's increasing ability to risk self-esteem when new and appropriate demands are made. The individual has a fairly confident sense of self which enables him or her to focus on new learnings and experiences rather than on whether or not the ego will be damaged.

Figure 1 illustrates the above variables with respect to the individual and career.

Descriptions of Category and Stage

These nine variables have been applied to create an adapted nine-position career model which describes the movement of a student from a simplistic categorical view of career, career counseling, and career decision making to a more complex pluralistic view of the same. A student's view of these areas affects the way that individual will approach the entire career-life planning process. As students move upward along the scheme, it is our contention that they will exhibit a more integrated understanding of the interrelationship between personal identity, values, and the entire career-life planning process and hence make more satisfying career commitments.

Dualism. The first stage is characterized by simplistic, dichotomous thinking about the career-life planning area. Lower-stage dualistic-thinking students are almost exclusively controlled by externals in their environment. Adhering to the belief that there is only one right career for them, they tend to turn to parents, teachers, counselors, interest inventories, the job market, and economy, as well as such factors as prestige, power, and financial reward, to define both self and the right career decisions. These students are lacking in the ability to analyze and synthesize material and exhibit only minimal processing of self in relation to the career decision-making process. For them, the career decision-making process exists only to the extent that one can turn to the Authority to provide the answer as to the right career. This Authority may be the counselor, the interest inventory, or any other external factor that would solve the student's dilemma.

Stage 1. The student has no dissonance in making a career decision, due to an absolute reliance on the suggestions of external authorities. No self-processing is evident. The student sees only one possible right career. The counselor is viewed as Authority.

Stage 2. The possibility of right/wrong career decisions is beginning to be recognized. This causes anxiety and leads to dissonance in the decision-making process. The student has only a minimal understanding of a decision-making process and only to the extent outlined by the counselor.

There should be only one right career. At this stage, processing by the

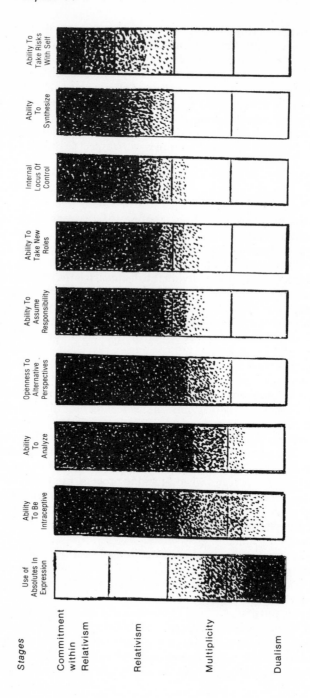

Figure 1. Variables of qualitative change according to the Knefelkamp/Slepitza model of career development.

student is only minimal and takes the form of dichotomous thinking. The possibility of right or wrong career decisions creates dissonance.

Because of the dissonance produced by the realization that others have made the wrong career decision, the view of the counselor and the counseling process is somewhat more tentative. Either the counselor as the Authority or the test as the Authority should provide the right answer. The process that the counselor outlines for the student must be simple, straightforward, and clear in order for the student to accept the counselor and the decision-making process.

Multiplicity. As students begin to become cognitively more complex, they become cognizant of the possibility of making right and wrong choices. This increased complexity creates increased dissonance, and, in an attempt to eliminate and reduce the possibility of wrong decisions, students turn to a decision-making process provided by the counselor. The locus of control, however, still rests on those external factors previously mentioned. Students are now able to include a variety of factors into their consideration and, as such, are able to analyze factors important to career decision making in greater detail. They begin to see a cause-and-effect relationship between these multiple factors and right career decisions. As the student matures in multiplicity, the decision-making process expands to include a wider variety of topics that carry different degrees of weight. It is important to note that the student shifts from a faith that one right career exists to be somehow discovered to a reliance on the *right* decision-making process to yield the right career. The student sees the counselor's role as providing that decision-making process.

Stage 3. Students realize a greater possibility of making right/wrong career decisions. This realization leads to increased conflict and anxiety and a recognition that the process of making a right decision may be more complex than originally perceived. The student's processing expands to include a greater self vis-a-vis others. The student is ready to begin elements of analysis in the decision-making process.

Students assume the attitude that others seem to have found the right career and that they will be able to as well. Underlying this conviction is the converse doubt that others have made the wrong decisions and that they may also. The educational/vocational decision-making process takes on a future orientation, a hopefulness that, in the end, a good decision will be made.

The right decision can be made through the combination of the educational/vocational decision-making process and the assistance of the counselor. The Authority is the process. The student views the counselor's role as providing the process and the student's role as participant in the process. Because the process includes such dimensions as values, information, and prioritizing, the student becomes aware of the quantity of components that can influence the decision-making process. Thus the student begins to analyze the career decision in more self-dimensions. The emerging focus becomes how the self and self-values relate to choosing a career.

Stage 4. For the student in Stage 4, right/wrong decisions are based on a more complex weighing of the components discovered in Stage 3. Multiple possibilities and multiple good choices exist. Students perceive that, with all of the quantity that exists, they need to prioritize in terms of both internal and external sources. The decision-making process becomes a complex weighing of factors with the hope that, in some cases, the right career exists and that it can be found through the process.

In Stage 4, the self is still not a prime mover in the decision-making process. Elements of self, however, need to be included with external factors in the decision-making process. The self is subordinated to the influence of tests, counselors, friends, parents, economy, and other external influences. The student does not yet accept full responsibility for choosing. At this stage the counselor is seen as the source for helping the student prioritize.

Relativism. As individuals enter relativism they experience what can be referred to as the *primary flip.* The student's locus of control has shifted from a basically external reference point to a predominantly internal one. For the student in dualism and multiplicity, teachers, parents, counselors, and other authority figures have been the prime resources in the decision-making process. As the student moves into relativism, these influences continue to be helpful resources, but the student now becomes the prime focus of the decision-making process. As students reach these higher levels of processing, they are able to utilize the skills of analysis in their approach to their own career decision-making process. They thus establish for themselves essentially a self-created decision-making process tailored to meet their own peculiar needs and interests. The individual is able to see a wide variety of legitimate possibilities and is able to appropriately detach from the decision-making process in order to proceed in an objective manner. Individuals in this category are capable of understanding and examining a variety of career possibilities, of dealing with the positive and negative elements of each, and of seeing themselves in a variety of examined roles. As students anticipate making a career commitment, they begin to be able to synthesize the many diverse and complex components of the process and to form them into their own resolution of the process. They are thus able to accept responsibility for their career decisions.

Stage 5. An exploring/doing stage, Stage 5 begins with a realization of the recognition of multiple possibilities and ends with the need to create personal order and clarification with respect to the decision-making process.

The self is now the prime mover in the decision-making process. Students own the decision as their decision. While the process to make the decision differs little from the process used in Stage 4, students now tailor the process to meet their own needs. They create the process with the assistance of the counselor, who is now viewed as an experienced, knowledgeable source and not as unquestioned Authority. The student has the ability to detach and analyze self and to systematically examine alternatives.

Stage 6. The student at Stage 6 has begun to tire of all the legitimate alternatives realized in Stage 5. Alternatives that were once seen as freeing in their quantity and legitimacy are now experienced as chaotic. The student at Stage 6 realizes that the only way to order the chaos is to choose; however, the student is not yet ready to commit the self to a career and thus reflect the necessity of making a commitment. In many respects, Stage 6 is a reflective stage enabling the student to: (1) establish ties between career and self, (2) vicariously think about the consequences of commitments to be made, and (3) confront the reality of the responsibility of commitment as the student's alone. The student sees the counselor's role as one of helping the student to engage in the reflective process. Although areas of interest in terms of career are closely linked to the concept of self, students still lack awareness of the implications of their own style and they thus continue to define career in terms of traditionally defined roles.

Commitment within relativism. At this point students begin to assume increased responsibility for the career decision-making process and not only are able to analyze the complexities of the issues in the process but also are able to synthesize the various factors into their own decision-making scheme. They begin to realize and experience the fact that choosing a career is a personal commitment of self. At first this is experienced as the feared narrowing of their world, but later commitment is often seen as the beginning of the expansion into a new world. Students experience the joy of watching themselves integrate self with what once was perceived as polarized choices. A second cognitive flip appears to occur when students experience a comprehensive integration of who and what they are with the style of their interaction with their environment. The theme "What I am about . . ." flows through the conversations and interviews of these upper-stage individuals. Students begin to see their role as an integration of who they are as a person and what that stance means in terms of one's values, purposes, and identity. This stance becomes highly individualistic when related to career. Career identity and self-identity become more closely intertwined. While forging their career identity, students forge for themselves a role in the world that extends beyond the confines of simple job descriptions. The student's values, thoughts, and behaviors become more consistent with one another, and at the same time the student is open to new challenges and changes from the environment.

Stage 7. Individuals in Stage 7 experience the integration of the self and the career role. Initially the student has a fear of narrowing, of being confined and defined by the role. However, in the latter phase of Stage 7, students experience the realization that they define the role. This realization leads to an affirmation of self and career and a new focus on individual style in how one acts—how one fulfills the role.

Stage 8. The individual in Stage 8 begins to experience all the consequences of the commitments made in Stage 7. The consequences are both pleasant and unpleasant, anticipated and unexpected. The consequences present new challenges to the definition of self and to the continuation of the commitments made. Individuals in this stage begin to truly experience the meaning of their commitments and are challenged to clarify once again their own values, purposes, and identity. Individuals are challenged to affirm who they are, what it is they believe, and how they will act in the world. Individuals in this stage experience a high degree of integration among all aspects of their life.

Stage 9. This stage represents a further expansion of one's self-created role. Individuals have a firm knowledge of who they are and how that affects all aspects of their life. Individuals at Stage 9 have an acute awareness of the interactive effect they have on other people, places, and things. They are aware of the effects they have on others and the effects that others have on them.

They constantly seek new ways to express what they are about and what that means for them. They are characterized by an active seeking out and processing of information from the environment, taking on more risks to their self-esteem in an effort to fully attain their potential. They are about new things, new challenges, new ways to interact but are tempered by an insightful realization of the potential positive and negative effects of their actions on self and others.

SUPPORTING RESEARCH

Predominant Stages in the Population

Work with this model has been conducted at both the University of Maryland and the Ohio State University over the last two years. Data has been collected through the use of written protocols and in-depth interviews. The data collected at both schools reveal the following predominant stages in respect to the career model in the populations listed in Table 1.

Table 1. Predominant population stages

Population	Stages
University freshmen and sophomores	2, 3
University seniors	3, 4, 5
First-year masters students in Educational Psychology	3, 4, 5
Advanced graduate students in Educational Psychology	6, 7

The Ohio State Project

In 1975, research was conducted at the Ohio State University that attempted to identify patterns of student behaviors in career decision-making classes and to examine whether or not those behaviors were characteristic of cognitive-stage level. The 35 students in the study were all students in career-development classes. They were all administered a written protocol from which career-development stage classifications could be attained. One aspect of the study required the class facilitators, all graduate students in counseling psychology, to complete rating forms in which they characterized each of the students according to six dimensions (student expectations of the class, student motivation, student attitude toward class structure, student view of career choice, self-awareness, and expectations about the role of the facilitators).

The results of the facilitators' evaluations of the Ohio State students in the career-development classes support the existence of the areas of qualitative change that were used as a basis for the career model. They also support the developmental movement within each of the areas as one moves from dualism to relativism. In the data presented below (N=35) Dualists (D) are Stage 2 and below and Transition (T) people are Stage 3(4).[1]

Area: Student Motivation
A. Student motivated to deal with career planning by external pressures (parents, peers, college rules, or grade in the course).

D = 68%   T = 33%

B. Student motivated to deal with career planning from an "internal need."

D = 32%   T = 67%

Area: Class Structure
A. Student learned most when class was fairly well structured. Student liked clear rules and guidelines.

D = 68%   T = 50%

B. Student learned most when class was fairly unstructured and students were allowed by self-direction to explore. Student enjoyed activities that required initiative and self-defined learning goals.

D = 26%   T = 50%

C. Student didn't get involved.

D = 5%   T = 0%

Area: Self-Awareness
A. Student is relatively unaware of self and career alternatives.

D = 21%   T = 0%

---

[1]"Stage 3(4)" is indicative of a stage of transition. The student is mostly reasoning at a Stage 3 level but also uses Stage 4 to a degree large enough to warrant its inclusion.

B. Student is somewhat aware.

$$D = 57\% \qquad T = 67\%$$

C. Student is highly aware.

$$D = 21\% \qquad T = 33\%$$

Area: Student View of Career Choice

A. Student tended to believe there was a "right" career for self. Student tended to depend on the "right" sources to identify the "right" career.

$$D = 47\% \qquad T = 0\%$$

B. Student tended to believe there were many careers that would meet his or her abilities. Student felt that the actual career choice was an awesome task and felt the need for much more explanations and experience so the wrong choice would not be made.

$$D = 15\% \qquad T = 13\%$$

C. Student tended to believe there were many careers that would meet her or his abilities. Student perceived the need to choose among alternatives and make initial commitments so he or she could more actively control the future.

$$D = 36\% \qquad T = 87\%$$

ISSUES TO CONSIDER

Our involvement with the creation of this model and our attempt to answer the questions it raises have given us a greater appreciation of the complexities of the career-development dilemma in the student's life. It is our conclusion that Perry's cognitive-developmental scheme was an excellent springboard for our work. However, a simple overlay of Perry on the career-development issue would not be sufficient to the task. What is needed is an adapted model—one that encompasses the concepts of cognitive-developmental theory and the unique and fascinating complexities of career development. Our work has led us to focus on the following issues.

Difference between Choice and Commitment

It is appropriate for the theorist and practitioner to ask what happens to individuals who make career decisions at various points along the continuum of development presented in the model. What are the essential differences between a career choice made in dualism and a commitment made within relativism? How are those differences operationalized in terms of the individual's interaction with the environment and the satisfaction derived from such interactions? According to Bodden (1970) and Bodden and Klein (1972), increased cognitive complexity yielded higher levels of congruence between occupation choice and personality choice. According to Holland (1966), this congruence yields greater satisfaction.

Movement from External to Internal Locus of Control

The results of our first two years' research tend to indicate that the prime factor separating the dualists from the relativists is locus of control. Individuals at each end of the continuum are confronted with the unsurety and confusion of making career decisions in a complex society. The primary difference between those individuals is found in the source to which the individual turns to deal with this uncertainty. Individuals at the dualist end of the continuum need to reduce the anxiety and confusion of choice by the discovery of the "truth." In seeking such a discovery, the individual turns to external reference points to define the "right" choice. The student at the middle and upper ends of the continuum considers external factors but also depends on self when meeting this same crisis. Such individuals are able to make decisions within the framework of doubt and risks and are able to assume responsibility for the consequences of such decisions. The dualistic-thinking student is unable to assume such responsibility or to take such risks.

The Fear of Narrowing and the Sense of Loss

In investigating how individuals approached the task of making commitments, we discovered a rather interesting paradox. In coming to commitment, students experienced the narrowing and associated fear and regret in choosing one alternative from among many. Indeed a true sense of loss was frequently expressed. It is true that to commit to one course of action is not to choose other courses of action. Yet in experiencing the ramifications of those commitments, we found that students experienced that which was once perceived as a narrowing as an opening that encompassed many aspects of the self. What was once regret became affirmation.

New Catechism Phenomenon

As we examined more and more of our data, we became aware of a phenomenon we had not anticipated: that of the students parroting frequently heard career-development maxims—the new catechism—when responding to the career protocols. It is a difficult task to distinguish between a statement that is truly relativistic and one that is written by a strict dualist who has memorized the current "truth" (e.g. "there is no right career for anyone"; or "many factors must be considered when choosing a career"). The phenomenon raises challenging questions. What method of data collection is most appropriate for guarding against this problem? How would one design career-development interventions that would foster student development and not simply the learning of a new catechism?

Description to Prescription

The movement from a descriptive model of student career development to prescriptive interventions designed to foster movement along the model is a step to be taken with deliberate care and caution. We see the need for continued work in the following areas.

1. The model needs to be tested on a wide variety of populations and with studies of a longitudinal nature.

2. The variables of qualitative change need further specification and validation.

3. A reliable, valid, and efficient instrument needs to be developed that will enable practitioners to place students along the developmental continuum.

4. Staff-development and counselor-education programs would be necessary to enable the counselor to work within the concepts of the model to promote developmental growth.

CONCLUSION

The model and the data presented in this article represent only our initial efforts at confronting the task of developing an accurate useful career decision-making model. It is important to us that our work be viewed in the context of previous work in career development and seen as a logical next step that builds on that development. And it is always useful to remember that students manage to remain larger than our categories and that it is the practitioner that is most helped by the existence of descriptive models. We remain encouraged by the results of the first two years and their potential usefulness to students of student development and practitioners of career development.

REFERENCES

Bodden, J. L. Cognitive complexity as a factor in appropriate vocational choice. *Journal of Counseling Psychology*, 1970, *17*, 364-368.

Bodden, J. L., & Klein, A. J. Cognitive complexity and appropriate vocational choice: Another look. *Journal of Counseling Psychology*, 1972, *19*(3), 257-258.

Ginzberg, E., Ginsburg, S. W., Axelrod, S., & Herma, J. L. *Occupational choice.* New York: Columbia University Press, 1951.

Harvey, O. J., Hunt, D. E., & Schroder, H. M. *Conceptual systems and personality organization.* New York: Wiley, 1961.

Holland, J. L. *The psychology of vocational choice.* Waltham, Mass.: Blaisdell, 1966.

Jepsen, D. A. The stage construct in career development. *Counseling and Values*, 1974, *18*(2), 124-131.

Kohlberg, L. Stage and sequence: The cognitive-developmental approach to socialization. In D. Goslin (Ed.), *Handbook of socialization theory and research.* New York: Rand McNally, 1969.

Loevinger, J., & Wessler, R. *Measuring ego development.* San Francisco: Jossey-Bass, 1970.

Perry, W., Jr. *Intellectual and ethical development in the college years.* New York: Holt, Rinehart and Winston, 1970.

Piaget, J. *The language and thought of the child.* London: Routledge and Kegan Paul, 1952.

Rest, J. Developmental psychology as a guide to value education: A review of "Kohlbergian programs." *Review of Educational Research,* 1973, *44*(2), 241-259.

Super, D. *The psychology of careers.* New York: Harper & Row, 1957.

Tiedeman, D. V., & O'Hara, R. P. *Career development: Choice and adjustment.* New York: College Entrance Examination Board, 1963.

Widick, C., Knefelkamp, L. L., & Parker, C. The counselor as a developmental instructor. *Counselor Education and Supervision,* 1975, *14*(4), 286-296.

Index